Made in Censorship

*The Tiananmen Movement in
Chinese Literature and Film*

Thomas Chen

Columbia University Press   *New York*

Columbia University Press wishes to express its appreciation
for assistance given by the Wm. Theodore de Bary Fund
in the publication of this book.

Columbia University Press
Publishers Since 1893
New York   Chichester, West Sussex
cup.columbia.edu

Library of Congress Cataloging-in-Publication Data
Names: Chen, Thomas, author.
Title: Made in censorship : the Tiananmen movement in Chinese literature
and film / Thomas Chen.
Description: New York : Columbia University Press, [2022] | Includes
bibliographical references and index.
Identifiers: LCCN 2021038579 (print) | LCCN 2021038580 (ebook) |
ISBN 9780231204002 (hardback) | ISBN 9780231204019 (trade paperback) |
ISBN 9780231555326 (ebook)
Subjects: LCSH: Mass media policy—China. | Censorship—China. |
Propaganda, Chinese. | Propaganda, Communist—China. |
China—History—Tiananmen Square Incident, 1989.
Classification: LCC P95.82.C6 C48 2022 (print) | LCC P95.82.C6 (ebook) |
DDC 303.3/760951—dc23/eng/20211109
LC record available at https://lccn.loc.gov/2021038579
LC ebook record available at https://lccn.loc.gov/2021038580

MADE IN CENSORSHIP

To the memory of my grandparents
Wang Shuying and Liu Yun

Contents

Acknowledgments

Long before the book, there was family. My grandparents Liu Yun and Wang Shuying raised me and are largely responsible for all that is good within me. My parents have always provided me with the room and resources to explore. Other family members instrumental in making this book possible include my aunt Eva and uncle Jack, as well as my cousins Liya and Su. In steadfast and selfless friendship, Ryan has been a brother for over twenty years. From Ithaca to Philadelphia, my wife Winnie is my reader, my counsel, my life partner. I've never been happier, growing alongside her with our kids, Nathaniel and Abigail, our blessing and our joy.

The idea for this book germinated at UCLA, where I spent my formative years as a scholar. I had the good fortune of working with many people whom I hold in high esteem. Robert Chi's scholarship is a paragon of erudition. In class, in his office, and over the phone, he showed me how to be the best teacher, reader, and writer I can be. No matter how serious and substantive our talks were, he always injected a sense of humor and levity. Kirstie McClure always pushed me to be a sharper thinker. Her dedication of time is without parallel. I am indebted to Efraín Kristal, whose breadth of learning, wisdom, and humaneness of spirit have served as a model from those graduate years to the present. Wang Chaohua continues to inspire me with her intellectual commitment. I am deeply appreciative of two "elder brother pupils," Brian Bernards and Nathaniel Isaacson, who offered pointers at key junctures. Last but not least, the memory of Michael Henry Heim is a perpetual source of inspiration. An incomparable translator who was at the same time the most learned and giving person, he will be remembered.

I am thankful to have colleagues at Lehigh who support my work in myriad ways. Connie Cook is that ideal senior colleague who gives me guidance and leeway in equal measure. The inimitable Mary Nicholas is unstinting, inside and outside the classroom. I am lucky to have Matt Bush as my mentor and friend. Olivia Landry couldn't have responded to my calls for help with more alacrity and discernment. Yinan He has been a valuable interlocutor across disciplines. From the book proposal to the chapters and everything in between, each of them read my writing meticulously and provided precious feedback. As departmental chair during the completion of the manuscript, Kiri Lee cultivated an environment that assisted my research.

Beyond Lehigh, Guobin Yang has fostered my professional growth ever since I interloped into his seminar. Andrew Clark generously shared the fruits of his labor. Qi Wang, Duan Jinchuan, Paola Voci, and Timothy Brook all helped me with sources. Belinda Kong lent her encouragement both early and late. Conversations with Xiaobing Tang clarified my thinking. I also want to thank colleagues in China, without whom I could not have completed this book.

An immense thank you to Christine Dunbar at Columbia University Press, who believed in my project from day 1. She ushered this book through the entire process with tireless advocacy and judicious advice. I can't imagine a more expert guide for a first-time author. I am also extremely grateful for the care and acumen the anonymous readers lavished upon my manuscript to make it better. What a gift.

Earlier versions of parts of chapter 4 appeared as "Blanks to Be Filled: Public-Making and the Censorship of Jia Pingwa's *Decadent Capital*," *China Perspectives* 1 (2015): 15–22; and as "The Workshop of the World: Censorship and the Internet Novel *Such Is This World*," in *China's Contested Internet*, edited by Guobin Yang (Copenhagen: NIAS Press, 2015): 19–43. I thank the French Centre for Research on Contemporary China and the NIAS Press, respectively, for permission to publish these pieces in revised form.

MADE IN CENSORSHIP

Introduction

Making the Censored Public

On June 4, 2007, exactly eighteen years after the Chinese government's violent crackdown on the 1989 demonstrations for social and political reforms that centered on Beijing's Tiananmen Square, a one-line ad appeared in the *Chengdu Evening News*. The ad, in the Sichuan province newspaper with a daily circulation then of around 200,000, read simply: "Saluting the strong mothers of 64 victims."

The number 64, which could refer to the number of victims, is here a digital disguise for June Fourth, as the student-initiated Tiananmen movement in which millions of citizens participated is known in the People's Republic of China (PRC). This sleight of hand helped the tribute sneak into publication. When the young clerk responsible for vetting the ads phoned the person who placed it, she was told it referred to a mining accident. Three editors at the newspaper were fired in the aftermath.[1]

That such an ad could appear in a Chinese newspaper is astonishing. The military crackdown of 1989 was followed by a clampdown on all unauthorized expression regarding June Fourth that has continued to the present. The classified ad is a reminder that, try as the Party-state may to "classify" the Tiananmen protests, people still think of creative ways to declassify them and to commemorate them in public.

As the anecdote about the ad illustrates, *Made in Censorship: The Tiananmen Movement in Chinese Literature and Film* is more interested in what is created than what is blocked. The main questions answered by this book are the following: In what ways does censorship condition contemporary Chinese cultural production, circulation, and reception? How should censorship be viewed differently? And what is the relationship between censorship and the public? This book's central argument is that censorship does not merely cross out or strike through; it also forms and fashions, molds and manipulates.

The reconceptualization of censorship as formative derives from Michel Foucault's writings on power, especially in his 1975 *Discipline and Punish* (although there, "censorship" remains strictly inhibitory).[2] In rethinking censorship since the 1990s as both repression and production, "constitutive censorship" scholars in the U.S. academy have also challenged the assignation of censors (the state, the church, etc.) to one side and artists (writers, filmmakers, etc.) to the other. The power to censor is decentered and dispersed, blurring the lines between an external power—composed of film censors, government officials, church authorities—that bans or restricts and the internal (artistic) expression of some subject.

In 1976, Foucault lamented that "we still have not removed the head of the king," meaning that analyses of power were still beholden to the concept of sovereignty.[3] More than forty years later, we now have. The provenance of constitutive censorship can be traced to the (neo)liberalizing West of the 1970s, where and since which time sovereign nation-states have receded behind transnational corporations, and the globalized market, more so than inquisitors and autocrats, has acted as the administrator of discourse. But to lop off the head of the king does not suit everywhere. My book intervenes in historicizing censorship theory.

Retheorizing censorship yields important insights for modern Chinese literary and cultural studies. Books and films are produced not despite censorship; they do not so much go around it as pass through it. Censorship is not a barrier that can be circumvented but a condition that imbues and transforms every text. But the danger of constitutive censorship lies in flattening all particularities into the same. In the dreadful words of Michael Holquist in his introduction to a 1994 *PMLA* special issue on the topic: "To be for or against censorship as such is to assume a freedom no one has. Censorship *is*."[4]

If censorship *is*, then it is not. As Frederick Schauer remarks, "[I]f the use of the word *censorship* presupposes that censorship is a relatively identifiable subset of the set of human activity, then it makes no sense to identify as such a subset something that is part and parcel of all human activity."[5] In a context such as the neoliberal West, where freedom of speech and of the press is guaranteed in constitutions and disputed in the courts, critique can and should turn toward censorship that is socially structured. In the context of post-Mao China, however, the Party-state is simultaneously residual *and* dominant, to use Raymond Williams's terms.[6] Current censorship theory spotlights the normative and the discursive, but the Chinese case demonstrates that what is at first decreed can become normative and beyond dispute. The distinction between structural censorship and regulative censorship cannot be so easily marked.[7]

In addition to the theory of censorship, *Made in Censorship* also makes a related intervention in contemporary China studies. There, as the eponymous country turns into an ever-larger financial powerhouse on the world stage, the emphasis has shifted to the PRC's involvement in global capitalism. With this move, the 1989 movement and massacre become but momentary in a postsocialist era when economics has tamed politics.[8] Scholars, including in the humanities, have challenged the fixation on famous events, such as June Fourth, in narratives about modern China. They identify another marker—1992, the year when market reforms deepened further—as the decisive moment not simply for society at large but specifically in the domain of culture.[9] And so it would appear retrograde to harp on Tiananmen, politics, and the Party-state.

Such scholarship is a welcome corrective to Western media portrayals that, influenced by holdover Cold War ideology of the totalitarian other, hype the idea of Oriental despotism. The Tiananmen movement may not explain all transformations in Chinese society over the last three decades, and economic reforms have indeed been pivotal in altering the fabric of everyday life. But Tiananmen illustrates something that economic reforms do not, namely, the continuously fundamental role of the political in present-day China. Political intensity lives on, to be resorted to and fanned in critical moments, as seen in the government's response to the COVID-19 pandemic (discussed in the conclusion to this book).

Once in a while, the political returns to assert itself, not so much undermining the everyday as sustaining it. Tiananmen is not momentary; it is a momentous exception that proves the Party-state's rule. The severity of control may vary with the wind, but what stays steady from Mao to now is the political, not fiscal, bottom line.

Although the Tiananmen protests have prompted much scholarship in the social sciences, literature and film produced in China that evoke this watershed have been accorded little attention. Belinda Kong's *Tiananmen Fictions Outside the Square* (2012) examines diasporic representations in novels. Her case studies, part of a sophisticated analysis of the politicization of this literary diaspora, are all drawn from without the PRC. My case studies are all drawn from within, not to cover a different terrain than Kong's but because the scope of materials undergirds my critical framework. These materials are "made in censorship" in a way distinct from those produced outside mainland China, including Hong Kong (which, despite recent depredations by the Chinese government, is still hanging on to an attenuated "semiautonomy").

The objects of study in *Made in Censorship* are picked for their exemplarity from a wide range of written and audiovisual sources, with a cross-media breadth that covers film, fiction, and online texts both rare and well-known.[10] Instead of a familiar focus on bans and elisions, each of the four main chapters gives pride of place to a distinctive aspect of what is generated through censorship, including the underground documentary, controversial best seller, and internet novel. Most unexpectedly of all, the book examines the Chinese government's literary and televisual propaganda. Why? Because the official narratives of Tiananmen, produced and disseminated under the direction of the state, are also part of my analytical purview. They, too, are "made in censorship," just like the unofficial narratives.[11]

The dual lenses of Tiananmen plus censorship are not haphazardly chosen. Tiananmen Square in 1989 is the most rigorously suppressed spatiotemporal coordinate in modern China. Yet even in the case of Tiananmen, censorship's relation to it should not be viewed solely as negation. Even inside China, Tiananmen is characterized not just by suppression but also by competing representations. *Made in Censorship* uses the taboo of Tiananmen as a litmus test to argue for censorship's reconsideration as a total project encompassing both proscription and propagation. In spite of the taboo, literature and film that re-create the event have never ceased to be produced and to play an important cultural role.

What merit is there to conceiving proscription and propagation under the single umbrella term of *censorship*? Here the Chinese term for censorship, *shencha*, offers insight. Literally, *shencha* signifies "inspection" or "examination." To be "censored," in Chinese, is to be inspected at the gate of public discourse. Not only what is examined and then barred from the public—a banned book, for example—but also what is examined and then allowed to go through—including propaganda—have been censored. Therefore, *shencha* corrects the current English term's nearly exclusive stress on the repressive dimension. It encompasses both prevention and promotion, its meaning not limited to the former. It is comparable to the English word *sanction*, where the sanctioned can be the forbidden and the outlawed, or the permitted, even protected. In this resignification, then, the marginalization and erasure of the Tiananmen movement from Chinese public discourse are a product of censorship, yes, but so are the top-down production and propagation of authorized accounts and ideologies.

In China, censorship as a function cuts across various state institutions. The government does not see denial/deletion as one thing and publicity/propaganda as another, but rather it sees both as parts of a whole.[12] The latest set of internet regulations from the Cyberspace Administration of China, effective since March 2020, testifies to the proscriptive and prescriptive dimensions of censorship.[13] The list begins not with content that "cannot be produced, reproduced, or distributed" but rather with content to be "encouraged." What falls into this category? It includes the "Thought" of President Xi Jinping, "socialism with Chinese characteristics," the Chinese Communist Party's (CCP) platform and policies, as well as unity and stability. And what counts as "illegal information" to be precluded and "harmful information" to be resisted? The former ranges from content that threatens national security to the dissemination of cults, superstitions, pornography, and violence. The latter comprises, among other things, clickbait, discrimination, vulgarity, and "improper" commentary on natural disasters. As one can see, the governance of the discursive environment straddles the political and moral domains.

By choosing the Tiananmen movement as my litmus test, do I not risk privileging the political in censorship? My counterargument is that Tiananmen precisely illustrates that the bottom line is politics—not economics, much less ethics—in contemporary China. The regime tries to wrap itself in the mantle of moral guardianship. It wants to conflate moral and political censorship so that today's "decadent" values might invoke from some quarters calls for "more censorship." Subversion, not perversion, is what it guards against.[14]

Marxist critique is right to point out a "material censorship" exercised by the market, wherein the press excludes not dissidence but, for example, the speech of the disadvantaged. The Chinese mediascape is no longer shaped solely by the state, to be sure. Commercial (social) media proliferate. But let there be no question of who rules the roost. In a 2016 visit by the now termless President Xi to three major state media outlets, he reminded them that they are all surnamed "Party."[15] One may add that that is why the "Party" in "Party-state" is capitalized.

What are the stakes of making in censorship? They consist in nothing more and nothing less than a politics of the public. Any invocation of the public, of course, implicates what delimits it, the private. What is more, the repressive aspect of censorship can be conceived as a making-private: ensuring that certain speech stays private or removing it from the public realm. But make no mistake that censorship's concern is primarily the public. We may not be entirely past the age when our diaries and letters are scrutinized for sedition (and we may not be far from a future when our thoughts are scanned for adherence to orthodoxy). Nevertheless, in the present, censorship perks up its ears in matters of public opinion, or when a public understood as a group of people, however small, is involved.

The productive aspect of censorship can be conceived as a public-making, therefore, in three ways, at minimum. First, public-making signifies the making public of what is kept under wraps, not least the operation of censorship itself, which is often shrouded in secrecy. Second, public-making is not a private undertaking. It points to the collaborative nature of working in censorship. While the names of writers and filmmakers may be singled out in the chapters to come, they should be considered a shorthand for the mode of coproduction under censorship involving, among others, publishers, editors, critics, audience members, and not least of all, censors themselves. Third and finally, whether it is the Chinese government or the independent film-maker, both aim at constituting publics as collectivities. The former, by waging media and educational campaigns, attempts to reforge a nation loyal to the party in the wake of massacre. It's in the business of "making the *censored* public," fixing the contour and composition of "the people" as it sees fit. The latter, meanwhile, endeavors to conjure forms of association and assembly alternative to the People's Republic, onscreen and off, online and off. In reanimating with recalcitrance a buried past, Tiananmen fiction and film "make the censored *public.*"

Since the beginning of the twentieth century, Tiananmen Square has played the role of a "primary site of public activity and expression."[16] After the establishment of the PRC in 1949, it became a locus of visual expression—parades, paintings, sculptures—in conjunction with political practice. Yet there is a tension built into its very structure: on the one hand, the square, the enlarged public space for the people instituted by Mao Zedong; on the other, Tiananmen, the Gate of Heavenly Peace from whose heights Mao's gaze and that of later leaders command the expanse below. In *Remaking Beijing* (2005), Wu Hung analyzes visual representations of Tiananmen Square, both official iconographies and unofficial recuperations of historical memory, including those that came after June Fourth. The artistic contestation of that space persisted through the crackdown because, as Wu perceptively observes, "the antagonism between the ruler and the ruled had been always there, in the very opposition between a public ground and a privileged platform."[17]

The political meanings of Tiananmen Square, old and new, are ever present in this tension. Wu attests that "the Square has been—and will continue to be—a prime visual means of political rhetoric in modern China to address the public and to constitute the public itself."[18] My book extends the means to the literary and the audiovisual because all artworks related to the Tiananmen movement exemplify a politics of the public in their address, whether summoning readers and viewers back into the fold of the nation, as in the case of the state propaganda analyzed in chapter 1, or creating discursive spaces of remembrance and reappropriation, as in the case of the fiction and film analyzed in chapters 2 through 4.

In *Publics and Counterpublics* (2002), Michael Warner cautions against a voluntaristic faith in public-making: "The making of a public requires conditions that range from the very general—such as the organization of media, ideologies of reading, institutions of circulation, text genres—to the particular rhetorics of texts."[19] It is an understanding in sympathy with Wang Hui and Leo Ou-fan Lee (in conversation with Michael M. J. Fischer), who make a similar point, although from the opposite angle, in "Is the Public Sphere Unspeakable in Chinese? Can Public Spaces (*gonggong kongjian*) Lead to Public Spheres?" (1994). They were responding in part to William Rowe's "The Public Sphere in Modern China" (1990), published a year after the first complete English translation of Jürgen Habermas's *The Structural Transformation of the Public Sphere*, as well as a year after the Tiananmen protests. Rowe maps the historiographical opportunities opened in Chinese studies by Habermas's book. Wang and Lee point out that, while Rowe finds socioeconomic parallels between European and Chinese developments, he takes less into account the historical changes in "communicative devices" and "linguistic, metalinguistic, genre, and institutional forms" that support Habermas's argument.[20]

Like Wu Hung, Wang and Lee are interested in the political potency of public space. They remark that in the mid-1980s, after the economic reforms were under way, there emerged a proto-public sphere in China in the form of new journals, art exhibits, and so on.[21] These new public spaces fostered the environment in which the Tiananmen movement arose. In their brief sketch of the post-1989 scene, they reference the pressures of the market that push newspapers to adopt tabloid tactics—for instance, columns on sex—in order to boost sales, as well as the appearance of new transnational spaces and electronic media. What remains to be fleshed out, and where I see an area for contribution in the field of modern Chinese literary and cultural studies, is the political edge of the public realm in the wake of the June Fourth crackdown. Market pressures and state censorship are ultimately incommensurable: only one of the two can lead to imprisonment. Even though censorship has become partly privatized, carried out by publishing house editors and web monitors hired by internet companies for whom the administrative may be the day-to-day, the mundane is precisely underwritten by the punitive to this day.

While Rowe's survey covers hundreds and indeed thousands of years, and Wang and Lee mainly consider the twentieth century, my study concentrates on the last thirty-odd years. In parsing the various forms of public-making in the chapters to come, *Made in Censorship* takes heed of both Rowe's level of inquiry—the socioeconomic transformations since the end of the 1970s—as well as Warner's and Wang and Lee's suggestions: from changes in the publishing and film industries with the deepening of marketization and privatization, plus the dawning and development of the internet, to the genres of literary reportage, "special topic program," dystopian novel, and blog. Both individuals (writers, filmmakers, critics, netizens) and institutions (the People's Liberation Army [PLA], the erstwhile General Administration of Press and Publications [GAPP], and the State Administration of Radio, Film, and Television [SARFT]) figure prominently. The inquiry extends across multiple media, from print to cyberspace, from television to DVD. I conduct close and sustained readings not just of key literary and audiovisual texts but also of censorship policies, critical debates, and online interventions. These multiple contextual levels inform my analysis of the contestation between authoritative discourse and the fiction and film that elicit the fractious significance of the Tiananmen movement.

With fiction and film as its objects of study, *Made in Censorship* pits works of art, or "fabrications," against the top-down "truth." The book underscores the creative act, illuminating the artistry and artifice involved in the making. The objects under consideration do not intervene strictly on the grounds of history and memory.[22] In rereading their reconfigurations of the past, each of the four chapters opens up other possible configurations for the present and for the future.

Each chapter treats a different kind of production. The book begins with mass production by the Chinese state. Chapter 1, "Rebuilding the Republic: State Propaganda in the Wake of Tiananmen," opens with a survey of the flood of literary and audiovisual materials issued by the regime after June 4, 1989. It then focuses on two case studies: a volume of literary reportage titled *Songs of the Republic's Guardians: Collection of Reportage Literature on Martial Law Troops' Heroic Deeds in the Capital* (*Gongheguo weishi zhige: Shoudu jieyan budui yingmo shiji baogao wenxueji*), and a television documentary called *Flutter, Flag of the Republic: A Record of the Quelling of the Beijing Counterrevolutionary Riot*

(*Piaoyang, gongheguo de qizhi: Pingxi Beijing fangeming baoluan jishi*) that graphically lays down the official line. Both materials, edited by the PLA in 1989, are representative of censorship as state propaganda, flooding the public sphere not to distract or to divert, in this case, but on the contrary to fashion a selective memory that tries to recall the people to the party's embrace and to restore the state's legitimacy after the massacre of civilians.[23] My reading of these works against the grain lays bare their contradictions more than thirty years later.

Despite the government ban on unauthorized articulations, Tiananmen film and literature continue to appear in China. Chapter 2, "Songs from Afar: Contesting the Official Narrative from the Periphery," looks at three works, one from each post-1989 decade: Wang Guangli's documentary *I Graduated* (*Wo biye le*) (1992), composed mainly of interviews of Beijing college graduates; Tang Xiaobai's fiction-feature *Conjugation* (*Dongci bianwei*) (2001), which follows the lives of a young couple in the winter after 1989; and Sheng Keyi's novel *Death Fugue* (*Siwang fuge*) (2011), part Tiananmen allegory, part dystopian fiction. The two films were independently produced and shot without permission, and the novel was published in mainland China only in a literary journal. Unable to be widely distributed, they nevertheless exemplify varying and evolving responses from the margins of the Chinese public sphere. In spite of and because of censorship, they challenge the authorized narrative, exposing the role of state violence not just in the massacre but also in the return to "normalcy" afterward.

Underground films and clandestine literature do not constitute the entirety of nonofficial Tiananmen-related narratives in China. The two films discussed in depth in chapter 3, "Transgressive Cuts: Making a Scene in the Postrevolutionary Age"—Stanley Kwan's *Lan Yu* (2001) and Lou Ye's *Summer Palace* (*Yiheyuan*) (2006)—do not fit the bill. Both fall within my rubric of "made in China/made in censorship." Shot surreptitiously in mainland China with a predominantly mainland Chinese cast and crew, *Lan Yu* concerns a decade-long romance beginning in late-1980s Beijing between two men. Released in one version in Hong Kong, it was later officially distributed in a differently edited DVD version on the mainland. *Summer Palace* tracks the tumultuous relations of a young couple from the late 1980s into the new millennium, and, surprisingly, it was filmed in China *with* permission. It was never released there, however, and the director was banned from filmmaking for five years. These two films can be accused of capitalizing globally on their sexual and political content. I argue, however, that in the context of post-Tiananmen China, such interpretations are amenable to the party-promoted position. It is the state itself that violently crushed the political demonstrations in 1989, subsequently diverting all passions into the sexual and the economic. My analysis recovers the political edge that has been ceaselessly blunted.

Chapter 4, "The Orthography of Censorship: Participatory Reading from Print to the Internet," moves to two novels where Tiananmen is present precisely as a mandated absence. Jia Pingwa's *Ruined City* (*Feidu*) (1993) is the quintessential work of literature of the early post-Tiananmen period. Narrating the downfall of a celebrated writer, it was banned the year after its wildly successful publication, not least, I argue, because of the blank squares—□□□□□□—that Jia inserted throughout the text to designate where he deleted words. *Ruined City* was unbanned in 2009, although with the blank squares removed from the reissued edition. As for Hu Fayun's celebrated *Such Is This World@ sars.come* (*Ruyan@sars.come*), which is set against the background of the severe acute respiratory syndrome (SARS) outbreak of 2002–2003, a netizen compared the version first published online in 2004 with the 2006 print edition. This collation epitomizes the active, collaborative production through censorship in the internet age. In addressing and engaging reading communities, both novels reenact the participatory publics that were displaced from Tiananmen Square in 1989.

Like SARS and the Tiananmen movement, the story of COVID-19 in China is one of both repression and creation. The silencing by authorities of a whistleblower, Dr. Li Wenliang, led not only to his death but also to the early unchecked spread of the novel coronavirus that eventually became a global pandemic. But in the conclusion to this book, I also discuss Chinese authors who have pointed out the propagative side of COVID-19 censorship, which spins the government response into tales of "socialist" triumph and popular "gratitude." Both Tiananmen and COVID-19 reveal that prohibition and proselytization go hand in hand. By tracing recent developments in official discourse, I observe a certain "opening up" of Tiananmen. But this shift, even if fully realized, would not signify the end of censorship. On the contrary, it signals a new weight placed on propagation in the overall project of censorship. While the focus of this book is on production within China, in conclusion I tease out the transnational implications of public-making.

The common belief is that Chinese state censorship has rubbed out the Tiananmen movement or that those who speak of it have to do so in code or overseas. *Made in Censorship*, however, shows that the fight is far from over and that its central arena is precisely the public in China. The etymology of the Chinese word for "public," *gong*, reveals a historical polysemy, from the common, communal, and collective to that which belongs to the imperial-bureaucratic state.[24] Today, the contestation over its meanings continues. In reimagining the memories of Tiananmen, the case studies in this book showcase not only their resonance more than thirty years later but also the continued consequence of public-making: who forms the public, what is accessible to the public, and how public memory is mediated.

The contestation is both binary and plural. It is binary because any unofficial revivification of the events of 1989, when they are—as is the case at present—under a near total ban, is necessarily oppositional. It would indeed be easy to designate as "counterproduction" the artworks that challenge the "reproduction" of censorship, or discourse like propaganda that duplicates the official line. But counterproduction connotes the automatic, as if the very éclat of censorship makes it self-defeating. Chien-hsin Tsai has astutely analogized the effects of censorship to that of autoimmunity, "in the sense that even as [state censorship] attempts to prohibit disseminations of proscribed ideas by controlling channels of communication, it simultaneously produces unexpected, self-debilitating results."[25] That censorship often draws attention to what it tries to suppress is certainly true, as several of the literary and audiovisual examples I examine attest. And it would indeed be convenient to apply the analogy to a narrative such as Hu Fayun's novel *Such Is This World* (discussed in chapter 4) of the Chinese government's failed attempt to quash reports of an epidemic outbreak. Yet autoimmunity's emphasis is on reflexive destruction, while what I highlight in my book is the making, the creative work required from all parties involved—artists and censors alike. The contestation is not a reflex but a response.

Other forces push for binaries as well in the discursive environment of the contemporary PRC, leading to the polarization of "you're either with us or against us." In the liberal worldview, a Chinese artist is either a freedom fighter or a toady to the regime, while in China any disagreement with the party line is frequently branded as treasonous. As Tang Xiaobing urges, "we ought to have a good sense of the relational difference between the mainstream and the marginal, the systemic and the sensational, the constituent and the provocative, the publicly expressed and the politically sensitive in our effort to piece together the many aspects of contemporary China."[26] A project on the Tiananmen movement in Chinese literature and film might be expected to be circumscribed within the marginal, sensational, provocative, and politically sensitive. Yet my book precisely defies this expectation because censorship entails the mainstream, systemic, constituent, and publicly expressed. Studying censorship, understood constituently and systemically, does not imply a fixation with the fringe. One must recognize that the regime itself tries to marginalize and privatize Tiananmen in memory when it was mainstream and publicly expressed in the event. That to evoke it is to provoke, to be insensitive, cannot be a given.

Made in Censorship cuts across these dyads. The contestation, while binary, is also plural because the opposition is not univocal. If we need a term other than *counterproduction*, we could do worse than *alter-production*. It captures better the heterogeneity of responses, which include direct opposition, doubtlessly, but do not comprise it solely. Analogous to the dynamic between Tiananmen Square and the Gate of Heavenly Peace sketched earlier, the two kinds of making in censorship, alter-production and reproduction, can be conceived as *x*- and *y*-axes, respectively, in a coordinate system. It might not be always clear where on the graph a particular act falls. If a literary editor rephrases a writer's reference to make it more obscure, is he functioning as the state's proxy? Or is he protecting the author while aiding in the publication? Reproduction can also turn into alter-production, as the example of state propaganda in chapter 1 shows, which becomes propaganda non grata when read today against the grain.

While the plotting of individual points may be difficult, the directions of the two axes cannot be more different. The reproduction of censorship operates vertically. A combination of coercion and commission serves as its binding logic: the former is the stick that ensures compliance, while the latter is the carrot, in the form of political or pecuniary capital, that sweetens the deal. Those lower on the axis may want to climb the hierarchy, but the hierarchical order itself is to be maintained. The alter-production of censorship operates horizontally. Its binding logic is obligation. Obligation rejects the hierarchical order. It is not motivated by any mandate or compensation. Instead, it is a tie into which one enters of one's own accord. The literature and film discussed in *Made in Censorship* obligate us, as readers, to partake in public-making that contributes to an alternative order. This obligation weighs on us, personally and collectively. To evoke or revoke, to delay or relay—we all have a part to play. It is not a one-state show.

Tiananmen itself was a broad-based movement that counted among its proponents many social elements in addition to students and workers, including state agents and party cadres. As Kirk Denton reminds us, "state discourse is not monolithic, immutable, or unresponsive to the dramatic social and economic transformations that China has experienced in the past three decades."[27] But just as members of the state, then and since, have contributed to alter-production, so should the reproduction of censorship be viewed not as the monopoly of the state. That means there are those who play along, whether "helplessly" abiding by the rules or actively reinforcing them, especially online. I am talking about search engines, networking platforms, and videophone services, for instance, domestic or foreign, that receive from the regime competitive advantages in the Chinese market over counterparts that do not act as its brokers. I am talking about so-called internet opinion companies whose "products"—online opinion reports, training, programs, robot commentators, and other public relations services—help government clients, from the local to the central, eliminate antigovernment information and boost progovernment opinion.[28] I am talking about members of the so-called 50 Cent Army, who are allegedly paid RMB 50 cents for every proregime comment they post—astroturfing for a paltry price. I am also talking about patriotic bloggers singled out for commendation by the state, which actively invites popular participation and collaboration in the production of propaganda.[29] This last group may not be driven by the profit motive, like the other individuals and entities. But they are not ingénues either. They cannot be unaware that the might of the state is behind them. Therefore, they speak with impunity.[30]

They do so for reasons far more complex than "brainwashing" by state propaganda and educational campaigns. That the Tiananmen movement is essentially absent from Chinese public discourse is not solely due to censorship understood as a twin project of prohibition and proselytization. Because of the ubiquity of the discourse of censorship in the popular media, its critical value has seemingly been exhausted. In *Negative Exposures* (2020), Margaret Hillenbrand uses the theoretical framework of "public secrecy" because the model of censorship "accords more power to the state than to the people in the management of troubled pasts."[31] But censorship, as my book argues, does not bespeak a monopoly of power by the state. As a power to delete and deny as well as to produce and create, it is leveraged by the state, but every person is part of the production. In my reconceptualization of censorship, power emanates from each of the artists and artworks I analyze.

According to Hillenbrand, censorship and amnesia cannot adequately explain why Tiananmen, for instance, is not present in public discourse: it is also because of the collective decision not to talk. But that begs the question: why is there a collective decision not to talk? That decision is overdetermined, to be sure: you talk, and you get punished; it conjures embarrassing or shameful memories for you; it could be pragmatic: not talking—or talking in the approved way—gets you rewarded; and it could be out of self-choice, wishing to move on. All these reasons are at play. Yet crucially, they are weighted differently. This overdetermination must not mask the fundamental imbalance of the various reasons. For one "reason"—the Party-state capacity for brute force—outweighs and tilts all others in its direction. In spite of this reason, however, people still talk in a discrepant manner. My study of censorship is as much about talking as about hushing and silencing, and this talking is not the opposite of censorship but is part and parcel of it.

The scales certainly seem tipped. On one side is a vast apparatus with plenty of carrots to offer, backed ultimately by the same big stick that struck down dissent in the first place. On the other side are individuals in networks both scattered and fragile, prone to disconnection, discouragement, and disappearance. As should be obvious, to emphasize the productiveness of censorship is *not* intended to sugarcoat it. In addition to its generative dimension, the destructive is still there, with death or long prison terms at one end of the spectrum. It would be callous to suggest that something like Foucault's "repressive hypothesis" regarding the relationship between power and sex in Victorian England applies to power and Tiananmen in China today. The massacre itself, on the night of June 3 to 4, 1989, is censorship's destructiveness executed to the extreme.

While not mitigating censorship's harms, *Made in Censorship* nevertheless denies political defeatism and fatalism. In the face of the imbalance, some still press for change. They challenge the ownership of the Tiananmen movement, which the regime tried to classify not long after the massacre. In declassifying Tiananmen, they affirm that, as event and experience, it belongs in the public and to the public. They give Tiananmen back to the Chinese public so that every reader and viewer can re-read it, re-view it, and re-appropriate it, despite and through censorship as a (de)formative force.

A certain circularity, which Michael Warner describes as a characteristic of any public, is inscribed in its very organization: "A public might be real and efficacious, but its reality lies in just this reflexivity by which an addressable object is conjured into being in order to enable the very discourse that gives it existence."[32] Address in this equation plays a seminal role. The role, as I see it in *Made in Censorship*, calls for a conscious righting of the scales. Barred though we may be from that physical square in Beijing, we can nevertheless take part in activating the potential in what Miriam Hansen describes as "a discursive matrix or process through which social experience is articulated, interpreted, negotiated and contested in an intersubjective, potentially collective and oppositional form."[33] Addressed by Tiananmen literature and film, I in turn now address the reader, you. A spiral dynamic grows out of the circular, as public upon public is forwarded to new addresses.

CHAPTER ONE

Rebuilding the Republic

State Propaganda in the Wake of Tiananmen

On the morning of June 5, 1989, a lone man stood not far from Tiananmen Square in the middle of Chang'an Avenue, the thoroughfare that cuts through the heart of Beijing. Just the day before, government troops had retaken the square by force, clearing it of the protestors who had occupied it in the hundreds of thousands since mid-April, demanding social reforms and political freedom. Now this solitary individual stood alone in front of a column of tanks. The lead tank tried to go around him, but he kept blocking its way, at one point even climbing onto the tank before eventually being spirited away from the scene by bystanders.

Captured by foreign reporters stationed in a nearby hotel, photographs and videos of the Tank Man have circulated worldwide ever since. That the man's identity and whereabouts remain a subject of speculation to this day has only inflated his iconicity. For many viewers, here was the dramatic conflict between Human and Machine, the individual and the state, bravery and brutality—crystallized in a single image. Besides these binaries, the Tank Man has also come to symbolize Chinese censorship. In the 2006 PBS documentary *The Tank Man*, a U.S. reporter shows Chinese university students a reproduction of the image and asks whether they can identify it. In confirmation of the reporter's suspicions, the students claim ignorance. Journalist Louisa Lim repeats the experiment in *The People's Republic of Amnesia: Tiananmen Revisited* (2014). Lim again questions students on Beijing university campuses on the Tank Man photo. Only fifteen out of one hundred recognize it.[1] The result of her test and the title of her book reinforce each other. At stake is the "amnesia" forced upon future generations of the Chinese. The interviewees—the same ages as those of the 1989 student protestors—are ignorant of their predecessors, preemptively cleansed of memories of them in their entirety.

The Tank Man, then, simultaneously signifies its wide currency outside China and its blackout within. That was not always the case, however. The footage broadcast around the world was actually played on Chinese television, too. Instead of being used as a shorthand for the clash between repression and resistance, this footage was presented to the domestic audience quite differently. This is the audio that accompanies the video: "Anyone with common sense can see that if our tanks were determined to move on, this lone scoundrel could never have stopped them. This scene recorded on videotape flies in the face of Western propaganda. It proves that our soldiers exercised the highest degree of restraint." This voice-over narration appears in the TV program *Flutter, Flag of the Republic: A Record of the Quelling of the Beijing Counterrevolutionary Riot*, produced by the People's Liberation Army (PLA) in July 1989 (figure 1.1). Outside China, through "Western propaganda," the Tank Man may perpetuate the liberal political worldview.[2] Inside China, however, the iconic image is just as amenable to a model of paternalistic governance. The stern male voice reinterprets—even though the meaning is self-evident to "anyone with common sense"—the confrontation between the state and the Tank Man as the forbearance of the father, on one side, and a renegade's brazenness, on the other. All challengers of state authority must be lone wolves because the broad masses of the people stand with the Chinese Communist Party (CCP) and its army.

More than a reframing of that encounter, the above excerpt indicates that total elision was not the only way the Party-state handled the 1989 protests. In addition to precluding alternative voices from domestic newspapers, airwaves, and screens, in the immediate aftermath of June Fourth the state launched a coordinated campaign in text, image, and sound to delineate and then disseminate its own narrative. The censorship of June Fourth has always been a total project of both proscription and prescription, prohibition and exhibition, silencing and speech. Government propaganda, of which *Flutter, Flag of the Republic*

FIGURE 1.1 The Tank Man, recast in *Flutter, Flag of the Republic* (1989).

is but one example, should not be viewed as the opposite of censorship. Rather, it is a crucial dimension of censorship itself, a dimension almost always overlooked.

This chapter focuses on literary and audiovisual propaganda produced in the wake of June Fourth by the PLA. The PLA itself illustrates the duality of censorship in its simultaneous deployment of both destructive and creative forces: on the one hand, it uses tanks on citizens; on the other, it uses its General Political Department and the numerous organs in news, publishing, education, and the arts under its control (including the newspaper *PLA Daily*, the journal *PLA Literature and Art*, the PLA Arts Academy, the PLA Song and Dance Troupe and Spoken Drama Troupe, the August First Film Studio, and the PLA Publishing House) in attempts to mold those same citizens.[3] Both case studies in this chapter issue from the PLA's General Political Department. The first, *Songs of the Republic's Guardians: Collection of Reportage Literature on Martial Law Troops' Heroic Deeds in the Capital*, was published in October 1989 by the PLA Publishing House. This volume compiles tales of sacrifice by the "Republic's Guardians," a decoration bestowed in part by Deng Xiaoping—chairman of the Central Military Commission and the ultimate arbiter in the use of force on June 3 and 4—upon soldiers killed or wounded during the crackdown. My second case study is a detailed evaluation of *Flutter, Flag of the Republic*, produced a mere month after June 4 by the General Political Department's Propaganda Division. This four-part documentary presents a chronological account, from the seeds of the protest movement to the resumption of control by the state.

After an overview of the overall print propaganda campaign, I return to *Songs of the Republic's Guardians*, analyzing the characterization of protestors "ignorant of the truth" in contradistinction to the exemplary soldiers. My analysis of that work's literary description of the soldiers' martyrdom is then followed by a critique of the trope's visualization in *Flutter, Flag of the Republic*. As my study demonstrates, the unruliness of images persists there, opening to multiple meanings in the documentary despite manipulation. False as both materials are in fact, they nevertheless bring to the fore what censorship produces, from memories tailored to collectivities shaped. The materials are treated neither as outright lies to be dismissed nor as historical records to be taken at face value. Instead, they are treated as fictions, that is, something made and fabricated.[4] This chapter uncovers their productive strategies and recovers their repressed truths.

PROPAGATING THE PROTESTS

The censorship of June Fourth—the prescription of the authorized line, the proscription of alternative accounts—began before June 4, 1989. The propaganda in the aftermath was a continuation and expansion of the campaign that started during the protest movement itself. With the conquest of Beijing and the rest of the country following June 4, however, the war of words ratcheted up. In addition to regular pronouncements from the recaptured press, the state churned out books and pamphlets quickly. Of the more than fifty titles I surveyed, nearly two-thirds were published in the second half of 1989. But the spate of publications was short-lived. A quarter of them appeared in 1990.

By 1991, the stream had slowed to a trickle. As far as I could ascertain, none came after 1991. (I will return to the timing of the propaganda's surcease at the end of this chapter.)

In terms of space, the production of materials, as well as their distribution through official channels, was widespread. Beijing was the hub, the center of both China's publishing industry and the protest movement. Yet publications issued from over a dozen cities throughout the country, from the northeast to the south, from the coast to inland areas. This geographical range reflects the reach of the demonstrations themselves, which extended to more than one hundred cities. While most non-Beijing books also concern mainly Beijing, some of them are decidedly limited in scope, dealing with local outbreaks.[5] A few Beijing publications, on the other hand, aim at audiences abroad. Printed not in the simplified Chinese script of mainland China but in the traditional script used in Hong Kong, Taiwan, and certain overseas communities, they explicitly state their addressees as "Chinese foreign nationals, Chinese nationals, and countrymen in Hong Kong, Macau, and Taiwan."[6] English translations of Chinese materials, meanwhile, came out of the government's Foreign Languages Press.[7]

Whether the targeted readership is foreign or domestic, there are, as I see it, five narrative modes at work in the entire corpus of June Fourth propaganda: imperative, pedagogical, retrospective, documentary, and artistic. They are not mutually exclusive categories, and they are certainly not exhaustive. In fact, all five are properties, to varying degrees, of every publication, including *Songs of the Republic's Guardians* and *Flutter, Flag of the Republic,* as I will show. Nevertheless, they not only provide here a provisionary typology of the mass of materials but also implicate distinctive functions and effects.

In the first mode, the imperative, I count propaganda of the heavy-handed sort. It speaks in directives. This mode takes its cue from the infamous April 26, 1989, editorial of the Party mouthpiece *People's Daily.* Titled "It is necessary to take a clear-cut stance against the turmoil," the editorial labeled the budding student protests as "turmoil" (*dongluan*), a term associated with the Cultural Revolution of 1966–1976 launched by Mao Zedong that had plunged the country into chaos.[8] Chaos would recur, sabotaging the economic and political advances made by the state since the late 1970s if the "extremely few people" (*jishaoshu ren*) agitating behind the scenes were left to their own devices. This minority flies the banner of democracy while "harboring ulterior motives" (*bieyou yongxin*). Against it, the broad majority of people must "take a clear-cut stance" (*qizhi xianming*) or, more literally, show the flag. Martial in rhetoric, the imperative mode brooks no opposition. A small but significant strain of propaganda in the wake of June Fourth manifests this mode.[9] It is in fact the mode underlying all state propaganda as command production.

The second mode, the pedagogical, teaches. It emphasizes enlightenment and elucidation, carried out in a didactic manner. Because students initiated the movement and populated its ranks, they are naturally the subject as well as the audience of many publications. One such publication, from the Beijing Communist Youth League, specifically aims at "league members and youths," while another trumpets its role in the "campaign to help primary and secondary school students study and develop 'love for the Communist Party of China, love for the socialist fatherland, love for the People's Liberation Army.' "[10] The Ministry of Education, for its part, made an effort to discredit the "elites" (*jingying*), both student leaders and intellectuals who supported the cause.[11] A major format was the textbook that collected "study materials."[12] But these textbooks were not restricted to use in the classroom. On campus and at work, mandatory "discussions" of June Fourth took place. Both the pedagogical and the imperative modes were characteristic of these sessions, which, far from being open discussions, lacked even, in James Lull's felicitous phrase, the "freedom of silence."[13] For those in school and in the public at large, catechism is a method of choice, as testified by the multitude of books in the form of questions and answers.[14] Each of the twelve chapters in *1989: Looking Back and Reflecting After the Turmoil*, for example, is organized around a single question, such as "What role did 'Voice of America' play in this turmoil?"[15]

Terms like *looking back* and *reflecting* in the title above are striking in their ruminative quality. Yet the gesture of retrospection is prevalent enough in the propaganda to warrant its own mode. Such words not only signal the past, as all the materials necessarily do, coming after the event. They also perform memory, or more exactly, "identification under the sign of memory."[16] They reveal an approach to June Fourth that is not of simple erasure but of recasting and realignment in the guise of remembrance. In an important article, historians Joseph Esherick and Jeffrey Wasserstrom analyze the 1989 protests as "symbol-laden performances whose efficacy lies largely in their power to move specific audiences."[17] The students, consciously or unconsciously, made use of a "repertoire" of actions and followed "scripts" both national and international, pitting their "theater" against state "ritual." But to extend Esherick and Wasserstrom, the propaganda state also tried to rewrite the students' scripts and sever certain associations. If the June Fourth movement of 1989 is to be located in history, government texts argue, then the connection made is not to the May Fourth movement of 1919, when another unresponsive Beijing government drove students to Tiananmen Square clamoring for science and democracy. The 1919 movement influenced generations of Chinese activists, including those who would later found the CCP. The student demonstrators seventy years later saw themselves very much in this lineage of political action, gathering around the Monument to the People's Heroes in the square where May Fourth is memorialized. But government texts attempt to tie them instead to the Cultural Revolution, as mentioned above, or situate them in the 1980s as the last straw in a decade of student protests, or as evidence of the increasing incursion of "bourgeois liberalization."[18] Retrospection here, like the pedagogy above and documentation below, is never neutral. To look back on the protests in the "proper" manner—for participant, sympathizer, or current reader—should be to repent. *Motherland, Please Listen to Me: Reflections of the Capital's College Students After the Turmoil*, again from the Beijing Communist Youth League, makes evident the note of suppliant remorse.[19]

Analogous to the retrospective is the documentary mode. It makes up the largest share of the propaganda. It consists mainly of the self-styled "record" or "chronicle" of riot-quelling and includes the "eyewitness account."[20] If the quintessential gesture of the retrospective is to look back, then the quintessential gesture of the documentary is to write down. The former performs memory; the latter, truth.[21] Like the retrospective, the documentary does not stoop to simple erasure. This time, however, it perpetuates the most outrageous distortions and omissions in the guise of inscription and testimony, mixing falsehoods with facts, taking images out of context. The documentary mode can get away with it because the Party-state, in addition to the presses, has at its disposal the guns. More than historiography is at play. The object of the game is not only to convince Chinese readers and viewers of the truth of what they are told but also to tell them the rules of the game they must play by.[22] All the better if they believe, but at the very least, they will learn what discourse is allowed in public and what is not.

Apart from chronicling June Fourth as a whole, a subset of documentary narratives focuses on the soldiers who took part in the seizure of Tiananmen Square and the quashing of the protests.[23] Within this subset I distinguish a fifth and final mode: artistic. This mode is characterized, to be sure, by the use of literary devices—symbolism, imagery, figural language. But just as decisive are factors external to the writing itself, such as publication by "literature and arts publishing houses,"[24] or titles that echo the literary canon, especially in the genre of reportage literature.[25] My first case study, *Songs of the Republic's Guardians: Collection of Reportage Literature on Martial Law Troops' Heroic Deeds in the Capital*, is drawn from this mode. Why? Because the book that is literary by self-presentation has even more license to be creative than accounts that advertise the truth. It is all the freer, then, to pursue its objective, which is the objective of all state propaganda, no matter the mode: to remold a people obedient to the Party and to remake the republic as the only valid public.

THE BENIGHTED CROWD

Songs of the Republic's Guardians comprises fifteen short-story-length pieces of reportage literature by nineteen authors on sixteen "Republic's Guardians" (as well as a few other "heroic" individuals and units). No editor is listed, although a preface, penned by a PLA general (Guo Linxiang), states that the authors are writers and journalists within the military. Who are they? Without detailing their names, some of them work in the political department—responsible for such tasks as propaganda and political education—of various PLA administrative units.[26] Others work specifically in the "Office of Literary and Artistic Creation," located within many PLA political departments.[27] Many are also members of the China Writers Association (CWA), which is not a civic association but a government-controlled organization whose membership—voluntary and competitive—is on the state payroll.[28]

Songs of the Republic's Guardians actually contains a piece on a military writer. It is not much of a portrait, however; all the reader essentially learns about the press officer (a certain Yu Ronglu) is that, after "thugs" and "masses" attacked and stopped the vehicle in which he was riding, he proceeded on foot to Tiananmen Square and got killed on the way. He is a cipher next to the function he served, as indicated by the title of the piece itself, "He Used His Life to Finish a Last News Item." Shortly before his death, he had apparently written "Suspicion, Understanding, Love: The Masses' Changing Feelings Toward Martial Law Troops in a Certain Beijing Suburb." Whether this article is descriptive or proleptic—trying to enact what it purports to report—it is a useful reminder that the war of publicity, censorship as the realignment of opinion, was waged from the beginning. The press officer continued to contribute to the state campaign after his death, and not just with the news of his own martyrdom. On his remains was allegedly found a manuscript titled "Soldiers: The Homeland's Interests Trump All Else," which was later published in the PLA newspaper.[29] "He used his life," and they used his death.

In *Doing Things with Words in Chinese Politics*, Michael Schoenhals argues that prescription is more effective than proscription in governing speech and therewith consolidating and preserving state power. No matter the author, certain phrases appear verbatim in every piece of *Songs of the Republic's Guardians*. These formulations (*tifa*) include "crowds ignorant of the truth" (*buming zhenxiang de qunzhong*) for gatherings of protestors or, alternatively, "thugs mixed into the muddle-headed people," which unfailingly foreshadows violence on the thugs' part. Whenever a "thug" (*baotu*) opens his mouth, it is almost always to shout in reference to a solider: "Kill him!" But if a soldier uses his gun at all, it is to "fire a warning shot into the sky." The repetition of these formulas throughout the collection bespeaks not just the careful inspection (*shencha*) of the pieces but also the very subsumption of authorship under a master code.[30] This is the extent to which propaganda production can be said to be "collaborative." The writers of *Songs* are themselves not granted immunity. They have to abide by the imperative of this code and not run afoul of it—knowing full well nonetheless both the disproportionate casualties suffered by the other side and the untold other stories of heroism and sacrifice.

Despite the code that governs the writing, it is possible to read *Songs of the Republic's Guardians* against the grain, turning it into alter-production. In many ways the genre of reportage itself makes this possible. "Reportage" is a leftist cultural legacy, coined in the 1920s by German communist writers from the French *reportage* to refer to investigative reports on the labor movement that were agitational in nature. Since its beginnings, "reportage literature" (*baogao wenxue*) has sought to construct collective forms of consciousness and identification.[31] Contradictions come to a head in *Songs*, however, where agitation and mobilization—in the form of the "extremely few people" "inciting" (*shandong*) the masses—are expressly bemoaned. Meanwhile, readers are bombarded with the most graphic depictions of civilian brutality and the passion of the PLA to move their sympathies to the military and to glorify the collective represented by the Party-state.

In terms of literary lineage, *Songs of the Republic's Guardians* harks back to two subgenres of early reportage: war and public demonstration. The conversion of everyday space into combat zones echoes the former, while the depiction of large gatherings of people recalls the latter. A passage on the peculiar challenge faced by soldiers displays both elements: "Their sacrifice took place neither beneath the enemy's knife nor upon a smoke-filled battlefield, but in Beijing, the capital of 1.1 billion people, on avenues with modernized buildings and facilities. What they faced was not a fully armed enemy wearing camouflage, but a bustling crowd wearing all colors of clothing, within which may be their friends, their brothers and sisters" (97). A city that in peacetime is the setting of "modernization" is thrown back in time, as it were, by the havoc wreaked by the unrest. The "Four Modernizations," in the domains of agriculture, industry, science and technology, and national defense, were officially implemented in the late 1970s.[32] This modernization program is now in jeopardy because the very seat of government is in jeopardy. But the threat is no ordinary one indeed. As the passage attests, the crowd is not armed, belying the legitimacy of its ultimate suppression by force. With "all colors of clothing," it also represents the broad, variegated base of the protests. The possibility that even the soldiers' families and friends may be participants indicates how widely supported they are. It is the military, therefore, that turned Beijing into a battlefield.

If the avenues of Beijing constitute a public space that needs to be reclaimed from a motley populace, then the central square to which they lead is even more crucial. Tiananmen Square became the epicenter of activity on April 15, 1989, when spontaneous tributes to the deceased former Party Secretary General Hu Yaobang, viewed as a reformer, soon swelled to mass demonstrations. Such uses of the square are unacceptable; it is strictly for picture-taking—or so presumes this statement from a deceased soldier's brother on a visit the two of them had paid during the protests: "We originally wanted to take photos in front of Tiananmen and send them to our parents. When we excitedly arrived at Tiananmen Square, we were shocked: all we saw were forests of tents, trash everywhere, all kinds of banners and flags waving chaotically, the sound of loudspeakers and shouts causing a headache. Huaiqing said to me indignantly: How did our capital get defiled like this!" (86). To take one's picture at Tiananmen and then send it to one's parents is more than an act of filiality. It is also an act of loyalty, the assertion of a "bond between the individual and the state."[33] The only occupation of the square allowed is the momentary one of standing in front of a camera. All other ones, especially those that might endure, are desecrations of a hallowed ground. The heterogeneity of that space at that time—with a multitude of banners flying in addition to the flag of the People's Republic of China (PRC), with loudspeakers in the hands of people and not just affixed to the top of light poles—stuns the soldiers, unaccustomed as they are to this kind of repurposing of monumental space. They may not have wound up taking pictures and sending them to their parents, but the above picture is a souvenir sent to the present, when the sanctified ritual of posing before Tiananmen has resumed its place.

Contrary to its early precedents, the reportage of *Songs of the Republic's Guardians* constantly deplores the public demonstration. The masses are merely "bustling," as observed above, or gawkers at the "bustling scene" whose involvement is the largely passive one of "joining in the bustle." Although crowds have been portrayed as acted upon rather than capable of agency since early China, their characterization in *Songs* conjures up the figure of the crowd as voyeur in modern Chinese literature.[34] In the canonical fiction of the writer Lu Xun, from the oft-cited "Preface" (1922) and "The Real Story of

Ah-Q" (1921–1922) in *Outcry* to "A Public Example" (1925) in *Hesitation*, spectators at execution scenes invariably exercise a cannibalistic gaze. Whereas Lu Xun, according to Haiyan Lee, shifts the lines of conflict from the state versus society to the crowd versus the individual, *Songs*, in turn, shifts them to the crowd versus the state.[35] It reverses the trend that Marston Anderson espies from the 1930s, when "the vengeful, persecutory crowds of 1920s' fiction, who had as often as not instilled feelings of terror in readers, were replaced by unified, purposeful political aggregations, that is, the masses."[36] In *Songs* the masses devolve back into mobs. Metaphors from those earlier days reappear, such as the elements of wind, water, and fire ("tide," "tempest," "torrent") and the animal and insect kingdom ("frenzied tigers," "swarms"). Individuals lose their minds, swayed by inhuman forces: "The innumerable heads under the streetlights were like a black river, swelling to and fro. As soon as the squadron neared Xidan, it was broken up and submerged by the black waves" (190). Thus does the figural language stigmatize the public constituted by the protestors.

Yet the seemingly natural phenomenon has an unnatural cause: guileful words sweep it into commotion. Earlier the pandemonium on the square repelled the two soldiers, and elsewhere the protestors are portrayed as incapable of speech, emitting mere noise: "all kinds of tones and pitches, hoarse, shrill, aged, puerile, mixed with shameless whistling, formed an ear-splitting wave of sound" (203). Complementing this portraiture is the imputation of rumor-mongering and lying to those "harboring ulterior motives," both student leaders and "thugs." Instead of causing a headache, their words inflame the gullible masses. Witness how two college students ply their trade, to the consternation of a soldier named Zhao Guohai:

> "City residents! Countrymen! We come from Tiananmen Square. We witnessed everything that happened there. We cannot but tell everybody with grief that the nation's heart, beating rapidly these many days for democracy, has just shed scarlet blood . . ."
>
> This extremely agitational speech, like smoke released from a magic bottle, spread its black wings wider and wider, soaring smugly high in the sky.

People's feelings were infected, from silence to vigor, from excitement to frenzy, eyes shooting sparks, teeth flashing light. The whole world seemed to be trembling from those teeth.

"You can't speak nonsense without evidence!" Zhao Guohai's hoarse voice interrupted the college student's speech. He knew the danger of his situation and even more the weight of responsibility he carried.

"Without evidence? This is a bulletin just come from Tiananmen Square. If you don't believe it, read it to everybody yourself."

The college student put the "bulletin" in Zhao Guohai's hand. Guohai returned it without looking at it. (206–7)

This excerpt stands out for its representation of college students. Other scenes of dialogue between them and soldiers in *Songs of the Republic's Guardians*, borrowing the catechistic format of the pedagogical strain of propaganda noted before, are in actuality question-and-answer sessions. Military cadres play the masters, while their pupils are reduced to responses like "These words made the college student blush and say repeatedly: 'It is so, it is so!,'" "Students and soldiers applauded together in agreement," and "Several students said with a smile: 'What you say is right, what you say is right!' " (240–41). In the encounter above, however, Zhao Guohai accuses the college students of "speaking nonsense." But by giving them, when they are presumably in a state of urgency, a highly stylized opening—"the nation's heart, beating rapidly these many days for democracy, has just shed scarlet blood"—the author implies that these rabble-rousers are only too artful in rhetoric, easily manipulating their audience. The author condemns the "extremely agitational speech," describing the listeners thus "infected" in monstrous terms, as frenzied beasts with flashing teeth and eyes on fire. The soldier Zhao Guohai, on the other hand, is the lone voice of reason amid a sea of rage. A member of the state apparatus assumes the role of defiant dissent.

But civilian blood *was* shed, if not specifically on Tiananmen Square, then all around it. And "people's feelings *were* infected." The passage documents this truth. What rises unbidden from the "magic bottle" is the genius of reportage as a genre, in the mobilization of the disaggregated into a collective. In the face of passion, Zhao Guohai supposedly appeals to rationality by emphasizing evidence. In the end, though, he is the one who refuses rather than refutes the evidence presented by the other side. His gesture of not looking is synecdoche for the Party-state's blinding of divergent political visions. The scare quotes around "bulletin" intend its duplicity.[37] The real fear, however, resides in the fact of its publication, its status as an alter-production in a mediascape previously monopolized by government organs.[38] Hearing a new speech, the people are moved "from silence to vigor." It is this movement that causes "trembling."

Who speaks for the nation is the heart of the matter. The college students call the crowd "countrymen," and the people they address include not only the actual audience gathered around them and not just the public that composes the ordained People's Republic but also an imagined alternative to that public that they seek to evoke into being. One of the state's primary tasks in the wake of June Fourth is to quash this plurality, especially in the very signification of "the people" (*renmin*). Another exchange, this time between a soldier and a Beijing resident, demonstrates what is at stake. The resident, referring to the crowds he sees, asks the soldier rhetorically, "Is the power of the people great or what?" to which the soldier replies: "Of course the power of the people is great, but can you represent the people? Can those who obstruct military vehicles and oppose the Liberation Army represent the people?" His questions render his interlocutor "speechless in response" (59–60). The soldier cleverly turns the issue into one of quality over quantity: those blocking the PLA's way may be people, and a lot of people, but they do not "represent" the people. For the determination hinged not on "the people" at all. It hinged on "power." The might of the military prevailed on June 4, 1989. Yet the outcome of the battle over "the people" remained uncertain. The Party-state was well aware that brute force alone could not rebuild the republic. Representation, as the soldier stressed, would be paramount to this project. And so, in addition to the aimless crowds, the vicious thugs, and the vainglorious leaders of the movement, *Songs of the Republic's Guardians* had to craft a pantheon of worthies, a model public in print to be emulated by the reading public.

The Chinese state cannot afford to purge the totality of protestors and sympathizers. That would mean millions of people. For theoretical guidance, it turns to Mao Zedong and his well-known distinction, in "On the Correct Handling of Contradictions Among the People," between antagonistic and nonantagonistic contradictions. Soldiers are therefore urged to "concentrate your hatred on an extremely few provokers and plotters of the riot and a small group of bad elements, strictly carry out orders, carefully distinguish between two different kinds of contradiction" (158). The antagonistic kind, vis-à-vis enemies of the people, can only be resolved through annihilation. The nonantagonistic kind, within "the people," involves reorienting those temporarily led astray. One scheme for achieving the latter is hagiography.

Partaking of the retrospective mode, *Songs of the Republic's Guardians* draws on the mythos furnished by the past exploits of the PLA. It constantly reminds readers of the fact that the PLA collective—and the CCP that it serves—has been in existence for a lot longer than the collective centered on Tiananmen Square. Repeated invocations of the army's history bind it irrevocably with the history of nation building. They include fighting in the Second Sino-Japanese War, or the War of Resistance Against Japanese Aggression (1937–1945); "volunteering" in the Korean War, or the War to Resist U.S. Aggression and Aid Korea (1950–1953); and contributing to relief efforts after the deadly Tangshan earthquake of 1976. Therefore, the soldiers carrying out the order to clear Tiananmen Square must be either combatting aggression or responding to disaster. They are carrying on the glorious mission of forging and protecting the PRC. And those who give up their lives in doing so, the martyrs of June Fourth, join an undying rank of 20 million who have previously fallen for the nation. This number, across time, dwarfs the number, across space, demonstrating all over the country. Thus is *Songs'* relationship to memory characterized not solely by erasure but also by reconstruction in the service of remaking the (re)public.[39]

Songs of the Republic's Guardians borrows not a little from the legend of Lei Feng (1940–1962), the PLA soldier lionized after death in periodic campaigns for his selflessness and service to the people.[40]

The Republic's Guardians, too, exemplify public-mindedness. They forsake the individual for the greater good, like the military police officer Li Guorui: "Thus towards his own pleasures Li Guorui is 'miserly;' towards the collective, however, he is 'generous.'" His family is not only a private sphere that needs to be transcended; Li revalues the word itself: "He loves his mother, who gave birth to him and raised him, but he loves even more the family that is the army" (176, 181–82). Affiliation—Party and army—overtakes filiation elsewhere as well, where another soldier is apostrophized: "But when family matters and army matters came into conflict, the pole on your shoulder would start to lean: the 'big family' far outweighed the 'little family.'" It would be a mistake, however, to assume that familial structures are accordingly crumbling. Instead, the "big family" is a continuation of the "little family," replicating the latter's line of authority. As the same soldier's mother relates, "When he was little he listened to me; when he grew up he listened to the Party" (147, 150). Over the course of natural development, the Party-army inherits the mantle of maternity.

Women do not fare well in *Songs of the Republic's Guardians*. Actual mothers, as opposed to the party surrogates, are always getting left behind. In one of the pieces, a certain political commissar does not go home to see his gravely ill mother but stays with the army in its time of need, while a soldier, on leave to visit his sick mother, rejoins his unit ahead of schedule. In two other pieces, daughters are "bestowed" by their parents upon the army following the brothers' deaths. Brides are not spared either. In a fourth piece, one of the soldiers protests to his superiors, who want him to stay behind with his fiancée: "Does my own wedding matter? Going to Beijing to carry out the order is the big matter" (38). The only kind of defiance allowed is that of obeying the command.

Sick mothers, dumped daughters, and spurned lovers are not the only women in *Songs of the Republic's Guardians*. None belongs to the pantheon, to be sure. Most preside instead over the domestic domain, either raising heroes and/or mourning their untimely deaths. Nevertheless, the collection supplements their function as conveyor belts—of young men into the service—by sometimes staging their own entries into the public. A woman can share the stage with a man, for example, by rescuing him.[41] Or she can follow in his footsteps. The fiancée of the soldier Ma Guoxuan, a twenty-year-old village girl, was suicidal when she first heard of Ma's death, personifying the type for whom romantic love is everything. But it comes as no surprise that she is successfully integrated by the end, deciding to join the army and thereby completing the same journey made before her by other female characters in literary and film classics from the socialist period.[42] In her own voice, she describes her transformation from a melancholic woman into an ecstatic revolutionary: "I have only one wish now: to take up Guoxuan's gun, carry on his legacy, and give all of myself to the Party!" (118). The party saved her life, and in return, she sacrifices her life for the party. A Communist variant of the Hollywood ending, the lovelorn girl has found love again.

Elsewhere, even though only the soldier Zhang Zhen is decorated as a Republic's Guardian, his sisters also receive commendation for their sacrifices behind the scenes. The author's praise of women quickly expands to this concluding panegyric: "I hope that whoever wishes to remember Zhang Zhen remembers also his younger sister Xiaojie, his youngest sister, as well as the numerous people who have nurtured and helped him. Since the names of these numerous people cannot all be remembered, please remember their generic name: the people" (136–37). "The people" reappears, linked to "numerous people." But numbers, as seen earlier, do not mean much. The protestors, no matter their number, can never constitute the people because they do not have the right to "name." This right belongs not to the author either, but to might, the authority behind the author.

Retrospection and documentation, and not simply forgetting and deleting, form the censorship project. "Remember," above, appears four times in two sentences. The repetition reveals the anxiety in *Songs of the Republic's Guardians* over memory and historiography, how June Fourth is passed down. The anxiety reveals itself again in a different scene, this time extending from the literary to the visual: "Some people are afraid of not getting into the foreign reporter's shot and getting forgotten by history; they willingly serve as extras for the foreign reporter, heading straight for the camera, smiling to reveal a mouthful of yellow teeth" (9). The foreign reporter records, yet in his film the Chinese figure not as protagonists but only as "extras," used by the reporter for his "foreign" narrative. "Extras" in Chinese (*qunzhong yanyuan*) literally means "crowd actors." Those who perform for a foreigner cannot be a part of "the people." The "yellow" teeth fawning for the camera's Western gaze is a not-so-subtle suggestion of (self-)orientalization. It soon becomes evident, however, who is the one "afraid" in regard to the camera and the history it documents. A military officer orders the foreign reporter, inside a car, to turn over his camera and film, citing martial law. When the reporter's Chinese interpreter tries to keep the car door closed, the military officer responds: "Are you a Chinese? If so, open the door." After he confiscates the equipment, "To his surprise, not a few people actually spoke up on the foreign reporter's behalf, rebuking [the officer] for interfering with press freedom." Livid, the officer again wonders "whether there is still a Chinese soul inside those people" (9–10). One's nationality is supposed to be the alpha and omega, and within the community projected by *Songs*, "press freedom" and "Chinese" cannot be imagined together. By defending the former, the interpreter as well as the others necessarily betray the latter. In fact, freedom in general is suspect, as in this depiction of an intellectual through the eyes and ears of a soldier:

> He heard some celebrities lecturing on freedom and democracy.
>
> Pushing up a pair of glasses on his nose with his forefinger, a lecturer hurled abuse at China's history, denounced China's present, and smeared the image of the Chinese nation. Whoever's words were the most cutting and whoever's abuse was the harshest received the most welcome applause and cheers. The fevered listening audience all raised their fingers in the shape of scissors, as if to cut something. (15–16)

The lampoon of the bespectacled intellectual is a familiar one in a Communist iconography that exalts the triad of the worker, peasant, and soldier. Like the two college students discussed previously, this "celebrity" knows how to work the muddle-headed crowd into a frenzy. The fingers making scissors is, of course, the V-sign, here viewed by the soldier with incomprehension. Together with "freedom and democracy," they compose a semiology that is not just foreign and unintelligible to the Party-state faithful but inimical to China itself.

As one of four people who staged a hunger strike on Tiananmen Square days before June 4, the intellectual Liu Xiaobo was a "celebrity" even in 1989.[43] *Songs of the Republic's Guardians* does not mention him by name, but he is the "madman" referred to here: "That madman who wants China to 'be a colony for 300 years' is sitting on Tiananmen Square. That is the most dangerous omen" (16). Liu's quote is taken from a 1988 interview with a Hong Kong magazine where, remarking upon the achievements of Hong Kong after one hundred years of British colonialism, he opined that China would need three hundred years of colonialism to attain something similar, given its size.[44] This provocative statement is presented as evidence that the leaders of the protest movement are compradors who would trade away China's nationhood, which was won under the leadership of the CCP from imperialist forces that had robbed China of the territory of Hong Kong in the first place.[45] A couple of pages later, the dyad of national peril and salvation is summoned again to mobilize patriotic feeling: "If the 'Eight-Nation Alliance' were to stage a comeback, if invaders snatched your ear and were about to slit your throat, you'd probably scream: 'Save me, Liberation Army'" (18). Comprising Austria-Hungary, France, Germany, Italy, Japan, Russia, the United Kingdom, and the United States, the "Eight-Nation Alliance" intervened in the suppression of the Boxer Rebellion in northern China, an uprising against foreign missionaries as well as native Christians at the turn of the twentieth century.[46] Now the alliance recalls not only the perennially imminent threat of foreign impingements on Chinese sovereignty but also a time of national weakness and shame. *Songs* reopens old wounds in cultural memory, the better to highlight the healer. The Liberation Army, confiscating cameras and pacifying protests, is actually the protector of the Chinese public and the People's Republic from exogenous injury and endogenous harm.

SCAR LITERATURE, SCAR TV

Imperialist depredations are not the only wounds that *Songs of the Republic's Guardians* rehashes for the post–June Fourth public. A surprising source of painful memory is the Maoist past. *Songs* unmistakably laments the hardships not of the "old society" of presocialist China commonly depicted in literature and film of the socialist period but of the socialist period itself. It was a time, recounts one of the pieces, of "'[r]ather socialism's grass than capitalism's sprout.' Each work point was worth five, six cents; a whole day's labor couldn't bring in half a yuan" (34). In repudiating the point system of agricultural labor allocation and incentivization, *Songs* points in retrospect not just to the poverty but also to the ideological straitjacket that constricted those years. It is emblematic of a postsocialist schizophrenia caught between a socialist aesthetic and capitalist ethic, with soldiers staying on as the literary heroes but with peasants and workers relegated to the role of villains. Of the four "thugs" captured and interrogated in another piece, three are urban "drifters" (*mangliu*), vagrants from the countryside with no job prospects in sight (13). Elsewhere, the troublemakers are again identified as "migrant workers from the outer provinces" (208). They have wandered far indeed from the land where they were once masters.[47]

Songs of the Republic's Guardians is willfully unaware that the Party-state, in unleashing a market economy, set these people adrift in the first place. Herein lies another of its contradictions. It tries to impress on readers how good they have it now compared to before the economic reforms, obviating the need for protest. Yet social problems appear even in this collection of reportage, as if influenced by the larger trends of the genre itself.[48] Unemployment, the rural–urban divide, and the breakdown of public welfare—all of which worsened in the reform era and fed the discontent of the 1989 protests—are but a few of the problems peeping through the cracks. Seeing an old man beg for food in a county seat, one soldier says to him: "Why did you come here for work? Can't you get rich by farming at home? . . . Even people in town are looking for employment; it's not easy finding work" (114). Rural poverty is again the issue when the soldier Zhang Zhen's sister Xiaojie—the subject of praise cited earlier—gets leukemia, and the family does not have money to pay for her treatment. The reforms of the 1980s boosted China's economic growth and efficiency. But they also effected dramatic societal upheavals. Inflation soared. The social safety net thinned. The "iron rice bowl" of secure employment cracked as factories weaned off the state fired, laid off, or simply did not pay their workers. The defects of the reforms were a major catalyst for the protests that paired social grievances with political demands, as in the widespread call for an end to rampant government corruption.

In lieu of attributing the movement to the structural cataclysms of the 1980s, *Songs of the Republic's Guardians* links it to another decade. The "10 years' turmoil," below, is the semiofficial designation of the Cultural Revolution of 1966–1976: "Our country already experienced the pain of 10 years' turmoil, which left in many people's hearts a scar hard to erase" (202). As another instance of "turmoil," the 1989 protests must not fester for another ten years. Yet by picking at that previous "scar," *Songs* consciously aligns itself with "scar literature" (*shanghen wenxue*), a wave of writing in the aftermath of the Cultural Revolution that was steeped in emotional trauma.[49] *Songs*, on the other hand, incarnates the trauma, graphically illustrating the corporeal injuries sustained by soldiers in quelling the unrest. The depictions are detailed and gruesome, full of burns, blood, and bullet-ridden bodies. To outmatch words and images that document the much higher number of civilian casualties, the collection offers eyewitness accounts from local residents, signed and dated, which directly counter the "rumors" that soldiers killed. Meanwhile, the portrait below vividly captures the violence committed against a Republic's Guardian: "On the early morning of June 4, a shocking and pitiful scene appeared at the Fuchengmen overpass: from the northern side of the yellow-gray cement railing was hanging upside down a body still breathing, mutilated in its entirety, its skull cracked open, its limbs broken, dark-red blood and white brains dripping from the bridge onto the cement ground below from time to time" (168–69). The picture is meant to elicit the most visceral responses from the reader, painting in brutal strokes the outrage that continues to be perpetrated. For the picture is not a still life: the body is still breathing, the blood and brains still dripping. If indeed the perpetrators hung the body on display, then this passage reenacts the spectacle, a piece of agitprop that, like the incendiary rhetoric attributed to student leaders and intellectuals, seeks to stir elemental passions.

In tandem with this individual portrait is a group sculpture of collective victimhood. While the former is "shocking," the latter invites the viewer to tarry. Behold this assemblage of heroes in agony: "The military vehicle has already been burned into a pile of coal. The burnt-black corpses of the five soldiers are embraced in unity. Perhaps they had hugged their burning comrades one by one and in the end came together, a collectivity of friendship burned to death" (23–24). In life the soldiers formed a military unit; in death the soldiers form an artistic unit. The fire has forged their eternal monument. As Haiyan Lee observes, "the aestheticization and de-individualization of death is indeed the essence of the military sublime."[50] The soldiers' final, awesome performance of togetherness is supposed to induce the reunification of its spectators. Should the latter need help, here is a template: "the hundreds of millions of viewers in front of the television nearly all gaped in shock at the crimes of the thugs. Their hearts trembled vehemently; tears flowed from the eyes of not a few people" (72). Not only does the writing evoke a unanimous viewing public into being, it enacts how its own public should react upon reading it. As with the two college students' "extremely agitational speech" of bloodshed on Tiananmen Square, the effect aimed for here is "infection."

As the above excerpt attests, the state campaign was cross-media in nature. The text of *Songs of the Republic's Guardians* not only limns gory tableaus of ecstatic martyrdom but refers specifically to its televisual counterparts. Reading and watching become mutually reinforcing practices that work in tandem to mold reception. The former bleeds again into the latter in the following: "At this moment, 7 p.m. on June 8th, 1989, China Central Television [CCTV] is broadcasting the news. If there are 1.1 billion viewers in front of the TV screen, one can say with certainty that, if they have not betrayed their conscience, all will feel shock and indignation" (54). These lines underscore the temporal dimension. A community dispersed all over the country is nevertheless united in China's only time zone, Beijing time. It is also connected by the tube. The news that a projected 1.1 billion people are watching is the *National News Bulletin*. Literally "news simulcast" (*xinwen lianbo*), the *National News Bulletin* is shown simultaneously at 7 p.m. every day by many if not most terrestrial channels in China. Since the early 1980s, it has been the only regular CCTV program to have "must carry" status across all broadcasters.[51] After June Fourth, watching the appointed show at the appointed hour becomes a public duty. The parents of one soldier demonstrate how to partake in this communal ablution: "June 15th, 1989, 7 p.m.: time for China Central Television's *National News Bulletin* . . . Husband Bo Shangxue and wife Li Aiqun, concerned very much with the development of the current political situation like every family all over the country, have also sat down early in front of the television" (71). If the TV is on at 7 P.M., one is perforce tuning in "like every family all over the country." To be sitting in front of the TV is also not to be back in the streets.

Besides the *National News Bulletin*, the state commanded special programs to drum its message into the viewership further. These programs, made for the small rather than the big screen, allowed for repeated, even continuous playing on TV without the need to organize required attendance at cinema screenings. For the most part, they were aimed at a domestic audience.[52] The circumstances of their broadcast are difficult to ascertain, but to surmise from the airing of one such program, episodes of a single program were shown one day after the other, including in prime time.[53]

Produced by the Propaganda Division of the PLA's General Political Department in July 1989, *Flutter, Flag of the Republic: A Record of the Quelling of the Beijing Counterrevolutionary Riot* comprises four episodes, each between twenty and thirty minutes, totaling a little less than one hour and forty minutes. The four episodes are, respectively, "The Turbulence's Sudden Rise," which covers the backstory of the protests up to the April 26 *People's Daily* editorial that branded them as "turmoil;" "The Tide of Turmoil," which brings events up to the declaration of martial law on May 20; "Truth of the Riot," which includes the military's reconquest of Tiananmen Square on June 3 and 4; and "Going Down in History," a paean to the soldiers who lost their lives. Under the cover of a straightforward chronology, they carry out the official verdict on the progression of the protests, from the comparatively mild "turbulence" to the loaded "turmoil," to finally "riot" (*baoluan*), which literally means "violent chaos," a teleology marked at the end by the apotheosis of the soldiers.

These four episodes of *Flutter, Flag of the Republic* may or may not have been broadcast in prime time one day after the other. What is certain more than thirty years after 1989, however, is that it is the one, of all the video propaganda produced by the Party-state in the wake of June Fourth, with the longest reach in time as well as in space. Like the other programs, *Flutter* is no longer welcome in the country of its birth. Instead, it lives on in exile—on YouTube, for instance. Yet it is transmitted there in truncated form. The portion edited out is precisely the Tank Man scene addressed at the beginning of this chapter. Who might have done it? Who might have uploaded the video on YouTube? And finally, what does it mean?

RECAPTURING THE MEDIA

Flutter, Flag of the Republic opens not with images but with text and speech. A white typescript appears against a blue background, read by an authoritative male voice. The text repeats the familiar formulation of the "extremely few people" behind the plot to stir up the masses. It implicitly admits to the effectiveness of this rabble-rousing: "some people are perplexed and confused to this day." Thus, this program is necessary to dispel the confusion, and it claims to do so by using "recordings on location" (*xianchang shilu*). But these pieces of visual documentation by themselves are insufficient. Ambivalent pictures need to be not only accompanied by narration but also prefaced by explanation. That is why the subsequent images are framed by this initial verbal instruction.

The white text on a blue screen recalls the *National News Bulletin* on the night of June 4, 1989. On the news that night was no footage of the carnage, no vehicles in flames, no sound of gunfire, no screams or howls. Yellow typescript on a blue screen merely stated that martial law troops had retaken Tiananmen Square in the quelling of the counter-revolutionary riot.[54] There was insufficient time then to edit a composite video that presented the military operation in a favorable light. A month's labor was required.

When *Flutter, Flag of the Republic* appeared on Chinese television in July, its first footage is precisely of the flag, namely, the flag-raising ceremony on Tiananmen Square on June 9. The scene, with a squadron of soldiers bearing the national flag and surrounding the flagpole, establishes that the public square, which students and citizens had occupied for seven weeks, was back in the possession of the Party-state. In place of the raucous performances that had been previously on display, a solemn ritual could once again be staged where the military, raising aloft the national flag to the music of the national anthem, played the protector and guarantor of the nation. Furthermore, it was a ritual to be recorded on location and broadcast to viewers all over the country.

The above text and scene occur as a prologue before the program title appears. Afterward is familiar archival footage of the founding of the nation, the ceremony on October 1, 1949, with Mao Zedong and other leaders atop the Tiananmen gatehouse and the masses in the square below. Attention immediately then turns to the Western powers that tried a variety of means, from military aggression to economic sanctions, to topple the Communist regime; failing, they eventually resorted to the strategy of "peaceful evolution," or subversion from within. In the context of this retrospection, *Flutter* brings up the dangers of foreign seduction, citing the creeping influence of "bourgeois liberalization" since the implementation of economic reforms in the late 1970s. Hostile forces worked tirelessly, such as the U.S.-government-funded Voice of America over the airwaves, to bring down the republic brought into being by the Communist Party.

Enemies reside both without and within. In conjunction with the narration of infiltration, images of books and journals pile on top of each other, indicating that the spread of noxious ideas through publications is responsible for the ideological perversion. Besides print media, *Flutter* also points to salons, forums, and conferences as other culprits in shifting the tide of public opinion. These are all semiofficial and unofficial spaces that emerged in the Chinese public sphere in the 1980s, alternative forms of communication and community that challenged the government monopoly on information and the top-down model of organization. They did indeed contribute to the conditions in which the 1989 movement arose. The connection between such forums and the protests was evident in the city of Shanghai, for instance, when the shuttering of the liberal newspaper *World Economic Herald* in late April led to demonstrations on the streets.[55]

In relation to the media, *Flutter* singles out two entities for condemnation, one directly, the other indirectly. The first, the astrophysicist and public intellectual Fang Lizhi, who openly espoused democratic reforms throughout the latter half of the 1980s, is accused of using his writings as well as university lectures to sow the seeds of political change.[56] The second is a TV documentary called *River Elegy*. The six-part "special topic program" (*zhuanti pian*) juxtaposed the values of unification and uniformity, symbolized by the Yellow River, whose basin was the cradle of Chinese civilization, with democracy, equality, and freedom, symbolized by the ocean. *Flutter* alludes to the latter when it charges the program with "promoting the West's blue civilization." *River Elegy* was a sensation when it first aired on CCTV in June 1988. A year later, in the aftermath of June Fourth, the station produced programs that attacked it.[57]

That the heterodox *River Elegy* could appear on national television at all signaled the contentiousness in the ideological realm by the late 1980s. To some, it signaled confusion. A revealing piece in this regard is "Television and the Orientation of Public Opinion," written by Beijing TV's station chief and published in a Beijing-based party journal in the June Fourth aftermath. Its title echoes language from *Flutter, Flag of the Republic*, where the protests, both eruption and escalation, are partly attributed to the "wrong orientation of public opinion." The station chief begins by pedantically postulating the superiority of television to newspaper and radio in reaching a mass audience. He then admits to the misuse of this powerful tool. Beijing TV placed too much emphasis on "culture and entertainment," at the expense of the public's correct stewardship.[58] Diversion, in effect, eclipsed direction.

If the station chief has recognized the mistake of prioritizing entertainment over edification, he has also taken to heart the principles of popular appeal. Learning the lesson, he proposes "a master strategy in television propaganda" moving forward. At the core of this strategy is the arousal of patriotic feeling. Love of nation, furthermore, is inextricable from love of the party and love of socialism. On these themes will be developed the "main melody of television propaganda." The "main melody" (*zhu xuanlü*), in its cinematic variation, will return at the end of this chapter. Here, it is important to accent the accompaniment to the melody. According to the station chief, the new propaganda, while perfect in doctrinal pitch, will "also have high artistic standards, be fresh and lively, variegated and resplendent, and enchant the beholder."[59]

These are high standards to satisfy. Does *Flutter, Flag of the Republic*, made by the PLA and not Beijing TV, do so? Regardless of its success, the comments above should orient attention towards *how* it says what it says. What it says, in part, is this: the demonstrations were not peaceful; the military response was called for; what started as "turbulence" quickly became "turmoil," which, in the days leading up to June 3 and 4, turned into a "counterrevolutionary riot." The protestors were wanton in word and deed, while soldiers exercised the utmost restraint. The ouster of the illegal occupation of Tiananmen Square returned that public space to the people and restored order in the capital and country.

How it says it is this. First, *Flutter, Flag of the Republic* shares many characteristics of the "special topic program," such as the use of archival footage and voice-over narration from a script. In this regard both *Flutter* and its ideological opposite *River Elegy* are examples of the "logocentric documentary" that prefers saying things over showing things, epitomized by the opening to *Flutter*—script on screen read aloud—discussed earlier.[60] But the verbal can dominate the visual even in an image, as in this shot (see figure 1.2) from *Flutter* where soldiers listen to the April 26 *People's Daily* editorial read by an officer. While the media at large, because of loosened controls during the earlier half of the protests, was able to express sympathy for the students' cause, rigorous discipline could be maintained within the military. Here the soldiers, rigidly seated, are presumably listening with rapt attention to

FIGURE 1.2 Soldiers receiving the April 26, 1989, *People's Daily* editorial.

the editorial. They, too, have been shaped by censorship, not just in the privation of other sources of news but also in the active inculcation of pro-party opinions and postures. Hierarchy and obedience are still the ruling principles in this high-angle shot, with the commandment cutting across the center.

In addition to on-screen text and archival footage, *Flutter, Flag of the Republic* also contains what it self-styles as "recordings on location." The shot of the soldiers in figure 1.2 is an example, as is the national flag-raising ceremony on the recaptured Tiananmen Square, already discussed. Descriptions of charred bodies, spattered brains, and dripping blood told the tale of PLA martyrdom in *Songs of the Republic's Guardians*. In *Flutter* the audience is treated to their visualization. Footage from the scene of death displays macabre still lifes of mangled forms and spilled entrails. Even the dead soldier's private parts—the clothes burned off—are shown for maximum effect. The frontal nudity is sanctioned not just because the subject is inanimate but also because it is art, portraying most explicitly the affront to dignity to which the soldier was subjected.

Such artful montages contrast sharply with images of the protests. By the film's own admission, the media, from newspapers to television, had in part sided with the mass movement. Therefore, in the aftermath of the crackdown, the producers of the film had to use footage shot by reporters who had previously played the role of not propagandists but publicists. In fact, *Flutter* itself contains fleeting images of banners floating above the crowd that call for press freedom. Other shots even show groups of journalists—including from *People's Daily* and CCTV—marching in solidarity. These snippets preserve in the official record not only a moment when state propaganda organs splintered and the uniform message fractured but also visual fragments of an alternative history that belie what the official record claims.[61] A plot fomented by an "extremely few people" has to confront the sight of a sea of people from all walks of life: students and professionals, workers and intellectuals, men and women, old and young. Countering the imputation of the movement to those "harboring ulterior motives" are flashes that show people contributing and collecting donations for the cause, residents encircling military vehicles, entreating soldiers to turn back or lay down their arms. On display, despite doubtlessly the most painstaking editing and rigorous vetting, are the spontaneous camaraderie and unbidden emotion of hundreds of thousands of people. Made by the military, *Flutter* is a work of command production, to be sure. Nevertheless, the sheen of alter-production gleams from its stitching together of manifold pictorial sources.

Pictures, however doctored, remain polysemous. How to rein in this unruliness? Through sound design. A confused murmur, as of cattle, furnishes the soundtrack of crowd scenes in *Flutter, Flag of the Republic*. Those capable of speech are guaranteed to have theirs torn out of context to expose their ignominy and perfidy. Most salient, however, is the voice-over narration. The script may be univocal in intent, but it is delivered by two voices, male and female. Stern messages, such as the opening text that frames the program to come, are declaimed by the man. He rebukes, he does not equivocate, and he tolerates no dispute. The woman, on the other hand, gets the more lyrical lines of the script. Over a sequence of troops pushing their way to the square despite the crowds and roadblocks, she rhapsodizes over their bravery. Over a shot of a soldier with a bloodied head, she laments his heartless treatment at the hands of thugs. Her voice evokes sympathy, while his aims for awe. She beckons the audience back into the fold of the party. He threatens it into submission. This two-voice approach is representative of the dual understanding of censorship as simultaneously no-saying and yes-saying.

The bombast and the bathos peak near the end of the documentary, in the segment of family members as well as strangers mourning the soldiers' martyrdom. Wrinkled fathers fight back tears; weeping mothers have to be supported on either side. Not to be outshone is the onlooker who dabs at his or her eyes with a handkerchief. These may indeed be sincere expressions of grief. Yet true emotion in the film cannot be separated from orchestration, in two senses of the word. First, the acts of mourning are grand affairs peopled by more authorities than the bereaved, as in the scene shown in figure 1.3. The uniformed men in the background, holding cameras that mirror the camera filming the scene, cannot but elicit docile bodies in the foreground, bent less in condolence than in subjection. Second, the entire segment, with both narrators at their histrionic high, is backed by swelling strings and a billowing chorus. Each of the Guardians' names is intoned—while stark silence prevails over the names of the uncountable and discounted dead.

The deaths of students, workers, and other citizens, which vastly outnumbered those of soldiers, can only be marked in private. Until they
can be commemorated in public, until their names can be recited aloud,
every beatification of the military hero, every lamentation for his loss,
can only be a sham.

In figure 1.3, the masses have once again found their allegiance.
Previously "ignorant of the truth," they are now enlightened by it, and
they pay it forward with their performance for the television audience.
At the end of the reportage pieces in *Songs of the Republic's Guardians*,
the masses act out for the reader an awakening, too. No longer a "black
river" or "black waves," they proceed in single file: "One group after
another, a mass of thousands upon thousands attended the memorial
service of martyr Yanpo" (196). Such gatherings coagulate naturally
from the heaviness of the recognition: "Cars slowed down passing
through here, going past gently; many bicyclists voluntarily got off their

FIGURE 1.3 Civilians bow before a makeshift altar for a martyred soldier.

bicycles here, coming before the martyrs' portraits to mourn silently. Here a spontaneous mass grieving continued day after day" (74). Like the composition of the picture above, the "voluntary" and "spontaneous" procession in the foreground is subtended by the imperative gaze in the back. In addition to casting the model of PLA soldiers in general and Republic's Guardians in particular, and in addition to linking party rule with national sovereignty by reactivating the collective memory of Western infringements, government propaganda remakes the (re)public by staging melodramatic mourning.

The commemorations "continued day after day." Then one day they stopped. They could not start again, even though they were far from complete. Both *Songs of the Republic's Guardians* and *Flutter, Flag of the Republic* make pledges of remembrance that, not long after their utterance, were broken, pledges like "Going Down in History," the title of *Flutter*'s last episode. And this one, from *Songs*: "The day of June 4, 1989 will be written weightily upon Chinese history" (60). Or this one: "A hero's statue should be made for the Republic's Guardians at Xidan Road in the capital: This statue will be grand and perfect, spotless and flawless, forever smiling on the passing pedestrians" (43). Less than three years after *Songs* and *Flutter* were produced, the state propaganda campaign ground to a halt. What followed was the razing of the statue never built, the near eradication of June Fourth's memory in its entirety—unauthorized *and* official—buttressed by different forms of party-approved production and propagation.

The state campaign was short-lived. According to the June Fourth historian Wu Renhua, the PLA General Political Department—the same department that produced both *Songs of the Republic's Guardians* and *Flutter, Flag of the Republic*—wanted to hold a celebration on the one-year anniversary on June 4, 1990. But the party's top leadership, including Deng Xiaoping, forbade it.[62] Wu dates the end of the propaganda campaign to around that time. But as outlined earlier in the chapter, the last state-sponsored publications about June Fourth appeared in 1991. Afterward, a near total whiteout set in. Even two government collections were banned, one for chronicling protests throughout China that belied their limited scope, the other for depicting the rage of a multitude of people—not "extremely few"—spitting on and cursing the intruding army.[63]

In the aftermath of the propaganda campaign, June Fourth may have disappeared. But the task of producing subjects loyal to the Party-state continues apace. What replaced June Fourth? In the film industry, it was the "main melody film." Even though the term was first used in 1987 to refer to edifying as opposed to entertainment fare, main melody films were heavily promoted only after the 1989 crackdown.[64] The Film Bureau ordered studios to make these films on revolutionary history, past party heroes and military martyrs, and the achievements of the economic reforms, although even there the depiction of the masses and collective action disappeared from the screen.[65] The films were guaranteed not only exhibition throughout the country but also attendance because schools and workplaces organized free screenings.[66]

A parallel substitute for the June Fourth campaign was a state campaign officially started in the same year the former ended. Not long after the crackdown, Deng Xiaoping had remarked that "during the last ten years our biggest mistake was made in the field of education, primarily in ideological and political education—not just of students but of the people in general."[67] The Patriotic Education Campaign, made official by two government documents in August 1991, thus responded directly to the anti-Communist revolutions of 1989. This campaign resulted not only in the rewriting of history textbooks but also in the building boom of museums, monuments, and other memorial sites, as Kirk Denton has detailed.[68] The campaign utilized not the Tiananmen Square "turmoil" but more distant fears that both *Songs of the Republic's Guardians* and *Flutter, Flag of the Republic* had invoked, namely, the humiliations China has suffered at the hands of foreign powers since the mid-nineteenth century and the sovereignty restored to the Chinese nation by the CCP.

Another 1991 development is no coincidence either. The number of military police officers in charge of the national flag-raising ceremony on Tiananmen Square increased from one to three in 1982. On April 15, 1991, exactly two years after the protests started with Hu Yaobang's death, the three-member "National Flag Group" expanded to a thirty-six-member "Protection Team." The ceremony also changed from an occasional event into a daily ritual.[69] Even the flagpole was raised from twenty-two to forty meters. But the 1991 elevation was not the final one. In 2018, responsibility for the ceremony transferred from the military police to the PLA. Now, the Protection Team is composed of sixty-six members from the army, navy, and air force.[70]

Such pomp could be innocuous under another circumstance. But what if state propaganda is understood not as the opposite but as a component of censorship? If *Songs of the Republic's Guardians* and *Flutter, Flag of the Republic* are products of the censorship of June Fourth, as I have argued, then so is the national flag-raising ceremony that takes place every dawn where the statue of the Goddess of Democracy once stood. The state's manipulation of the memory of June Fourth did not end with the surcease of the propaganda campaign. Rather, it took on everyday as well as momentous, spectacular forms. The latter, such as the 2015 Victory Day parade marking the seventieth anniversary of the end of World War II and the 2019 National Day parade on the seventieth anniversary of the PRC's founding, may grab the most attention. But every public pageantry performed on Tiananmen Square, however quotidian, constitutes censorship as long as the protests of 1989 are disavowed. It is not fortuitous that *Flutter* opens with footage of the flag-raising ceremony and ends with the image of the fluttering red flag.

Flutter, Flag of the Republic, in addition to its TV broadcasts, was once distributed on video by the Beijing Higher Education Audiovisual Publishing House. Today, it can no longer be found in China, not on any of the Chinese video-sharing websites. As mentioned earlier, it can be found on YouTube, although this online version has been tampered with. The Tank Man scene broached at the beginning of the chapter—with the declamation against the "lone scoundrel"—has been edited out in such a way that the removal is not immediately noticeable.[71] Was the person who first posted the video responsible? Or did the officially distributed video already contain the deletion?

In any case, it appears to be an admission of defeat on the part of the editor. The effort to promulgate one reading of the Tank Man is ultimately abandoned due to the persuasiveness—and pervasiveness—of another. The Western reading—the courageous individual standing up to repressive state power—has won. The Tank Man scene from *Flutter* and also the Tank Man image cannot be found using Chinese search engines. Censorship of the Tank Man, then, can be conceived in at least three ways. First, censorship as erasure, in which Chinese college students interviewed by foreign journalists cannot recognize the iconic photo. Second, censorship as propaganda, in which Western and Chinese state media project their own interpretations to shape how the Tank Man is received. And third, censorship as productiveness, in which the multiple versions of *Flutter, Flag of the Republic*—with and without the Tank Man—lead further to the latter's fetishization.

The truncated version of *Flutter* has one more implication. In the immediate post–June Fourth period of 1989 to 1991, Party-state propaganda was indeed monolithic and top-down. But it did not stay that way. Propaganda has evolved to "have high artistic standards, be fresh and lively, variegated and resplendent, and enchant the beholder," as the Beijing TV chief prophetically noted in 1989. And it has also decentralized. The identity of the publisher(s) of *Flutter* on YouTube may be unknown, but many of the comments, in Chinese, are pro-Chinese government. They bash the distortion of June Fourth by the Western media, oblivious of the irony of speaking—on a Western media platform blocked in China—about a memory forbidden by the Chinese government. The propagative and denunciative capacities of censorship have exceeded the Chinese state and exceeded its borders. Supplementing the command production from its institutions are brokers who relay its narrative far and wide.

CHAPTER TWO

Songs from Afar

Contesting the Official Narrative from the Periphery

During graduate school, I spent an academic year in China on a Chinese government fellowship. I had cast my research project as a historical study of film censorship from the early twentieth century to the present, so whenever I met with a certain professor at the host university, we would discuss my findings as well as relevant articles that he frequently shared with me. Toward the end of my stay, I finally confided to him my interest in June Fourth literature and film produced in the mainland. At the time he merely nodded, not taking up my revelation. I thought I had misplaced my trust. But in our last meeting, apropos of nothing, he brought up the author Sheng Keyi: "She is a very talented writer who deserves more attention," he said. This remark did not strike me then. Only back in the United States did I discover that, in addition to fiction published in China in books I was familiar with, her latest novel appeared in a Chinese literary journal. That novel is *Death Fugue*, an allegory of June Fourth.

The restrictive aspect of censorship is manifest in the professor's initial response of silence. As my experience illustrates, however, censorship is just as productive of workarounds both artistic and everyday. In spite of the Chinese government's taboo on June Fourth, I was able to conduct research in China—on a government fellowship, no less—by way of a somewhat specious project proposal. In spite of the same taboo, the professor still managed to alert me to Sheng's novel. But the taboo should not be regarded as something solely side-stepped. In spite of it, as well as because of it, a whole stratum of art is formed of which *Death Fugue* is but one example: writing that is set at a temporal, spatial, or referential remove, and films shot mostly indoors, at night, or on the move, with a dearth of crowd scenes. Such art is shaped through censorship's heat and pressure like diamond, emerging sharp and iridescent with facets cut on the edge between restraint and transgression.

The three case studies in this chapter have this hard and hard-won luster. Censorship does not relate to them as an exterior force. Rather, their aesthetics are forged by it through and through. The first, Wang Guangli's documentary *I Graduated*, was shot without permission on and off Beijing university campuses in 1992. It comprises mainly interviews with graduating seniors who experienced June Fourth as freshmen. The second, Tang Xiaobai's fiction feature *Conjugation* (2001), was likewise shot without permission in Beijing and independently produced. Its central characters, of the same age as those in *I Graduated*, try to cope in the wintry aftermath of the massacre. And the third, *Death Fugue*, could be published in mainland China only in a 2011 issue of the literary journal *Jiangnan*: over a dozen presses rejected Sheng Keyi's manuscript.[1] Set alternately in "Beiping" and a dystopia called Swan Valley, the novel weaves the story line of a protest movement in 1989 with other narrative strands in subsequent decades, all the way up to 2039. All three works skirt around Tiananmen Square, both figuratively and literally, transformed in the process of this circumvention.

Yet their aesthetics cannot be conceived solely in terms of circumvention. We are familiar with the Straussian notion of the author in a dangerous time "writing between the lines," encrypting a message whose meaning can be deciphered by "trustworthy and intelligent readers only."[2] With regard to the June Fourth literature produced in the People's Republic of China (PRC), the scholar Belinda Kong is right to home in on the deployment of aesthetic strategies of "evasion" by mainland Chinese writers.[3] The previous chapter on June Fourth propaganda demonstrates, however, that frontal assault, and not evasion, characterizes state-commanded literary and audiovisual production. The three case studies of this chapter show, besides evasion, an aesthetics of confrontation and disclosure.

Each of them constitutes a unique act of recalcitrant remembrance that not only ruptures the June Fourth moratorium placed on the Chinese public realm following the conclusion of the propaganda campaign in 1991, as detailed in chapter 1, but also disputes the official memorialization promulgated until that year. Each reveals the role of state violence not just in the crushing of the 1989 protests but in the aftermath as well. The millions of participants and supporters did not simply reembrace the party, recognizing their mistakes. Neither did they choose to move on, getting on with their lives while putting the event behind them. Violence enacted upon the people—and not upon the "martyred" soldiers—was a constitutive element of the turn. People have not voluntarily forgotten or lost interest. Their disinterest and forgetfulness stem from twin factors, the repressive and the constructive. The former spans the spectrum from manuscript rejection to imprisonment and death. The latter assumes the form of censorship's reproduction: not just the propaganda materials in print and on TV examined previously but also required "discussions" of those materials in the classroom and in the workplace, regular and regulated pageantry on Tiananmen Square, and the rewarding of those who cooperate—instances of authorization that are every bit as violent as proscription and erasure. It is the duality of "sanction" that molds the post–June Fourth era.

I Graduated, Conjugation, and *Death Fugue* are self-reflexive in this regard. They depict the precarious conditions of their art. *I Graduated,* a film in part about the attempts to make a film, records the film crew's run-in with authorities. At the heart of *Conjugation* is a disappeared guitarist whose songs can no longer be heard. And the protagonist of *Death Fugue* is a poet who has given up writing in the wake of the crackdown. All three of them betray an ambivalence toward their very endeavor, caught as they are between the rock of systematic expunction and the hard place of resource-rich state campaigns. But therein lies the poignancy of their position. They do not ring out with the triumphalism of party screeds. Neither are they hampered, however, by a cynical or defeatist fatalism. On this perilous perch, they await an encounter with the audience.

This chapter first follows the camera in *I Graduated* from dorm rooms ultimately to Tiananmen Square. It then picks up the camera in *Conjugation* that tracks, on the move from beginning to end, the transitional moment of the massacre's immediate aftermath. The chapter finally shifts to *Death Fugue*, which itself shunts between reimagined places past and future. These three case studies, one from each of the three post-1989 decades, show the intractability of June Fourth more than thirty years on. The Party-state may try to pin its story as the only history and then quash that history entirely. But discrepant versions and visions continue to be generated, constituting an alternative archive to be opened to the Chinese public. Just when one thinks that all will stay still, a movement stirs from the unlikeliest of places.

LEAVING THE CAMERA ON

In the immediate wake of June Fourth, the retrenched state media fully implemented its productive capacities, as we saw in the previous chapter. It churned out vast amounts of articles, books, and TV programs that saturated the news, schools, and workplaces with essentially one message: that the protests had gotten out of hand and had to be put down, that the real heroes are the soldiers, and only their sacrifices are to be extolled. In addition to the inundation of this message, a tightening gripped the public sphere to the preclusion of alternative accounts of June Fourth. Propaganda of the heavy-handed sort was not the only fare. Also promoted was the "main melody" (*zhu xuanlü*), or cultural production that sang of a glorious revolutionary history or the wonders of the economic reforms.

Despite these strictures, however, discrepant narratives of June Fourth continued to be recounted. In response to the strictures as well as the command production, many artists chose the way of rupture, leaving the system to make art on the sly. It is not a coincidence, for instance, that Chinese independent cinema was born right after June Fourth. Both Zhang Yuan's *Mama*, the first independent fiction-feature in the PRC, and Wu Wenguang's *Bumming in Beijing*, the first independent documentary, appeared in 1990. The latter originated as a project commissioned by China Central Television (CCTV). It started in 1988 but was finished later at Wu's own expense.[4] Shi Jian's documentary *Tiananmen* (1991) also began as a CCTV-commissioned project that was eventually completed at the director's expense. It is an eight-part series about everyday life in Beijing that, like *Bumming in Beijing* and unlike the state-produced documentary *Flutter, Flag of the Republic: A Record of the Quelling of the Beijing Counterrevolutionary Riot* (analyzed in the previous chapter), features interviews with ordinary people. June Fourth is conspicuously absent from both *Bumming in Beijing* and *Tiananmen*.[5] Their historical importance lies in their venture outside the state system, bypassing official review and distribution altogether.

In this context appeared Wang Guangli's *I Graduated* in 1992. Wang graduated from East China Normal University in Shanghai in 1989, the year of June Fourth. *I Graduated*, his first film, was shot in Beijing with a borrowed video camera in one week of July 1992. As an early title card states, the documentary is dedicated to the class of Chinese college students who graduated in 1992, as well as "all those concerned about their destiny." What is the significance of this class? It was the last graduating class to have experienced June Fourth while in college. Students in the class would have been freshmen during the protests, which started in mid-April 1989.

Yet this context is not evident from the beginning of *I Graduated*. After a stylized prelude of song and tinted images (to be discussed later), the film opens onto a crowd of students busily moving out of their dormitories. The shaky images from a hand-held camera weave through the heaps of bags and boxes, accompanied by the ambient sounds of the general hubbub as well as the public address (PA) system broadcasting the news. Then, as if in a flashback, the audience is shown how the film crew got inside the gated campus in the first place. In a continuous shot, the image treads unsteadily into a restaurant, while a subtitle informs the viewer that this is the only entrance to Peking University that bypasses security. The shot moves through the dark interior of the kitchen and out into the light of a back alleyway. Here it pans to the left before an off-screen voice calling, "This way! This way!" directs the image to the right. Also heard off-screen is a woman's voice asking: "What are you guys up to?" "Looking for a friend" is the faint reply. The image tracks shakily down the alley, which eventually leads to a throng of bikes parked in front of a dorm.

These scenes signal, right from the start, the break that *I Graduated* makes from the kind of documentary filmmaking represented by the state-produced *Flutter, Flag of the Republic*, examined in chapter 1. First, there is no nondiegetic music or voice-over narration dictating the reception of the image. Ambient noise provides the synchronous soundtrack instead: the commotion of students packing their belongings, the PA system, the off-screen chatter. Second, the action is unscripted and not pieced together with archival footage. In going through the restaurant, the image captures, in passing, customers and employees minding their own business. Both the wrong turn taken by the camera operator and the woman's inquiry off-camera accentuate the utter spontaneity of the filmic moment. And third, the shooting is consciously subjective, with the point-of-view angle frequently jolted as the viewer follows along. The presence of the camera, therefore, is not masked but brought to the fore. Rather than proffering the film in the guise of omniscience and the authoritative take on June Fourth, the director leaves in the missteps. Yet it is precisely in the wrong turn that the purported honesty of this approach to filmmaking resides.

At the same time, the continuous shot displays the audacity of the project. It alerts viewers to the obstacles to the shooting while at the same time flaunting the overcoming of these obstacles. Censorship, one could say, does not deter the filmmakers but spurs workarounds that are included in the artwork itself as part of the production. In this way does *I Graduated* evince not so much evasion as exposure, making public the mechanisms of security that guard the college campus.

From the alleyway, the shot enters a male dormitory and ascends a staircase. No artificial lighting aids the viewing, neither in the staircase and hallways nor in the dorm room of the film's first interviewee. An element of the unplanned characterizes even the interview. The first thing the subject says is that he thought the interview, though prearranged, would not take place because the film crew would not be able to enter the campus. This impromptu impression persists because both the interviewee and the presumed camera operator remain standing, with the former shifting his weight from foot to foot while the image constantly repositions itself. Only midway through this segment does a crew member remember to close the door, which slowly whimpers shut. Only then does the sound of speech become clearer.

The interviewee does not introduce his name. He says he entered Peking University in 1988 and majored in French in the Department of Western Languages and Literatures. He is noticeably jittery, whether in anticipation of graduation or in reaction to being filmed. He seldom faces the interviewer, all the while fidgeting a cigarette in his fingers. Only at the end of the segment, over his freeze-frame, does a caption in English reveal his name. He is identified as L. D. He actually entered Peking University in 1987, not 1988. He attempted suicide in 1989 and then left school for a year. After graduation, he would start teaching at a university.

The freeze-frame is the first instance of obtrusive editing in *I Graduated*. There have been many cuts, to be sure, but here Wang Guangli pauses what has hitherto been unrehearsed action to deliberately interject the filmmaker's power to shape time. No longer is the viewer limited to a subjective lens liable to stumble and err. Instead, Wang names the interviewee with godlike prerogative. The former's knowledge exceeds even the narrative framework, informing the viewer of what took place after graduation. Most significantly, of course, is what happened in 1989. By shifting his matriculation a year forward, L. D. clearly wanted to conceal his suicide attempt. Yet the director contradicts this time line and—with or without L. D.'s permission—reveals a secret of utmost intimacy. Thus does Wang cast his project as an excavation of buried truth, positioned on the legal and ethical edge. His is an indiscretionary documentary, not to be forestalled by campus security or concerns for privacy. Regardless of the ethical implications, he makes known that he will not shy away from the truth, that any and all prevarications will be unmasked.

Why did L. D. elide the year 1989? The filmmaker in effect poses this question to the viewer by articulating the discrepancy with the interviewee's time line. With the caption, the audience is introduced to the subterranean impact of June Fourth (after all, 1989 is mentioned only in a subtitle), a cataclysm that made a then college sophomore try to kill himself and the aftershocks of which reverberates, as attested by those cigarette-fumbling fingers.

Another question resounds: What drove June Fourth underground? Whereas the destructive dimension of censorship had eliminated June Fourth from the Chinese public sphere by the time *I Graduated* was made, as the previous chapter shows, the documentary testifies that it has not vanished from people's minds. Needless to say, the tremors course through more than one individual. *I Graduated*, after all, is a class portrait. It even includes someone who is not a member of the same class, or any class. He is H. J. G. He would have also graduated in 1992 but withdrew the previous year from the China Youth University of Political Studies, where Wang Guangli was teaching at the time. His head perpetually down, a guitar laid at his side, and sitting on the floor of a bedroom, H. J. G. admits in his first segment that he should have left school in 1989. Here he does not equivocate, giving no other reason than what he calls the "student movement." He wanted a "complete break" from the "regime" (*tizhi*)—educational or otherwise—and from his former life.

H. J. G.'s unbosoming makes the most explicit reference to June Fourth in the early part of *I Graduated*. It occurs at the end of the first of the film's five interview sections, each of which revolves loosely around a particular topic. The first section, where L. D. and H. J. G., among others, first appear, serves as a kind of introduction to interviewees who will reappear in later sections. Depression, love and sex, study abroad, and June Fourth are the topics of the second, third, fourth, and fifth sections, respectively. Along with the divulgences in the first section, June Fourth, then, bookends the entire documentary. Not only is it reinvoked, it is given another name, not "turmoil" or "counterrevolutionary riot"—the monikers bestowed by government boilerplate—but "student movement" (*xuechao*).

Immediately after H. J. G.'s mention of the student movement comes the film's first sectional interlude. The shot is back on the grounds of Peking University, this time literally on the ground. The crew has been caught by campus security, and the camera operator has put the camera on the ground. The camera stays on, however. It records—in addition to a close-up of the security personnel's feet—their communication through walkie-talkie static. It stays on, waist-level, when the crew is escorted to the campus security office, picking up along the way a news broadcast over the PA system that happens to be about crime and punishment. It even stays on in the office itself, where the camera, placed on a desk, captures a bureaucrat, unaware that the camera is filming, in a medium shot that cuts off at his eyes (figure 2.1).

The conversation between the official and the crew reveals that the latter has been caught before, the first time for supposedly taking graduation photos. This time the crew is again on the premises without permission, armed with an apparent letter of introduction that was never

FIGURE 2.1 The university official, in a medium shot, which is cut off at the eyes. The image is from the film *I Graduated* (1992).

approved, as the official points out, by the university or the university's Communist Party branch. As with the scene that takes the viewer into Peking University through a restaurant, Wang Guangli leaves in footage that shows the work, so to speak. He brings to light the barriers as well as dangers inherent in the filmmaking yet shares with the viewer how to transcend them. Therefore, these barriers no longer stand before his enterprise like gatekeepers but instead become elements absorbed within *I Graduated* that only redound to the film's fecundity.

More than the cleverness of the crew—feigning innocence, the ruse of the letter of introduction—is at stake. Effrontery is on display in the act of not turning off the camera, defiantly yet coolly documenting not only the encounter with the officers but also their foolishness, from the guards bumbling into their walkie-talkies to the paper pusher with his brain cropped. They unwittingly become part of the production, players in the drama Wang Guangli is directing between the "regime"—to use

H. J. G.'s term—on the one hand, and independent filmmaking, on the other. From the ground, the camera has risen to occupy the same plane as the bureaucrat's face, from a surreptitious shot of feet to a level affront.

In a documentary otherwise lacking in conflict, such a scene functions as reversal—as the people behind the camera are "interviewed" and not the other way around—as well as suspense of the unscripted kind. The "recordings on location" (*xianchang shilu*) claimed by the People's Liberation Army (PLA) to compose its TV program *Flutter, Flag of the Republic*—where the only cameras allowed are those recording people making obeisance to revolutionary martyrs (see figure 1.3)—do not warrant the name in comparison with the improvisation in contingency of *I Graduated*. The scene's placement right after H. J. G.'s interview creates another productive tension: June Fourth and the security apparatus are linked in the narrative, as if the former's mere mention by H. J. G. prompts the latter's swift response, making explicit that the state apparatus is what forestalls challenges to the narrative of "turmoil" and "counterrevolutionary riot." This placement not only indicates that the student movement is taboo but also suggests that its omission from the first interviewee's (L. D.'s) own account may result from more than private reluctance. The violence of repression lurks beneath the repression of violence.

The security apparatus returns in the fourth interlude, before the fifth and final interview section on June Fourth, thus giving the documentary a chiasmic structure. This time, however, security forces do not consist of guards on campus but the military police on Tiananmen Square. As outlined at the end of the previous chapter, a "National Flag Group" composed of three military police officers formerly in charge of flag ceremonies on the square expanded to a thirty-six-member so-called Protection Team on April 15, 1991, exactly two years after the 1989 protests began. *I Graduated* shows the Protection Team in action—not raising the flag, however, but lowering it. Goose stepping and shrilly shouted commands resound before any image fades in from a black screen. Still shots appear next, washed out to near black and white, first of Tiananmen hung with Mao Zedong's portrait, then of crowds of men, women, and children gathered in anticipation, some with cameras of their own. Video footage of the ceremony follows, awash in a dark orange that deepens in places to vermillion. As the flag is furled, the shot moves in, capturing the movements carried out by an officer with martial precision. The scene ends with the sound of command and marching again as the Protection Team bears the bundled flag toward Tiananmen and Mao.

The fact that Wang Guangli and team are able to film this scene at all surely required some subterfuge. Picture taking from a certain distance is permitted. Wang's crew not only records, however, but does so in obvious proximity. Operating independently, they would never have had such access. The closing credits, however, reveal a clue. Shi Jian is listed as the executive producer and coproducer of *I Graduated*. He himself completed in 1991 the eight-part documentary series *Tiananmen*, as mentioned earlier, with equipment from CCTV, where he worked. One can safely surmise that he used his CCTV credentials in 1992 to facilitate the filming of the flag scene in *I Graduated*. Two years later he would do the same for Duan Jinchuan and Zhang Yuan's *The Square* (1994), whose crew, under the guise of accompanying a CCTV crew headed by Shi Jian himself, interviewed police officers in charge of safeguarding Tiananmen Square. They were free to shoot there as they wished.[6] All of these filmmakers used state resources to collaborate on alternative production.

In stark contrast with *Flutter, Flag of the Republic*, where the audience is treated twice to the solemn elevation of the national flag along with the striking up of the national anthem, in *I Graduated* the ritual is reversed, the descent of the flag playing out in near silence against the background chatter of spectators, the quivering flagpole, and an occasional brutal blow as the officer ties up the flag. The goose stepping and the commands are much louder in comparison. They ring over still shots of crowds that, on first glance, may be taken from the 1989 movement. One onlooker even flashes the V-sign, a gesture so prevalent among June Fourth demonstrators that it had to be singled out for mockery in the PLA-produced *Songs of the Republic's Guardians: Collection of Reportage Literature on Martial Law Troops' Heroic Deeds in the Capital*, as described in the previous chapter. The color of the memories of 1989 may have faded to black and white, but the sky over the square is dyed red in bloody remembrance of the night of June 3 to 4. While the stridency of a police state has since then drowned out other voices from Tiananmen Square, Wang Guangli effects here a not-so-subtle subversion of official iconography in image as well as sound. Subterfuge is a prerequisite, as noted above, yet most impressive of all is confronting a state ritual in close proximity and then turning it upside down.

GOODBYE, GOODBYE

The flag-lowering interlude marks the film's transition to the June Fourth interview section. From the most surveilled space in China, Tiananmen Square, the scene returns to the sanctuary of the college campus. Right away the spectator is greeted with the buzz of cicadas and the voice and sight of a student met before, sitting outdoors. She is L. X. T., a Tsinghua University architecture student. In earlier segments, she expressed her views on cohabitation and study abroad. What she says in this section is even more personal. She recounts the story of a family friend, a classmate of her older brother's, who lent her books when she was little. On the night of June 3, 1989, his wife, pregnant at the time, was coming home. He became worried after hearing reports on CCTV and went out to meet her. While he was walking, a bullet went sideways through both of his eyes, blinding him. He has visited her family a couple of times since then, assisted by his wife, to ask about her older brother.

The mourning of the bereaved, in *Flutter, Flag of the Republic*, is staged as a public pageantry, buttressed in postproduction by an emotive voice-over and a swelling chorus with strings on the soundtrack. L. X. T.'s pain in *I Graduated* is profoundly solitary. She is outdoors and alone. The shot zooms in on her face as she relates the friend's blinding and zooms in further to an extreme close-up of her own eyes as she fights back tears. Those eyes, by turns blinking rapidly, averted, and shut, almost fill the frame when she says falteringly: "What I mean is . . . I've felt all that." Only the suddenly deafening noise of cicadas pierces the ensuing moments of silence. While the Republic's Guardians are treated with the hero's fanfare, their lives and deaths suffused with lofty purpose, senseless destruction marks the life of the young man—like the uncountable civilian casualties of June Fourth—in L. X. T.'s remembrance.

In recounting the blinding of a family friend three years ago, L. X. T. presents more than a factual truth. Her emotions attest to a moral truth: that civilians, not the military, were the victims of violence both directed and indiscriminate. But she does not wallow in emotion. Neither does Wang Guangli cut away at the climax. The shot continues, and as L. X. T. continues after collectng herself, it retracts to a medium close-up. She goes on to describe what happened after June Fourth. The university carried out an "educational" campaign, with mandatory "discussions" and reports in which students had to give an account of their actions during the protests. The atmosphere was tense for three to four months. Then normalization set in. The administration did not punish the students too severely, and they got on with their lives and studies. Seldom do they talk about June Fourth now. But they still think about it, says L. X. T. And it changed them.

Students may have moved on, as if things have returned to normal. Rarely do they mention what happened. But the reason they do not is not that June Fourth was a forgettable, insignificant moment in their lives. Rather, it is because of the bullet. For not just the blinded soon-to-be father was affected, and not just his family or L. X. T.'s family. The bullet tore through all of them and left its indelible mark. They all are part of the toll of the massacre, not just the hundreds of lives lost but also the innumerable lives changed forever. There is no talk of redress. Instead, the people themselves are made to bear the burden, exemplified by the unseen image of a woman assisting her blinded husband.

Rather than redress, talk took the form of organized "discussions," as L. X. T. relates, in all likelihood based on the kind of "study materials" compiled by the Party-state that was surveyed in chapter 1. Thus, the censorship of June Fourth, to reiterate, consists not solely in negation: the killing on the night of June 4, 1989, or the silencing of its memory thereafter. The proactive propaganda campaign to shape June Fourth's discourse—this, too, is censorship. The mandatory writing of reports on one's actions—this, too, is violence, here not as destruction but as coerced production. Silencing in this reconception is not so much the opposite of speaking as working in tandem with speaking: the subduing of recalcitrant voices alongside the reproduction of authorized discourse. Together, they constitute the total project of censorship. L. X. T.'s classmates do not talk about June Fourth because they would rather stay silent when the only acceptable words are lies.

As described in chapter 1, students and their feelings were a central target of the state media campaign in the wake of the 1989 movement, in two ways. First, their feelings had been "incited" (*shandong*), according to propaganda such as *Songs of the Republic's Guardians* and *Flutter, Flag of the Republic*, by the agitational speech of "extremely few people": liberal intellectuals, student leaders, foreign agents. That is why students needed to be subjected to a reeducation that taught them the "truth" about the "counterrevolutionary riot." Second, the Party-state itself pulled out all the stops in its own tried-and-true method of "emotion work."[7] Graphic depictions of the soldiers' martyrdom accompanied by the weepy arrangements mentioned above worked in concert to provoke the protestors to collective penitence.

Interviewees in the June Fourth section of *I Graduated* directly or indirectly respond to such tactics. Like L. X. T., their memories counter the claims of the government campaign that "extremely few people" fomented the protests, a radical minority against "the people," who stood with the party. A Peking University student named Y. D. T., from the shadows of a lower bunk, adamantly denies the imputation that students were "incited" into anything. He and his classmates acted, in the Arendtian sense, from a sense of social responsibility, going seven days without food. H. J. G., who earlier looked disconsolate when he brought up his dropping out of school, is now visibly animated. He gets "worked up" whenever anybody maligns the student movement. His life was saved by friends and classmates who risked their own lives in doing so. His is an alternative account of heroism, starring not soldiers but his peers—an account preserved by *I Graduated*.

An example of "emotion work" at its most damning is the interview of W. J. F. A caption in a previous segment of the film states that he joined the Chinese Communist Party (CCP) in 1989 and was assigned a job in Beijing upon graduation from Renmin University. In the June Fourth section, he at first appears to talk about something irrelevant, namely, job placement. Speaking with quiet assurance and a measured pace, he says he has always been steady in action and thorough in thought. Despite not being the best student, he ranked the highest on the university's job placement list.[8] One's academic record and "overall behavior" formed the basis for the ranking, he explains, the latter category a catch-all for one's politics, conduct, and relations with others. His success in 1992 owes in no small part to a decision made three years previously in the realm of politics. He "ardently" joined the party in

1989, among the first students to do so after June Fourth. The "ardor" he references is a knowing jest; he unabashedly admits that it was a "means" and not an "end." According to him, everybody understands the distinction: the former accounts for 90 percent of party applications, the latter, 10 percent. But these numbers alone do not fully evince W. J. F.'s calculation. Passion and its mobilization lie at the heart of the CCP. W. J. F. played along with a show of fervent feeling, recounted in the most subdued manner.

As a whole, *I Graduated* comprises more than June Fourth testimonies. It is not a "special topic program" (*zhuanti pian*) on June Fourth but paints a generation. It is a group portrait like *Songs of the Republic's Guardians*, but its main characters are ordinary students, not movement leaders, dissidents, or heroes. A few of them were devoted to the protests, to be sure, but they are not anointed as freedom fighters with solely the democratization of China on their minds. They play the guitar, opine on love, watch porn. One of the film's funniest moments exemplifies at the same time its extemporaneity. Just as Y. D. T.—who went on a weeklong hunger strike during June Fourth—is talking about sex, another student barges into his dorm room. Off-screen, the student hems and haws. Eventually he reveals that he has a porn tape and is looking for a place to play it. Y. D. T. rules out an old professor's home: the venue is hardly convenient. Leave it to college students, however, to find ways to circulate and consume forbidden films.

The group portrait of *I Graduated* is decidedly backward-looking in orientation. Absent are the rousing, forward-facing platitudes of commencement speeches. What weighs heavily is the sense of loss and farewell—to innocence, to youth, to community. After the final interview section on June Fourth, the shot dawdles in the now-empty dorms. Then in the train station, the new graduates send each other off. It is a deeply affecting scene, the valediction both collective and individuated: a bevy of arms clutching through the train window; a bespectacled face streaked with tears; a group gathered around a guitar player, singing of parting. Finally, over an image of a solitary smoker on the platform lost in thought, the last song of the film begins.

The song should strike a chord, for it is the same one with which the film opened. The closing credits would identify the musician as none other than the young man interviewed with a guitar perpetually at his side, H. J. G., or Huang Jingang. His song, "Goodbye," starts with a plucked guitar. Huang adds his voice to the melody when the title card fades into a tracking shot of a fenced sports field. Tracking shots of imposing dormitories and an enclosed construction site follow, similarly forbidding to Huang the dropout. Both voice and melody are plaintive while the images are filtered through nostalgic yellow. The lyrics are not so much sung as chanted, in a spoken-word style. They express loss and leave-taking, interspersed with evocations of azalea-covered hills and a head of long hair. "My beloved, goodbye, goodbye" is the falsetto refrain.

The first verse and refrain transitioned to the scene on campus of students packing their belongings. From the solitary smoker on the train platform, the refrain in its reappearance transitions to the second verse, sung over a night shot traveling down what turns out to be Chang'an Avenue, the avenue bisecting Beijing that passes by Tiananmen Square. The lyrics are now more narrative. Huang fixates on 1989, as reflected in the anaphora of four successive lines:

> In those days the organization criticized my unsteady stance and
> stammering
> In those days my brothers and I depended on each other for survival,
> often thinking of collective suicide
> In those days I was denounced harshly, but girl, you didn't say anything
> In those days my brothers and sisters were pure and without blemish

Huang remains immersed "in those days," which could refer to both June Fourth and the immediate aftermath, when life and death were at stake. The "organization" (*zuzhi*) in the first line signifies the CCP system of governance, here specifically the party branch at Huang's university. Huang's "unsteady stance" knowingly violates the injunction of the *People's Daily* editorial of April 26, 1989, titled "It Is Necessary to Take a Clear-Cut Stance Against the Turmoil." Again, what the Party-state demanded was not silence but rather the production of speech that performed the speaker's fealty. Huang's "stammering" and the girl not saying anything, then, represented acts of resistance to censorship. But if Huang was subject to reprimand, he was also not alone. He had family outside the organization. Now removed in time and space from his "brothers and sisters," however, he can recover that solidarity only on solo guitar: "I will miss you all, and write and sing songs for you from afar."

As Huang sings, the image continues down Chang'an Avenue in a single shot. Near the end of the song, the shot turns right. It then pans left as the music stops, capturing in slow motion a group of people scrambling across the street in darkness. The shot freezes over these figures, many of whom are clad in white. Meanwhile, the sound of heavy vehicles gets increasingly louder. It extends into the credits, gradually decreasing in volume until the film is over. This sound is not of tanks or armored personnel carriers bearing down on Tiananmen Square. It is wind blowing on the microphone. The crowd crossing the street is not running in panic from gunfire. They are high schoolers on their way to catch the flag-raising ceremony at dawn. The entire sequence, in one shot, was filmed in July 1992 by Wang Guangli and a camera operator in the early morning hours from a taxi.[9]

Recall the shot that led viewers into Peking University by way of a restaurant. Now the filmmakers are shooting guerrilla-style, in the dark and on the move. The shot is an unambiguous visual and aural re-creation of the night of June 3 to 4, 1989. A journey that started with the return to campus has to return, ultimately, to Tiananmen Square. The prelude played over yellow-tinted images of dormitories and then a construction site, designating a trajectory from school to society. The postlude, played in the dark, suggests that all roads lead back to the square. As with the earlier black-and-white image of the spectator giving the V-sign at the flag-lowering ceremony, the final shot of *I Graduated*—a freeze-frame of young people running near Tiananmen Square at night—can be viewed as a June Fourth memento bequeathed to the present. Without a budget—much less official permission—to re-create that night, the filmmakers creatively used the available resources.

But both still images are just as amenable to a different interpretation. The high schoolers, after all, are running to witness the solemn ceremony of the raising of the national flag. Do these students remember that a mere three years ago, students not much older than they also ran near Tiananmen Square, not toward a state ritual revamped precisely in the wake of June Fourth (as detailed in chapter 1) but away from gunfire? Or has the Party-state propaganda campaign in the media and "patriotic education" succeeded to such an extent that not just they but also the crowd at the flag-lowering ceremony, young and old, no longer remember? Can these people be members of the same viewing public of *I Graduated*?

TENSES IN TENSION

There is another 1992 graduate of Peking University whom Wang Guangli did not interview. In fact, she majored in French in the Department of Western Languages and Literatures, exactly like L. D., the first interviewee in *I Graduated*. She is Tang Xiaobai. She made her own first film, a fiction feature, in 2001, nine years after Wang's documentary. It was also independently produced, the director's Tang Films Ltd. registered in Hong Kong. It, too, was shot in Beijing without authorization. And it, too, concerns college graduates after June Fourth.

Why is Tang Xiaobai's film called *Conjugation*? Like the director herself, the female protagonist, Xiaoqing, is studying French in college.[10] Early in the film, an instructor teaches in class the *plus-que-parfait*, or pluperfect, illustrated on the blackboard with the breakdown of "had spoken." The instructor describes this tense as pertaining to an action completed before a past action. She is played by Tang herself (figure 2.2).[11]

FIGURE 2.2 Tang Xiaobai, the director of the film *Conjugation* (2001), teaches French in a scene from the film.

Conjugation (*dongci bianwei*) in Chinese literally means "verbs changing positions." That the director chooses tense, not mood, person, number, or voice, to illustrate conjugation bespeaks the importance of time in the film. At the end of the French class, the instructor explains to the students why there are so many lessons to review: "because of the suspension of classes last semester, the curriculum was disrupted; we have to catch up." The film opened with three successive white titles on a black background: "The Year 89," "Winter," and "Beijing." "Last semester," then, refers to the spring of 1989. But the student protests that then gripped the nation are not mentioned. The logic of events, the "because," stops at the "suspension of classes." Students are now expected to make up for lost time so that nothing will be amiss. They will have caught up when no disruption could have taken place at all. In this way does the past impinge upon the present, and the future cancels out the past.

Not that the Tiananmen movement is on Xiaoqing's mind. In class she is not taking notes on verbs—literally "movement-words" in Chinese—but rather jotting down nouns: items such as towels, detergent, and condoms that she and her boyfriend, Guo Song, need to purchase for their new home, a rented room in a Beijing alleyway. She is preoccupied by the present and not the past or pluperfect. She is the one who has undergone conjugation, having "changed positions" from the square she once occupied to the studio she now wants to furnish, her attention absorbed by the private realm in lieu of the public. When she does review French later in the film, she uses binoculars to look at the Post-it Notes she affixed to the studio ceiling. Instead of providing a distant view, whether into the future or into the past, these binoculars are trained on verbs in the present tense. She is behind in her lessons. And she is nearsighted indeed.

If tense is chosen to illustrate conjugation, why is the pluperfect chosen to illustrate tense? From the perspective of this 2001 film—or from the perspective of any subsequent audience—the plot takes place in the past of winter 1989. The past perfect, that which took place before this past, is precisely the Tiananmen Square protests of the preceding spring. The conflict of *Conjugation* lies in its tenses, so to speak, which Tang herself embodies. She is the director who returns to the past or, rather, the past of the past, the event not pictured that set the story in motion. She is also the figure of authority who wants to speed along in order to overcome the past, the pedagogue drilling the pluperfect conjugation of "to speak" whose placement before the blackboard visually bars speech. Speech is precisely located in time only in the pluperfect, centered in space on a public square. That space-time is precisely no longer spoken about.

This conflict between forward acceleration and backward pull is evident in several places in the film. At the factory where Guo Song works, a placard counts down the number of days until the Asian Games of 1990, which Beijing hosted from September 22 to October 7 of that year.[12] The first time the placard appears, 282 days are left; a later shot of the countdown shows 264 days. This future-oriented number goes down, while an ascending one, the number of days since June 4, 1989, is not counted. A party cadre at the factory lectures Guo Song on the importance of the upcoming Asian Games. She orders him to participate in a dance group that will compete with other groups for a spot in the opening ceremony. She names two imperatives for college graduates like him recently assigned to the job: "sense of organization" and "discipline." The next time Guo Song is in the factory, he is indeed rehearsing the group dance. Although visibly disgruntled, he has nevertheless fallen into line, his body partaking in movements "organized" and "disciplined." He is forced to physically act out his reintegration into the body politic. The party cadre's command is a form of censorship, here not as proscription but as prescribed performance in an authorized production.

The cadre is not explicitly prescribing the memory of June Fourth, neither is she simply directing Guo Song to the future of the Asian Games. Her words draw upon a past too, the same past of revolutionary heroism exploited by *Songs of the Republic's Guardians* and *Flutter, Flag of the Republic*, discussed chapter 1. Sense of organization and discipline are not broached haphazardly. They are the exact two qualities mentioned in a scene halfway through the 1956 film *Battle on Shangganling Mountain*, a Communist classic about the Battle of Triangle Hill (1952) in the Korean War—or the War to Resist U.S. Aggression and Aid Korea, as it is officially called in China. When the dashing company commander leaves the mountain stronghold of Shangganling without permission to take out enemy bunkers, his superior, the division commander, scolds him over the phone: "In the face of this cruel battle, we need even more a heightened sense of organization and discipline." Adherence to hierarchy is a greater virtue than valor.

Conjugation's reference to *Battle on Shangganling Mountain* is far from fortuitous. Later in the film, when Guo Song and his friend Tian Yu are in the latter's home talking and watching TV, *Shangganling* is being broadcast. Playing alongside their conversation is the famous song "My Motherland," sung by the nurse and soldiers yearning for home as they are holed up in a cave. After Guo Song falls asleep on the couch later in the night, Tian Yu watches the scene toward the end of the movie where the PLA's double, the People's Volunteer Army (PVA), is about to retake lost positions. The shout "Company Commander, let the people of our motherland hear the news of our victory!" is followed by the sound of machine gunfire. These are the last words the soldier Little Yang proclaims before he blocks an enemy bunker's gunfire with his chest so that his company can overrun the position. The episode is based on the real-life heroics of the famed Korean War martyr Huang Jiguang.[13]

Tian Yu, watching *Shangganling* in the winter of 1989, is not going to reprise Little Yang's role. But the rerun, coming after the crackdown, works in tandem with TV programs such as *Flutter, Flag of the Republic*. It reminds the viewing public of the sacred duty of soldiers in the PVA as well as the PLA to defend the nation. Those whom they fight have to be the enemy, whether encroachers from without or counterrevolutionaries from within. *Conjugation* shows, as the previous chapter testifies, that in the immediate aftermath of June Fourth, TV programming glorified soldiers and their selfless sacrifice and (re)called the audience to the republic forged in the flames of war and to the canonical tradition of obedience to organization. "Organization" (*zuzhi*) in party parlance, as seen in the earlier discussion of Huang Jingang's "Goodbye," refers to the CCP itself, that originative organization. To have a sense of organization, then, is to be endowed with party sense.

After June Fourth, declarations both in public and behind closed doors of one's allegiance to the regime were demanded first from national- and provincial-level officials and military commanders.[14] They were succeeded by "similar performances in schools, factories, research institutes, and administrative bodies across the nation as virtually every urban citizen was required to account for his or her actions since April and publicly announce solidarity with the new hard-line policies."[15] In *I Graduated*, the interviewee L. X. T. mentioned "discussion" sessions at her university where students had to confess their errors. In *Conjugation*, Guo Song's participation in the command production that is the factory dance would qualify as penance. What is more, the transplantation of sense of organization and discipline from *Shangganling* to *Conjugation*, and from the mouth of a division commander to the mouth of a factory cadre, indicates the militarization of society in post–June Fourth Beijing. The cadre even speaks of the dance group in terms of a "phalanx." From *Shangganling* to *Flutter, Flag of the Republic*, from professions of loyalty to confessions of wrongdoing, censorship reveals itself less in silencing and confinement than in authorized forms of speech and sociality.

Guo Song is now expected to acquire soldierly virtues, when soldiers were the ones who displaced him, Xiaoqing, and their friends from that public space par excellence, Tiananmen Square. In place of the bullet-ridden body of Little Yang in *Shangganling*, however, *Conjugation* holds open a space for a body that is never seen. It is not present and so cannot serve as a model to imitate or emulate, whether in a spectacular dance or in a spectacular death. Instead, belonging to the pluperfect, it haunts the narrative past, in reference not so much to its own person as to a people, a body public that, along with him, went missing.

THE DISAPPEARED BODY

Remainders from the crushed movement litter *Conjugation*'s landscape. After the initial titles of "The Year 89," "Winter," and "Beijing," the film opens with a tracking shot of a public bus depot. As the shot scans the buses parked for the night, a couple on a bicycle emerges from their midst: Guo Song pedaling slowly, Xiaoqing seated in the back, holding onto him. Then they stop, and Guo Song goes from bus to bus trying to open the door. He eventually manages to do so, and through the windows the audience dimly sees the two of them making love inside. Only then does the movie title, *Conjugation*, appear.

This opening scene, with Xiaoqing and Guo Song riding a bicycle in the dark, is a succinct metaphor for underground filmmaking as a kind of alter-production. *Conjugation* is set mostly indoors or at night. The shooting is on the move from the start, guerrilla-style, operating under cover of darkness. Like the couple then breaking into a bus to make love, it is characterized by contravention, in defiance of restrictions imposed. There can be no crowd scenes out in the open in broad daylight. The one exception is the factory group dance in which Guo Song is forced to join, although even this takes place in what appears to be an enclosed space. The suggestion is that, after June Fourth, all public gatherings have to be party-approved. The rest of the film shows the main characters isolated and vagabond: in the interiors of the café and rented rooms or in moving vehicles—bicycle, taxi, the back of a truck.

Like the camera itself, the two lovers are in motion from the very beginning, "movement words changing positions." They are conjugating in a bus because they do not have their own place yet. But they may be drawn there for another reason, too. During the Tiananmen Square protests, public buses were stationed at the northern end of the square, where they were used not only as transportation but also as dorms, canteens, student command headquarters, and medical clinics for hunger strikers.[16] They are therefore a reminder of the time and place where Guo Song and Xiaoqing met and of the passions of that spring. Where a multitude of bodies once huddled, however, only two now hug. Outside the bus and showing the windows' partitions, the shot frames an enclosure where the couple engages in the most private of acts in the most public of sites.

In the next scene, Guo Song and Xiaoqing are again on the bicycle, this time moving into a rented room inside a family compound. As they enter the passageway of the residence, the radio is heard faintly in the background. It is difficult to make out the news broadcast against the street noise and dialogue, but snippets can be gleaned. They include "troops garrisoned in the capital," "People's Armed Police Headquarters," and "cutting down on expenditures." The sound of the radio fades and disappears while Guo Song and Xiaoqing are inside their new room.

The scene exemplifies the film's meticulous sound design. The radio broadcast publicizes a socialist ethos of frugality and, more important, the physical presence of a state that has reestablished "headquarters." The listener is reminded that martial law, instituted on May 20, 1989, remains in place in Beijing, and that this law has teeth in the form of weapons. The broadcast's fade out is also no happenstance. The director draws attention to it because next, the landlady sends her son out to buy new batteries for the radio. That the state broadcast fails to reach Guo Song and Xiaoqing's room implies that the young couple have found a sanctuary that would shield them from external interference. But at the end of the film, to be discussed later, the radio will reappear to suggest that no space is safe from encirclement.

It soon turns out that even the private realm is precarious. When Guo Song and Xiaoqing return home one evening, the landlord tells them that the police will be coming later to check on IDs, rooting out "random elements." The term typically refers to those without a proper *hukou*, or residency status, but as cohabiters without a marriage certificate, Guo Song and Xiaoqing too belong to this category of the population that lacks stability. They go back out into the night and wind up again in a public bus. But this time the bus is more than a love nest. Initially used as shelters, medical stations, and student headquarters, as noted above, public buses were ultimately used as barriers against tanks on June 3 and 4, 1989. In addition to camaraderie and excitement, therefore, the buses conjure the dead. The second time in the bus, Xiaoqing hums Taiwanese singer Chyi Chin's "Probably in Wintertime," a song about missing a loved one to whom the first-person voice hopes to come home "probably in wintertime." Xiaoqing suddenly stops humming and says to Guo Song that she just thought of "Foot Finger." Then, for the first and only time in the film, dissonant music mixed with ambulance sirens gets louder and louder, while the image zooms out from the couple to a long shot of the bus's dark, otherwise empty interior.

Who is Foot Finger, this person known only by his nickname?[17] This is the second time in *Conjugation* that he is mentioned. Earlier on the same day in a playground, as Xiaoqing is listening to a long-haired guitarist perform another Chyi Chin song, Tian Yu tells Guo Song that he would not have hired this guitarist for the café he is opening "if Foot Finger were still here." Later in the film, after another friend brings up Foot Finger during a hotpot dinner at Tian Yu's home, Guo Song says: "Too bad we can't hear Foot Finger's songs anymore." Foot Finger, then, is always associated with music and its absence. He is missed because he is missing. And it is already wintertime in 1989. The strident ambulance sirens puncture any possibility of his return.

If forward and backward gazes are embodied in the figure of Tang Xiaobai as drillmaster and director, then song and silence are disembodied in the figure of Foot Finger. Time and again, Tang marks Foot Finger's loss. Yet her representation of this loss cannot be more different from what is found in *Flutter, Flag of the Republic. Conjugation* utterly eschews the "scar" schema, sketched in chapter 1, of trauma plus melodrama. Here is no blood or gore, no flashback to the moment of martyrdom, no spectacle of any sort. Foot Finger himself—like June Fourth—is never depicted, much less in deified mold. In lieu of the effusive strings, chorus, and voice-over narration that accompany the mourning of the "Republic's Guardians," Tang Xiaobai proffers a discordant soundtrack that, combined with the distancing effect of the retreating shot, provokes the opposite of absorption. The parents of dead soldiers, in *Flutter, Flag of the Republic*, receive condolences from party leaders at state functions. The parents of Foot Finger, on the other hand, receive nary an explanation from school officials, other than "disappearance," when they come to Beijing to inquire after their son. Like him, they are not even pictured. And without a body to grieve over, all they can take away is his picture. These evocations of Foot Finger, which remind viewers that not just soldiers lost their lives, point to him as the locus of an alternative memory of June Fourth.

Tiananmen Square is where Foot Finger was lost. It is also where Guo Song and Xiaoqing gained each other. During the hotpot dinner when Foot Finger is briefly remembered, the friends talk about how the two met there the summer before. Guo Song's landing of Xiaoqing is attributed to his "grand performance of romantic passion." It was a "performance" in the sense that, when the curtains came down on June 4, 1989, Guo Song as well as Xiaoqing and friends did not continue to act. Like the vast majority of people who once took part in the protests, they tried to move on with their lives, putting the show and its bloody finale behind them. But this moving on, unlike June Fourth itself, was not a voluntary movement. The curtains dropped on them like a cudgel. Forced off the square, they had no choice but to "change positions."

Guo Song changes position. Unable to suffer any longer the bossy cadre—who in another scene reiterates the "significant and profound historical meaning" of the Asian Games, which would let the whole

world see "the cohesion between our Party and the Chinese nation"—
he quits the factory job. No success story ensues. He goes from the rock
of an imposed collective to the hard place of the privatized. Tang does
not paint the self-employed adrift in the postsocialist sea in glamorous
terms. Guo Song is forced to hawk scarves on the street. At first reluctant out of self-esteem, he eventually hollers out the wares. The director
proceeds to slow down the image track so that his gestures no longer
match his voice. She then adds nondiegetic music. The effect not only
jars but also resonates visually with the factory dance rehearsal, where
he moved in step with other employees to the instructor's call. A slash
of red cuts across both frames. As one scholar observes, both the group
dance and the scarf selling are degrading performances.[18] Guo Song's
stage has shifted from Tiananmen Square, with hundreds of thousands
of others, to factory grounds, conscripted in a troupe, to back street,
alone. In the wake of the massacre, no alternative form of publicness is
allowed to exist: either the "organization" or private enterprise.

Xiaoqing changes position too: she quits school and begins to work
in Tian Yu's café. Yet she continues to evoke an event that refuses to
remain in the past and constantly barges into the present. Just as the
long-haired guitarist substitutes for the absent Foot Finger, so is Xiaoqing, whom Guo Song gained on the square, a substitute for Foot Finger,
whom everyone lost. In one scene, Tang even groups Foot Finger and his
two surrogates together. Xiaoqing asks the guitarist in the café to play
more Chyi Chin music, saying that a friend used to sing his songs really
well. When the guitarist asks about the friend, she replies that they got
to know each other in the summer: "But not long after we met . . ." She
does not finish this sentence. Only after a while does she add—holding
a candle in vigil, as it were—"They say he disappeared."

Xiaoqing may have replaced Foot Finger, but she does not remove
his place. The "they" in "they say he disappeared" is purposely vague. It
could refer to the authorities because "disappearance" is the explanation
school officials gave to Foot Finger's parents. Or "they" could refer to
Guo Song and his friends, who, in their disposal of a legacy from June
Fourth, become complicit in the disappearing of Foot Finger.

That legacy is a box of donations collected during the protest movement, kept in Tian Yu's apartment. The donations are brought up indirectly and directly throughout the film as the friends grapple with the

legacy now that the movement is over. What to do with the money? Split it up? Turn it over to authorities? In the end, though, after Xiaoqing tells Guo Song that she is pregnant, Tian Yu in the next scene takes the box from under his bed and distributes the money among the friends. Contributions from the people in support of a collective cause, therefore, are ultimately divided by a coterie.[19]

This private appropriation parallels that of other assets in the narrative, including chairs for Tian Yu's café from the school where he used to teach. But more is at stake than even postsocialist plunder. It is underwritten by the state's ruthless scattering of the public spirit that momentarily reigned on Tiananmen Square. Whereas citizens once gave selflessly to a purpose larger than themselves, individual interests—with the crushing of communality and the continuation of martial law—have retaken precedence. The doling out of the donations among the friends bespeaks the betrayal of the movement's ideals as well as Foot Finger. Just as the latter's death is of no account to officials, so do his friends no longer count him.

After Guo Song takes his share of the money, the scene shifts to a clinic where Xiaoqing gets an abortion. The two then ride home in a taxi after the procedure (figure 2.3). The soundtrack is completely muted.

FIGURE 2.3 After Xiaoqing's abortion in the film *Conjugation*, she and her partner, Guo Song, ride past Tiananmen Square in a taxi.

They pass Tiananmen Square on their left. Guo Song's eyes look away; Xiaoqing's, at first closed, open feebly. The next shot shows Tiananmen, the Gate, seen through the right-side window. This point-of-view shot indicates that their gazes are actively avoiding the square. It was where their love began, but they drive by it now when their love (child) has just been aborted. *Abortion* in Chinese literally means "artificial miscarriage." Part of June Fourth's legacy, the donations collected on behalf of the protestors as a whole, is used for the unnatural, premature curtailment of life—like the lives of Foot Finger and hundreds of others. The "grand performance of romantic passion" of the spring has been subdued to wintry silence.

How to explain Guo Song and Xiaoqing's averted gaze? One could opine that they voluntarily do so, trying to put the past of June Fourth behind them. But the sound design suggests otherwise. Neither the averted gaze nor the silence is natural. Tang Xiaobai's blatant muting of the soundtrack underscores the muting of memories of the terminated movement. There is violence in the utter silence, a nondiegetic intervention that signals not only artifice but also force. Along with orienting young people toward participation in approved activities celebrating "cohesion" between the party and the public, along with the reruns of red classics that glorify soldiers and their selfless sacrifice, the state deafens with repression. These are the twin dimensions of censorship: prohibition plus propaganda. Tang shoots Tiananmen Square from a moving vehicle, like the filmmakers in *I Graduated.* The square is off limits to alter-productions like theirs, approachable only tangentially.

The contradiction of sound and silence constitutes the leitmotif of *Conjugation.* In the film's penultimate scene, Tian Yu tells the guitarist he hired to stop playing because the café-turned-hotpot restaurant has no customers and, what is more, his music is ugly. This music, associated with Foot Finger and the spring of 1989, is now bereft of a public. Taking its place in the next and final sequence is a familiar sound. Guo Song and Xiaoqing are moving out of their rented room, and they do so in the same soundscape in which they moved in: state radio. The news broadcast here, in contrast with earlier, is loud and clear. It announces the impending lifting of martial law in parts of Beijing on January 11,

1990, in consideration of the "great victory" of "stopping the turmoil" and "quelling the counterrevolutionary riot." The announcement concludes with an oblique reference to the wave of revolutions that by then has swept the Soviet Bloc, including Poland, Hungary, and East Germany: "No matter what kind of turbulence occurs in the world, we will unswervingly walk down the socialist path."

The radio broadcast is associated with the family compound where it is first heard at the start of the film. When the sound reappears at the end, it again apparently emanates from the residence because it begins while Guo Song and Xiaoqing (with the landlord's help) are loading their belongings onto a truck. But what starts out diegetically soon becomes not so much nondiegetic as supradiegetic. The radio announcement, without interruption, follows Guo Song and Xiaoqing onto the truck that then carries them down a bumpy road. It continues even after the image goes black. In its first instance, the radio ran out of battery power. Now it is seemingly not subject to material constraints, forever trailing the couple. The words of the state, then, do not merely bracket the film. Their concluding iteration portends omnipotence, omnipresence, and endless duration in time.[20] June Fourth is never spoken of by name by Guo Song, Xiaoqing, and their friends; the closest is "last summer in the square." Meanwhile, the official media has no qualms about labeling it "turmoil" and "counterrevolutionary riot." Suppression is always paired with amplification.

Guo Song and Xiaoqing are in motion from the very beginning, when they are biking through the bus depot. They use their bike again to move into the rented room. After the abortion, the two of them are moving, passively borne along in a taxi past Tiananmen Square. Now, as they sit in the bed of the truck, they do not touch each other, in motion without emotion, carried again listlessly, this time we know not where (figure 2.4). The bars at their back are a visual motif that recurs throughout the film. They suggest not only the forbidden and the forbidding but also the captive. Guo Song and Xiaoqing have no wings. But like Walter Benjamin's angel of history, they, too, are facing backward as onward they jolt, their belongings strewn before them like ruins. They are swept into the future's "homogenous, empty time" on a postsocialist path they cannot escape.

FIGURE 2.4 Xiaoqing and Guo Song ride on a truck filled with their possessions after moving out of their rented room.

Tian Yu's business venture has failed. Guo Song and Xiaoqing have become estranged. And Foot Finger is dead. The last place and time all of them were together was Tiananmen Square in 1989. But their "movement-word," once whole, has since then undergone conjugation and disintegration. The "they" of the friends are displaced and dispersed as the "they" of the state apparatus consolidates its numbers. When the factory cadre is lecturing Guo Song for the first time in her office, other officials are seen. The second time, she reminds him that "so many pairs of eyes in our factory are staring at you." The threat of ferreting out "random elements" is relayed first by the landlord, then by the land-lady, and finally by a police officer himself. The radio announcements switch between male and female voices. There is no place where Guo Song and Xiaoqing are immune. They are outlasted and outnumbered. The republic goes from strength to strength by continuously shattering other publics.

This is the somber note on which *Conjugation* ends. But another story within this story gives glimmers of hope—even if it, too, is ultimately ambivalent. While working at Tian Yu's café, Xiaoqing tells customers a series of three stories.[21] In the first installment, told to three men at the bar, a woman abused by her husband kills him with a knife but then does not know what to do with the body. In the second installment, told at a later time to a single customer at his table, the woman chops the corpse into pieces and stores them inside a pickling pot underneath the bed. Xiaoqing also introduces here the woman's two-year-old son, who at the time has yet to talk. In the third and final installment, told while Xiaoqing is in bed with that previous customer, the woman tells people that her husband has "disappeared." At first, they do not believe her, but as time passes, they start to, and then "after more time has passed, nobody brought up this disappearance any longer." Years later, even the woman herself no longer remembers clearly. One day, the dead man's sister visits and asks about her brother. The woman replies that he disappeared a long time ago; everybody knows that: "She said it with her heart at ease, because she thought nobody would know the truth." But in the middle of a meal, her son— who has been mute all these years—suddenly speaks: "Is dad's meat inside the pickle pot ready to be eaten?"

A current of violence courses through *Conjugation*, from Foot Finger's disappearance to the silencing of the Tiananmen Square sequence. Xiaoqing's tale and the film's editing rework the theme of killing and concealment to hint at a broader complicity beyond the state and the massacre. Her development of the story is influenced by developments in the larger story. After the first installment, she finds loose bills in a drawer at home and suspects that the donation money has been split among the friends. So when she next resumes the story, the dead husband is chopped up like the donations and, like the donations box, kept under the bed. Part of Guo Song's portion was used to pay for Xiaoqing's abortion (*duotai*), whose *duo* is homophonic with *duo*, meaning "to chop." The third installment occurs only after Xiaoqing has learned that Foot Finger, or rather his parents, did not receive a portion of the money. As Xiaoqing is telling this final installment, Guo Song is seen in the kitchen of the café-turned-restaurant, first sharpening a knife, then shaving red slices of mutton that fill the screen. Like the woman in the story, he wields a knife, guilty, by association, not of actual murder but of disappearing Foot Finger a second time.

The woman's story of her husband's disappearance is received over time with disbelief, then belief, and finally apathy. In the aftermath of killing, her strategy is not silence either but persuasion. A lie repeated often enough and with conviction is eventually bought and, what is more, forgotten. Yet the ending of Xiaoqing's tale allows for a certain optimism. *Conjugation* appeared in 2001. One could say that for twelve years, Tang Xiaobai, like the boy in the story, was mute. But just when one thinks that the truth would be buried forever, that all have already accustomed themselves to mendacity and apathy, someone speaks up— precisely one who was seemingly too young to know anything. To the contention that what was lost in 1989—a few hundred lives—was negligible, as expendable as a "foot finger," Tang responds that this foot finger is connected to a foot, this foot to an ankle, this ankle to a leg, and so on. It is a part that points to the whole to which it was attached. The director, too, is but a unit, yet she enacts a remembering of what was dismembered, a recollection of the split apart. Carried irresistibly forward, she nevertheless returns to the past in an effort to pick up the broken pieces.

Just as the characters were driven from Tiananmen Square, so was *Conjugation* displaced from where it was shot, having to move to Hong Kong to be postproduced and distributed. Where will Tang Xiaobai's story be heard? The space in which Xiaoqing speaks, from the café to a hotel room, turns private. Xiaoqing's audience shrinks as well: her listeners go from three to one to none because the man in bed may well be asleep. Even the light of her cigarette as she concludes her tale is but a faint reminder of the candlelight she held earlier while recalling Foot Finger to the long-haired guitarist. Her tale concludes with a question: "Is dad's meat inside the pickle pot ready to be eaten?" While the boy's question echoes the allegorical cannibalism in Lu Xun's "Diary of a Madman" (1918),[22] the tale as a whole resonates more strongly with "The New Year's Sacrifice" (1924). There the protagonist, Xiang Lin's wife, tells the story of her son's death to fellow villagers, who are at first sympathetic. They become apathetic and then annoyed, however, as she repeats the story again and again. It is another set of questions that trails Tang Xiaobai's film: Will it, too, go the way of Xiaoqing's storytelling and Foot Finger's songs? Will it, too, be deprived of a public, in terms of both space and audience? Will it—like Xiang Lin's wife's loss, along with other June Fourth narratives of loss—eventually fall on deaf, nay, antipathetic ears?

> Those who have suffered spiritual disorder and chaos often become
> silent afterwards. Their earlier zeal has died; their beliefs wander off
> like stray dogs. They allow the heart to grow barren, and the mind to be
> overrun with weeds. They experience a sort of spiritual arthritis, like a
> dull ache on a cloudy day. There is no remedy. They hurt. They endure.
> They distract themselves in various ways, whether by making money, or
> by emigrating, or by womanizing. (location 34)[23]

These lines may well describe the main characters of Tang Xiaobai's
Conjugation. Their "grand performance of romantic passion" during
June Fourth cut short, their friend Foot Finger "disappeared," they have
no choice in the wintry wake but to cope. And so they move on from
Tiananmen Square: Tian Yu and then Guo Song go into business, and
Xiaoqing even has an affair. She and Guo Song, by the film's end, have
literally become silent. Not only are they muted while passing by the
square after Xiaoqing's abortion, but they are also deafened into speech-
lessness in the last scene on the moving truck by the radio broadcasting
the Party-state message ad infinitum.

The above lines are actually the opening paragraph of Sheng Keyi's
novel *Death Fugue.* They signal from the beginning, therefore, the novel's affinity with *Conjugation* as well as *I Graduated.* The unnamed
"they" indicates that *Death Fugue* will paint a group portrait like the
two films did. The novel, too, is set "afterward." In the aftermath of what,
one does not know: the "disorder and chaos" have yet to be specified.
But the aftereffects are specified, and they parallel the downward trajectory limned in *Conjugation.* In place of the energy and enthusiasm of
earlier, disappointment and despair have descended. "They" as a result
turn to distractions to numb the pain. Both the repetition of "spiritual"
(*jingshen*)—in fact, the first word of the novel in Chinese—and a figural
language of desolation and abandonment make clear that the unnamed
trauma is not physical. It has to do with the mind, heart, and beliefs.

The vagueness of the writing in *Death Fugue* is a circumstance of
its publication. State propaganda, like the kind examined in chapter 1,
could designate the "counterrevolutionary riot" directly. *I Graduated*
and *Conjugation*, although shot in Beijing secretively—mostly indoors,
in the dark, or on the move—could also afford to be direct to a degree

because they were never intended for wide release in China. The former film contains June Fourth testimonies, as detailed earlier, while the latter opens with the setting of "The Year 89," "Winter," and "Beijing" in successive title cards. *Death Fugue*, on the other hand, was intended for domestic readers. It appeared in a 2011 issue of the mainland literary journal *Jiangnan*, which is cosponsored by the Zhejiang province branch of the China Writers Association (CWA).[24] Although over a dozen Chinese book publishers turned down Sheng's manuscript, the facts that it passed censorship understood as inspection (*shencha*) and that it appeared in China at all meant that the author could not but write coyly.

Thus, Sheng announces this setup from the start. The novel begins in a country called Dayang whose capital, Beiping, is homophonic with the name of Beijing from 1928 to 1949. In Beiping is a public square called Round Square, with a size of 500,000 square meters—approximate to Tiananmen Square's at roughly 440,000. In late May 1989, a ten-meter-tall statue of a woman holding a torch, made mainly of Styrofoam plastic with plaster over it, was assembled on Tiananmen Square.[25] There it came face to face with the portrait of Mao Zedong hanging on the city gate of Tiananmen. This Goddess of Democracy was razed in the early morning hours of June 4. On Round Square, too, in 2019, there appeared a statue of a woman holding a torch. The *Death Fugue* statue, however, does not constitute a counter icon on the monumental space of the square. Sheng describes it as a public-address station of sorts, spewing out propaganda slogans, news, the weather, and poetry.

The allusions to the 1989 movement do not end there. In fact, the novel's primary plot revolves around a so-called Tower Incident. A nine-story-high tower of excrement of mysterious origin appears one day on Round Square. It causes a stir, and the government's handling of it—removing it swiftly and issuing a quick and unconvincing verdict on its provenance (a gorilla!)—leads to demonstrations. Dayang's government has control over the media. On the day after the tower's removal, newspapers across the country carry nearly identical headlines. Official reports echo unmistakably the rhetoric of Party-state pronouncements on June Fourth. As with its historical referent, the radio blames the Tower Incident on a minority of schemers: "If the small group of hostile elements in the capital take this opportunity to make trouble, they will be detained and severely punished!" (location 148). This small group is responsible for duping a larger populace: "ignorant people had been incited into rallying at Round Square, and they were destroying the public peace" (location 219). "Incitement" (*shandong*)—a charge frequently leveled against the 1989 protestors in propaganda pieces and explicitly denied by a student interviewee in *I Graduated*—reappears here. And the Round Square protestors, like those of Tiananmen Square, are violently repressed in the end.

Despite these thinly veiled parallels, *Death Fugue* is cagey in its representations of time. It may lead off in Beiping, but *when* it is located is more difficult to pinpoint. Only after readers do some math with the details sprinkled over the chapters can they sort out the various temporal threads, of which there are three main ones: 1989, the year of the Tower Incident; 1999, the "afterward" in which the narrative commences; and 2039, the perspective from which the narration occasionally speaks. (A fourth, in 2009, will be discussed later.) *Death Fugue* thus has a tense structure similar to that in *Conjugation*. In both, 1989 signifies the past perfect, with 1999 as the past and 2039 as the present in the novel. But not only does the 2011 *Death Fugue* exhibit a backward pull like *I Graduated* and *Conjugation*, it also concurrently projects into the future. Its scope is much broader than that in the two films, which focus on June Fourth and its immediate aftermath. Sheng reaches backward and forward more than two decades in each direction.

When the narrative commences in 1999, the reader is introduced to the protagonist, Yuan Mengliu, as one of the "they" of the opening paragraph. He is someone who, having experienced "spiritual disorder and chaos," distracts himself afterward, in his case, with womanizing. Now in his thirties, Mengliu works as a surgeon. He fusses over his health and keeps his appearance as immaculate as scrubs. Yet his physical well-being is a mere salve to unremitting spiritual impairment. "As a healthy person, Mengliu had no hemorrhoids, no beliefs, no ulcers, no ideals" (location 66; translation modified). He was not always this way.

Like Tian Yu, the teacher turned café owner, and Guo Song, the student turned factory worker then street hawker, in *Conjugation*, surgeon is Mengliu's adopted profession. Ten years earlier, in 1989, he was a well-known poet. He did not use to care about his appearance, writing poetry all night long, unshaven, with tousled hair. What is more, poetry for him was not solely an individual pursuit. Together with Heichun and Baiqiu, he belonged to the celebrated Three Musketeers. The three of them had sworn brotherhood, with the common aim to "awaken slumbering souls with poetry."[26] They were part of a general artistic and cultural ferment that reigned in those days. This ferment was not limited to "society." Literary salons were held at the Green Flower Bar, run by a man who turns out to be Mengliu's father, but state institutions played an equally vital role. Mengliu worked in the literature department of the National Wisdom Bureau of Young Elites, or the Wisdom Bureau, which had over 50,000 members in Beiping alone in dozens of departments. Outside the Wisdom Bureau were two long walls, dubbed the double-tracked wall, which functioned as a forum where discussion and debate took place. These various spaces were instrumental to the tenor of the times, when intellectuals were held in high esteem.

This is the context in which the 1989 Tower Incident arises. Because of the lack of transparency in the authorities' response, the tower of poop takes on a larger significance. As someone writes on the double-tracked wall, "there will come a day when even the sun above us will be covered up by them" (location 209). The resistance gathers steam, and both Heichun and Baiqiu contribute poems. Mengliu, however, stays on the sidelines. And so does Qizi—at first. Mengliu meets Qizi, who also works in the Wisdom Bureau, in an interrogation room where they and others are detained for their participation in a demonstration. But Mengliu was merely a curious bystander, and according to Qizi herself, she was simply lonely and bored after breaking up with her boyfriend. The two become a couple and are far from ardent activists; their plan was to go abroad together. Only after a fight with Mengliu does she throw herself into the movement, eventually becoming one of its leaders, along with Heichun.

With the persistence of the protests comes the tightening vise of the state. In addition to its censorship of the news, cited earlier, it starts to impinge upon cultural production. This is what happens to Baiqiu's poetry as the pressure mounts:

> Up until then Baiqiu's poetry had merely received criticism or warnings, and rejection by people with ulterior motives. Now it was all completely banned—though the word "banned" may be

too politically charged. To put it more precisely, no media source would publish his work. The editors stammered and stuttered, dodging behind various pretexts. Even those intellectuals who had previously valued Baiqiu's poetry quite highly now began to have reservations. (location 1157; translation modified)

The proscription does not materialize in any official ban. It might originate with the state but does not stop with state institutions and agents. Instead, it is much more insidious, emanating as a kind of ether that envelops editors, publishers, and critics at large. Even Mengliu's father, the owner of the Green Flower Bar that serves as an intellectual gathering place, no longer wants Baiqiu reciting there.[27] Baiqiu's poetry is deprived of both a reading and a listening public.

Baiqiu knows the source of this change. A line of poetry in his suicide note reads: "I see soldiers on patrol in my verse, searching everyone's conscience" (location 2935). The patrol's reach extends beyond the poet to "everyone," all potential readers who are preemptively vetted. And it is ultimately soldiers and the deadly force they represent—not the reillumination of the benighted masses, as state propaganda would have you believe—that are responsible for ending the protests, Baiqiu's poetry, and Baiqiu himself. Repression here is real: words forestalled from the world, a life lost.

Baiqiu's suicide prefigures the violence of the military crackdown. Qizi and Heichun disappear without a trace. A stray bullet kills Mengliu's half-sister. His father dies in prison. But Sheng Keyi never portrays the violence directly for reasons readers can guess. Mengliu is not present at or around Round Square on the night of the crackdown: he fell asleep at home. So Sheng evokes the mayhem of that night throughout the novel with a language suffused with the macabre: birds whizzing by with the sound of bullets, sail boats whose masts point skyward like tanks with their cannons. She also paints the massacre's aftereffects on Mengliu's psyche. Once in a while, those effects become decidedly somatic. At "the juncture of every spring and summer"—that is, around the time of June 4, 1989—he would experience an illness accompanied by hallucination: "He saw bodies lying in a disordered heap on the ground. The sun scorched them so that the people were faint and dehydrated."[28] The faint and dehydrated people on the ground recall the hunger strike undertaken by Tower Incident—and June Fourth—protestors. Although physically unscathed himself, Mengliu cannot escape these images. Elsewhere his morbid cast of mind is expressed in the olfactory: "A faint smell of blood was detectable, sometimes seeming to come from the flora and fauna, sometimes from the sewer, and sometimes from a certain class of people who couldn't seem to rid themselves of it no matter how often they bathed, applied perfume, or covered it up with gorgeous clothing" (location 303). The roads that formerly cracked under tank treads may have been repaired, and the buildings that were once riddled with bullet holes may have been fixed, but a decade after the crackdown and the cleanup, a whiff of the carnage still lingers in Mengliu's nose, no matter how thoroughly surfaces around him have been scrubbed. These sense memories are very much involuntary: Mengliu has no interest in preserving them. He, too, can be counted among the "class of people" who, with a perfumed exterior, try to mask the chronic stench.

Why does a whole "class of people" not want to remember? Blood is why. And blood is why Mengliu became a surgeon. When his anesthetist asks him why he no longer writes poetry, he glimpses a hairpin on her head and is overwhelmed by associated images: "The red hairpin flashed, catching the light's glare, and suddenly it was as if the sky was on fire, gun smoke filling the air" (location 1135; translation modified). That night of bloodshed is why Mengliu abandoned poetry. But there is another reason he stopped writing. He has blood on his own hands. He was not in Round Square on that night with Qizi and Heichun. His betrayal of them, to his mind, compounds his betrayal of the mission of the Three Musketeers, which is to arouse people from their torpor with art. In the aftermath he traces the opposite trajectory of the writer Lu Xun, who at the beginning of the twentieth century turned from medicine to literature in order to rouse the dormant masses from the "iron house," that most famous imagery in modern Chinese literature, from Lu Xun's 1922 preface to his short-story collection *Outcry* (1923).[29] At the century's end, Mengliu ditches the pen for the scalpel. His abandonment of poetry is a metaphor for what the massacre did to the life of the spirit in contemporary China.

Baiqiu's suicide as well as Qizi and Heichun's disappearance marked the turning point. Poetry for Mengliu no longer calls up anything but death, illusion, and futility. Ten years after the Tower Incident, he has long given it up. He is far from the exception, however, and is instead representative of a new rule:

> Poets suffered a worse fate than the common people. They were even regarded as rogue elements, who were fanning the counter-revolutionary flames. They were good-for-nothings, and that's why many remade themselves as businessmen. Now they were bosses, entrepreneurs and merchants, burying their poetry beneath their pillows, not bringing it even a half-step out of the bedroom. They were duplicitous all day long, expressing scorn for poetry when they were out drinking with friends, their poems—suppressed by cash—becoming coarse doggerel. All their elegance was pretense. They gradually fell in love with this life, disguising themselves as the business elite. They maintained an ambiguous attitude and a discreet distance from the affairs of the nation, holding tight to their women and children, while they watched the stock market as if their lives depended on it and engaged in their spare time in a little antique collecting, or calligraphy, or landscape painting. The book they never tired of reading was the passbook to their bank accounts. (location 4155; translation modified)

Just as Tian Yu and then Guo Song in *Conjugation* went into business, so did the poets in *Death Fugue*. Sheng explicitly uses the word *suppression* (*zhenya*) to account for poetry's degradation into doggerel. A word linked with military-political force, here it is tethered to *cash*, as if the lure of lucre brought about the downfall. Yet the earlier charge against poets of instigating "counterrevolution" reveals the primacy of the political-military dimension. Under the threat of subjugation, poets had to go into hiding. Their reemergence as merchants is but an epiphenomenon. Crushed are their concerns for the public, reduced now to the hearth and home, the *oikos* in the economic. What artistic endeavors they still pursue are mere pastimes that decorate their bourgeois lives like frills, which complete their metamorphosis from the cultural into the business elite.

One poet in *Death Fugue*, however, betrays more than art. Active during the Tower Incident, Jiawan reached out to a friend and fellow protestor named Mogen in the summer after the crackdown for the purported purpose of doing something "for the sake of their fallen class-mates" (location 2962). He claimed to have left the "Plum Party" and quit his government job. Under the pretense of starting an underground newspaper for popular agitation and linking up with foreign organizations, he managed to get Mogen sentenced to five years in jail for leaking state secrets. Jiawan was recompensed for his service. He started a successful pharmaceutical company and married the daughter of a senior government official. He still found time to write though, namely, "lyrics praising the political apparatus" (location 2990). In Jiawan's case, then, his poems were not "suppressed" by cash—or by force, for that matter—but inspired by power and its nexus with profit. For his troubles, he even received Dayang's highest poetry prize upon his death.

Mengliu's forsaking of poetry, Baiqiu's ban, and above all the latter's suicide demonstrate the destructiveness of censorship. Jiawan's opportunism, on the other hand, reveals that the total project of censorship comprises a creative dimension as well. Alongside the stamping out of the "counterrevolutionary" kind, the penning of panegyrical poems garners awards and rewards. That poetry can be used so instrumentally bespeaks its value to state legitimization. Mengliu does not partake in this campaign. As he says, "Poetry has become a whore's cry" (location 5123). His refusal to take up the pen again can be seen, in this light, as the refusal to blaspheme the memory of the Three Musketeers. When to be a poetically productive member of society means selling out one's friends and principles, then to be adamantly unproductive constitutes an assertion of freedom.

ART AND ARTIFICE

Death Fugue takes its title, of course, from Paul Celan's eponymous poem. Written in the immediate aftermath of World War II, "Todesfuge" conjures the dehumanizing horror of the Nazi death camp in incantatory rhythms. For Sheng Keyi to call her novel by the same name is to draw an immediate parallel between the Holocaust and June Fourth. Not that Sheng is equating the genocide of millions of people over several years with the killing of hundreds mainly over one night. In an interview, she once posited the questions that for her connect the novel to the poem, and June Fourth to the Holocaust: "After a spiritual massacre, are there any survivors? Who are the survivors? What do they do? How do they face themselves and life again?"[30] The weight of the comparison rests on the "after." What is the life of the spirit in the aftermath of catastrophe? Mengliu as well as Jiawan are the author's responses to these questions. But these two characters alone do not tell the whole story.

While not as elaborate as a fugue, the construction of *Death Fugue* is nevertheless intricate. It is divided into two parts. Chapters in the first part alternate between 1999 and 1989. In the 1999 thread, Mengliu falls asleep in a rowboat one day only to wake up and find himself in a land called Swan Valley. The rest of the 1999 thread as well as the entirety of the second part of the novel are set in that valley. Sheng facilitates this otherworldly turn in the narrative with references to literary utopias both Chinese and Western. Swan Valley, like the idyllic Peach Blossom Spring in Tao Yuanming's famous fifth-century fable, is reached by boat. When Mengliu first arrives, he sees children playing with jewels as if they were trifles, much like in Eldorado in *Candide*. Before long, however, familiar dystopian motifs take over. Drawing from canonical works such as Yevgeny Zamyatin's *We* (1924), Aldous Huxley's *Brave New World* (1932), and George Orwell's *1984* (1949), the author depicts a polity characterized by totalitarian faith in technology, pseudo-scientific reason, and the perfectibility of human beings. The state motto—"Ensuring a quality population starts with good genes"—entails omnipresent surveillance, ordained marriage, and artificial insemination along with a ban on sex, not to mention the dumping of "low-quality" babies in a trash pit. Along with the wiping of people's memories, control of the media, and sophistic contortion of words and their meanings, Swan Valley thus functions in *Death Fugue* less as an alternative to Dayang than as its eugenic counterpart.

It comes as no surprise to readers in the last chapter that Qizi, Mengliu's ex, is the leader of Swan Valley. In the novel's penultimate scene, she reveals to Mengliu that her legs were crushed by a tank in the Tower Incident crackdown. Heichun was severely burned. The two of them, with the help of Mengliu's father—who would be imprisoned as a result—managed to escape. They founded Swan Valley, Heichun drafting before his death its constitution, "The Genetic Code of the City-State." Having championed democracy and opposed authoritarianism in

Dayang, the two bring a despotic streak to their governance of the new world. Sheng Keyi thereby implies that we are corrupted by what we fight against. Like *I Graduated* and *Conjugation*, her June Fourth allegory does not pose a counter-romance to Chinese state narratives, with student protestors exalted in lieu of soldiers. Rather, the author raises a theme distinct even from the two films. The films bemoan the loss of idealism among young people after the massacre; *Death Fugue* suggests that idealism itself can be a double-edged sword. The same zealous ideals and beliefs that galvanize support and carry revolutions forward, that make their leaders such charismatic figures, are the same zealous beliefs and ideals that brook no dissent, that employ extreme methods in their implementation. Swan Valley and the People's Republic of China alike were founded with the best of intentions.

The whole time that Mengliu is in Swan Valley, he is variously cajoled, threatened, and abused physically into writing poetry again, namely, a paean to his adopted land. Yet Mengliu resists this form of censorship to the end. He holds poetry in too much esteem to sully its name by accommodating the state. In doing so, he not only redeems himself from the breach of the Three Musketeers' promise but also shows that he has hung on to certain ideals after all. And Qizi validates his obstinacy, declaring in the novel's penultimate scene: "Power, beauty, physical torture—you've withstood them all. You refused to write poetry. You have proved yourself a poet" (location 5406). The double-crosser Jiawan may have been officially recognized as such, but it is Mengliu who, first introduced as an almost antihero (apolitical womanizer fastidious about his body), ultimately embodies a rebuke of the spiritual treachery of the times.

Death Fugue, however, does not conclude there. Another meaning of *fugue* is a period of amnesia caused by trauma, a dreamlike state characterized by wandering from home. The novel ends with an "Epilogue" set in 2009. The Swan Valley episode was all a dream: Mengliu woke up in the rowboat in which he had drifted off. Ten years later, he is at a party on a cruise ship. He is writing poetry again, despite not being able to publish. He even "edited an unofficial poetry journal, collecting a variety of voices, and also self-printed his poems in chapbooks, giving them to those who needed them, and reading from them at private gatherings." Poetry readings are no longer events, as in the heyday of the Three Musketeers, but Mengliu nevertheless persists not only in self-publication and distribution outside official channels but also in the convocation of disparate yet sympathetic voices. More fundamentally, "he had belief again, which was to be, with a noble and solemn simplicity, an ever alert poet, and to leave true traces in history."[31] Twenty years after the Tower Incident, that stray dog named "belief" has come home. Mengliu may not have resumed the ambition to "awaken slumbering souls," but at least he himself vows to stay "woke."

What to make of Mengliu's return—after a temporal hiatus and an oneiric sojourn—to consciousness and to poetry? He is not content anymore to fight compulsory speech with silence. He is actively engaged in the inscription, in the face of censorship as proscription plus propaganda, of "true traces in history." What is he doing on a cruise? At the soirée is a forum on "artistic freedom and urban violence," at which the following is pronounced:

> "To liberate a person's thought isn't easy, because this sort of liberation requires one to walk out of the circles of tenderness and enticement, and then to question authority itself."
>
> "The past should not be forgotten. Sometimes art is the only means by which we may find out the truth, and a flexible tool we rely on for communication. Some may think that freedom of expression depends upon one's environment, but I want to say that, for poets, writers, and artists, the environment shouldn't be the real issue. The real environment is in your mind. If you have a flame in your heart, then you can make any kind of water boil. If you have enough talent, you can walk a covert path to freedom."
>
> Their voices, amplified to fill the room, were brimming with an embellished beauty. (location 5509; translation modified)

These are the last three paragraphs of the novel. The two quotations express lofty thoughts: on the remembrance of the past, the privilege accorded art in the pursuit of truth, and the ardor that illumes everything. In the grand assumption of individual responsibility, they express Mengliu's renewed belief that, no matter how constraining the external environment, no obstacle is too high to overcome as long as he remains internally free. It is a message of hope, of the triumph of mind over matter that the author herself seems to have borne out. With *Death Fugue*, Sheng Keyi was able to "walk a covert path" and usher into publication—in mainland China—an allegory of June Fourth. Try as the Party-state might to bury the traces, Sheng is able to excavate this memory with her "flexible tool."

The novel's final line, however, casts the preceding sentiments into doubt. It is not Mengliu who intones them, but unidentified speakers. Their voices, furthermore, are doubly imbued with artificiality, both "amplified" and "embellished." Might they be painting too rosy a picture of creativity and creation? Does it indeed come down to talent, one's artfulness in tiptoeing through a minefield of taboos? Or could the truth be "embellished" beyond recognition? Just prior to the forum on "artistic freedom and urban violence," Sheng Keyi presents another artist and his work. Dadong was first mentioned in the beginning of the novel as Qizi's ex-boyfriend who almost blew himself up fabricating antiques. Now, in 2009, he has become a man of repute who made a fortune in the antiques trade and wanted to "try his hand at running a film company" (location 5497). He has organized the gathering on the cruise ship, where he announces that his company's first film project has finished preproduction. The movie, *The Genetic Code of the City-State*, with Steven Spielberg as director, is to be a "reflection on the 'Tower Incident' " (location 5500). Mogen, who was framed by Jiawan, is the scriptwriter. Mengliu would serve as the literary consultant.

What kind of movie would *The Genetic Code of the City-State* be? Is the big-name Hollywood director of *Schindler's List* brought in to turn the Tower Incident into another commercial product of sentiment and spectacle? Would the film ignite a popular and critical debate on public memory and mass-mediated culture?[32] Mogen and Mengliu's involvement suggests that the effort would be sincere, but not Dadong's, despite his declaration that the movie would be a "reflection." After all, the producer, merely "trying his hand" at film, was formerly known for fake antiques. He has since met with success, much like that other fabricator—Jiawan—of verse. Artifice, not art, is recompensed in post–Tower Incident Dayang, whether in 1999 or in 2009.

And so it is in 2019 as well. A faux Goddess of Democracy statue went up that year in Round Square, we might remember, broadcasting the weather, news, propaganda, and poetry. One can be sure, though, that the poems it amplifies are not those of the Three Musketeers but rather "lyrics praising the political apparatus." We might also remember that, in relation to the 2011 novel, there is another future frame of reference. In 2039, the year from which *Death Fugue* is narrated, the profit-seeking zeitgeist of 1999 has all the more materialized. Whereas poetry readings and intellectual debates effervesced at the double-tracked wall in 1989, that space, fifty years later, has "filled with so many posters advertising random products that the wall has virtually disappeared" (location 118). The submersion of the double-tracked wall is symptomatic of a larger flood. A church destroyed during the Tower Incident crackdown was eventually demolished to make way for a commercial building, with the entire street turned into a shopping promenade. Can a flame in your heart make this deluge seethe?

In the year 2039, whose poems will be published? Jiawan's or Baiqiu's? What will be shown on TV? *Battle of Shangganling Mountain* and other programming that ensconce the party in the national imagination? Or *I Graduated* and *Conjugation*? Which songs will be heard? *Songs of the Republic's Guardians*? Or those by Huang Jingang and Foot Finger?

This is the diluvian ethos in which Mengliu takes up the pen again. It is the same ethos in which Sheng Keyi took up her pen. *Death Fugue* cannot be accused of "embellished beauty." Readers may be heartened by Mengliu's recommitment to literature, but the future in store presents a bleak picture indeed. Mengliu is unaware of this future, and thus one could argue that his born-again belief is blind. Yet Sheng is outside the irony. She envisages this future. And despite the post–June Fourth environment she finds herself in, despite state censorship's double-pronged project of destruction and diversion that she has to contend with, still she writes.

Death Fugue is not a facile equation of the Holocaust with June Fourth. The title signifies the necessity to write in the wake of catastrophe. For Sheng Keyi, the stakes acquire a different exigency. As in the Holocaust's aftermath, there is the question of the efficacy of culture in the face of brutality: "poetry isn't as fast as a bullet; poetry is not as cruel as the muzzle of a gun" (location 908). There is also the debate over whether it is possible or ethical to represent atrocity, and how.

But an additional, third dimension is representation through censorship understood as both repression—the rejection of Baiqiu's poetry as a stand-in for the rejection of Sheng's own manuscript—as well as production—Jiawan's "lyrics praising the political apparatus" as a stand-in for all puffery in the official media. The prism of censorship crystalizes Sheng's response: June Fourth may be impossible to represent, but it is not only necessary but ethical to do so. When the Party-state is actively trying to make the event a forgotten one, one has to reimagine it.

Wang Guangli, director of *I Graduated*, was a college senior in Shanghai during the 1989 protests. At the same time, the director of *Conjugation*, Tang Xiaobai, was a college freshman in Beijing. Sheng Keyi was not in college then. The youngest of the three, she was sixteen years old and living in a village in Hunan province. She found out about the protests in Beijing on a neighbor's black-and-white TV, which presumably broadcast programs similar to the state-produced *Flutter, Flag of the Republic*. It was only years later and far from home that she learned more about June Fourth from someone who had been on Tiananmen Square as a university student.[33] Just as the heretofore mute boy in Xiaoqing's story in *Conjugation*—who was seemingly too little to understand anything at the time—was the one who broke the truth of murder, so a village girl far removed from the event itself wound up writing a novel that resuscitates the memory of the massacre.

Each of the three works examined in this chapter issues from a peripheral position. As independently produced films shot without authorization, *I Graduated* and *Conjugation* have never been shown in Chinese theaters or on Chinese television. They can only circulate in limited circles, with screenings in small venues advertised in online bulletins. *Death Fugue* could not be distributed as a book in mainland China. The novel's manuscript was turned down by over a dozen publishers. Each of the three works evinces a certain self-reflexive doubt about its prospects in the public sphere. Will *I Graduated* ever have as much of an audience as the national flag-lowering and flag-raising ceremonies captured in the documentary? Will a state radio broadcast always drown out a film like *Conjugation*? And will advertisements and the "faint smell of blood" work together to cover up *Death Fugue*?

Pessimism is present, and so is cynicism: in the student in *I Gradu-ated* who, for a good job, joined the CCP right after June Fourth; in the prize-winning poet, Jiawan; in all the poets turned businessmen who nevertheless still dabble in art. But there is persistence, too. *I Graduated* continues to be screened, from Beijing to Hangzhou, from cafés to film clubs, including at Peking University, celebrated in Chinese social media as the "elegy of an era." In Chinese social media, people still recommend, request, and share *Conjugation*. And we already know—or don't—who recommended *Death Fugue* to me.

That such art is made and disseminated at all is a testament to the audacity of will. At the same time, it owes its being and becoming to censorship. Against the official accounts of shots fired only into the sky, it recounts the blinding bullet. Against depictions of the repentant people laying wreaths before "spontaneous" memorials to fallen soldiers, it pays imaginary tribute to all the casualties that cannot be openly mourned. Against the triumphant trumpets of the national anthem, it strums a solo guitar. Yet this seemingly solitary music is part of a larger ensemble spread across space and time. The ensemble includes Wang Guangli, born in the 1960s. It includes Tang Xiaobai and Sheng Keyi, born in the 1970s. It also includes me, born in the 1980s, and the professor at the host university, born in the 1950s. And it includes all those born in other decades who add their voices to the chorus, online and off. Like the musician Huang Jingang in *I Graduated*, we all "write and sing songs for you from afar."

CHAPTER THREE

Transgressive Cuts

Making a Scene in the Postrevolutionary Age

Scandal sells, so goes the truism. What is less self-evident is that the scandal of censorship sells even better.

The scholar Richard Burt has perceptively remarked upon the "fetish of censorship," whereby a cultural product—say, a banned book—accrues value as it is displaced from its place of origin and consumed unevenly across the global capitalist system: "Displacement is not just about more or less narrow kinds of readership and access, but involves a differential system in which texts circulate and become exchangeable by becoming cultural and economic capital. It involves the commodification of small differences meant to increase the text's value."[1] By the "commodification of small differences," Burt means a publisher's marketing of an edition, for instance, as the "complete" or "uncensored" version. This process is especially salient in a cultural marketplace dominated by the West, which capitalizes on repression in the East broadly conceived, from the Middle East to the former Eastern Bloc.

The "fetish of censorship" seems to apply seamlessly to contemporary China, from which cultural contraband emerges with a halo of scandal. Yet this chapter complicates Burt's concept in arguing that such critique of the commercialization of censorship in the global exchange plays precisely into the hands of the Chinese government. The Chinese government trumpets this economic reading all the while muzzling the political reading, which is this: the regime fixes the parameters of public discourse. When artists, activists, and intellectuals cross these boundaries, it prescribes their speech. It then accuses these speakers of profiting from controversy to ride on the Western circuit, when its own strictures, in banishing such speech (and sometimes the speaker) from its jurisdiction, set this circuit in motion in the first place. It takes advantage of the West's branding of dissent as dissidence to persuade its own nationals to regard these speakers as traitors currying favor with the enemy, looking for lucre and plaudits abroad. It cultivates the dichotomous scenario that Pierre Bourdieu once cautioned against, a discursive field where all speaking positions are reduced "either to silence or to shocking outspokenness."[2]

In the previous chapter, I examined artworks from the periphery: two films—*I Graduated* and *Conjugation*—shot secretly and a novel—*Death Fugue*—published in mainland China only in a literary journal. None of them have been widely distributed or discussed in popular media. But the marginalized does not comprise the totality of alter-production related to the Tiananmen movement. By contrast, this chapter and the next investigate film and literature, respectively, that garnered a lot of attention. The two films that are the focus of this chapter, Stanley Kwan's *Lan Yu* (2001) and Lou Ye's *Summer Palace* (2006), are unapologetically outspoken. Both courted controversy. China's first-ever Gay Film Festival was cut short after screenings of *Lan Yu*, which had been shot without permission. *Summer Palace*, though shot with permission, premiered abroad without first passing domestic censorship review (*shencha*) and thereby incurred a five-year ban on Lou Ye and a producer. Unlike *I Graduated* and *Conjugation*, which were made underground and essentially remained underground, *Lan Yu* and *Summer Palace* made a scene.

In both productions, the workings of desire take apparent center stage while the public and the political are sidelined.[3] *Lan Yu* concerns the decade-long romance starting in the late 1980s between two men. *Summer Palace* tells a love story that also spans over a decade, from the late 1980s to the early 2000s. Yet both films preserve reminders of the revolutionary moment that was the Tiananmen movement as well as of censorship, as if to say that, because of the massacre and the compromised conditions of their own production, their subjects can only indulge in sex and consumerism while alternative passions can be but glimpsed. As seen in chapter 2, where the "moving on" from Tiananmen was reinforced by force, so the case studies in this chapter demonstrate that people did not ditch politics "naturally." Activism was crushed, while commercialization and the integration into global capitalism were actively promoted by state policy.

Selling out—of their art, conscience, and country—of which the Chinese government accuses disobedient artists, is the very direction the government has been pushing culture toward since market reforms in the 1980s, and even more so after 1989. Shifting attention away from political suppression, it wants public discourse to fixate on the monetary motive, the imputation of self-interest, while self-interest at the expense of the public good is what it tacitly permits. With a stick in one hand, it keeps shut the door on revolutionary expressions, while with the other hand it dangles the carrot of riches. Cashing in is the mandate from on high, captured in the motto of the era *yiqie xiangqiankan*, a double entendre homophonic for "all look forward" and "all look toward money." The capitalist ethos is rampant precisely because of the quashing of a social movement that centered on a public square, and the state will eagerly encourage the private as long as no publics alternative to the republic form. This is the real relationship among censorship, productiveness, and commercialism: not "censorship is productive commercially," but "censorship is productive of commercialism."

This chapter begins with the depiction in *Lan Yu* of the closure of mass activity, the replacement of revolution with romance. The crowd hasn't been supplanted only by the couple, however; the prominence of the coterie in the film betokens the transition from "comradeship"— understood as queer sexuality and insurgent solidarity—to cronyism, that state-capital nexus. Nevertheless, the consequence of the Tiananmen movement is irrepressible, even in the mainland Chinese DVD version of the film from which the Tiananmen sequences in the original are cut out. The analysis then shifts to *Summer Palace*, in which crowd scenes, including the night of the crackdown, are depicted. Despite criticism from some quarters that it depoliticizes the protests in favor of profiting off sex, I argue that the film, in a postrevolutionary spin on the revolution-plus-love narrative formula in modern Chinese culture, shows that the regime itself crushed the revolution and its collective bonds, physical and spiritual. Both *Lan Yu* and *Summer Palace* may open themselves up to the criticism that they are selling sex. But the biggest pander behind the scenes is the regime, which channels political ways of being together into sexual ones. It may pose as a prude, but the truly threatening form of sociality in its eyes is not sex, gay or promiscuous, but the crowds of Tiananmen Square, who represent an alternative sociality subversive of the crony capitalism in command.

INCONSEQUENT CUTTING

What is the role of the Tiananmen movement in *Lan Yu*? According to Stanley Kwan, it is a crucial one. The relationship between the two main characters, Lan Yu and Chen Handong, is at first characterized by the exchange of sex for money and vice versa. A poor college student from the northeast, Lan Yu is set up with the businessman Handong by Liu Zheng, an acquaintance of Lan Yu's and an employee of Handong's. Then comes Tiananmen, which "turned out to be the moment of their commitment." The event itself may be "just background" to their love story, says Kwan—the protests and the crackdown are only adumbrated in the film—yet it propels the two men into a new chapter of devotion.[4]

It turns out, however, that the director's descriptions are not entirely accurate. In Tiananmen's aftermath, Handong does not commit to Lan Yu. He buys for Lan Yu, who is now a college graduate, a car and a villa, but these gifts, although more extravagant compared to the money and clothes he gave in the beginning, do not betoken a watershed in their relationship. In fact, a few scenes after Tiananmen, Handong meets a woman he will marry in hopes of starting a heteronormative family. During the subsequent breakup with Lan Yu, Handong shouts: "I spent a lot of money on this damn house! How are you going to repay me?" Lan Yu responds by taking off his pants and asking: "What position would you like, boss?" Money and body are still the bases of reciprocity. Not much has changed since their initial breakup, before Tiananmen, when Lan Yu caught Handong with another man. At that time Handong roared: "You think Liu Zheng can find you another client as lavish as I am?" Lan Yu's mock self-degradation post-Tiananmen reverberates from this earlier insult.

If, as a political event, it is "just background" and, as a moment in the love story, it has no decisive consequence, Tiananmen in *Lan Yu* is nevertheless significant because it signals the foreclosure of mass action in the postrevolutionary age. In the first scene of the Tiananmen sequence, it is daytime on June 3, 1989, and the fan is blowing in Handong's office. He complains of the air conditioning not being fixed, and when an employee explains that a strike has been going on in Beijing for weeks, the businessman replies: "On strike? Fake fucking altruists! Aren't there other workers? Besides those strikers, are all the workers in the capital fucking dead?" Tiananmen was a broad-based movement, although it was student-led, in which many social elements participated, most notably workers.[5] Handong's comments testify to its wide support. He cannot comprehend these "altruists," however, people who would risk their livelihoods—and lives—to stand in solidarity for a public cause.

If this cause affects his life at all, it does so only as a nuisance. In the next scene, later in the day in the same place, he and his associate Liu Zheng are talking in the foreground while commotion in the street outside is faintly heard. For the two of them, the protests constitute precisely "background" noise, preoccupied as they are with private concerns. Only when Handong's brother-in-law, Luo Daning—played by the producer Zhang Yongning—pays a visit (as Liu Zheng leaves) does the movement impinge upon Handong. Daning tells Handong that Tiananmen Square will be cleared that night and, more important, that he saw Lan Yu there picketing. That night Handong drives out in search of his ex-lover, whom he has not seen in months. Gunfire and explosions crackle, and from inside his Mercedes, he sees a rush of people bike past him, some carting casualties. Handong is not among them because he is shielded in his sedan; he is not part of the crowd moving collectively in the opposite direction.

In the end, it is Lan Yu who finds Handong. The latter has fallen asleep at the wheel, parked outside Lan Yu's dorm on a deserted campus. They embrace. Seeing Lan Yu a little scraped, Handong hugs him again. The next shot is of the two of them in each other's arms in bed, presumably in Handong's apartment, with Lan Yu weeping. The director has accomplished the remarkable feat of not simply singling them out but isolating them visually from the mass activity. Handong literally approaches Tiananmen in his vehicle but only in order to locate the one individual that matters to him. Lan Yu, as Daning informed Handong, picketed in the swarming square. But when he next shows up on-screen, he is by himself. Neither protagonist is depicted with the crowds of people. The brute scattering of a collective of thousands from Tiananmen Square and its environs culminates in the reconnection of two bodies.

If Lan Yu's tears result in part from getting back together with his first love, it is safe to assume that they are also occasioned in part by the bloodshed he witnessed. In other words, he is crying not just for himself and Handong but for a collectivity. He cries for its dispelling, which is also its death. This is the last time in the film that fellowship is pictured, when multitudes act in unison, fleeing the violence while not leaving behind the fellow wounded. A radio announcement finishes the Tiananmen sequence: "June 4, 4:30 a.m.," which is when troops surrounding Tiananmen Square began to advance toward the Monument to the People's Heroes, where the last group of protestors was holding out. Thereafter, Tiananmen vanishes completely from the film, leaving no imprint or echo.

This is the *Lan Yu* that premiered in Cannes in May 2001 and that opened in Hong Kong in November of the same year. A month later it was screened on the mainland, albeit briefly. The only public exhibitions took place during China's first-ever Gay Film Festival from December 14 to 23, 2001, in Beijing, at Peking University, Tsinghua University, and nearby coffee shops.[6] The organizers of the festival, students of Peking University's film association, had reached out to producer Zhang Yongning for a 35mm print. Tickets to *Lan Yu* sold out.[7] The Chinese media had reported on the film when it won four Golden Horse awards in Taiwan a week before the Beijing festival. Now numerous outlets covered the festival itself.[8] No cuts must have been made to the *Lan Yu* print. Several articles mentioned the full-frontal nudity.[9] One reporter even brought up the Tiananmen sequence.[10] Not long after the screenings, however, authorities at both Peking and Tsinghua cut short the remaining campus events, and the rest of the festival had to relocate to the coffee shops.[11]

In early 2002, Zhang Yongning applied to China's Film Bureau for the mainland theatrical release of *Lan Yu*. Approval, however, was not granted.[12] Only in 2006, five years after its original release, were video compact disc (VCD) and DVD copies of the film officially distributed in China.[13] The 2006 version was authorized, but it was edited.

Three scenes are missing from it. The first one is the nude scene involving Lan Yu and Chen Handong—played by Liu Ye and Hu Jun, respectively—on their first night together. The second one is in the scene when Daning visits Handong's office on June 3, 1989. The part where he talks about the clearing of Tiananmen Square is removed; he only mentions that he saw Lan Yu there. The third one is the entirety of Handong driving out in search of Lan Yu later that night, their reunion by the car, and Lan Yu's weeping in bed. The edited version jumps from Handong's room on the night of June 3 to a scene that could be as many as three years later (if Lan Yu was a freshman during the protests). The couple are in a car Handong bought for Lan Yu as a graduation present, on their way to the villa that Handong also bought for him. The radio is playing "How Can You Bear Seeing Me Sad?" This love song by the Taiwanese singer Huang Pin Yuan (from his 1990 album *Thoughts of a Man in a Supporting Role*) comprises three choruses that contain a total of eighteen instances of "you" and "I." It is nearly the only song in the entire movie—nearly, because another song is heard but faintly, and one other song (discussed later) is found only in the mainland version of *Lan Yu*.

That faintly heard song appears during the Tiananmen sequence in both the 2001 and 2006 versions. After Daning's visit, Handong is still in his office, lost in thought. From the open window, we hear "Unity Is Strength." A People's Liberation Army (PLA) song from the early 1940s, it was popular throughout the socialist period. It was also one of several left-wing songs sung by students during the 1989 movement. What distinguishes it from "How Can You Bear Seeing Me Sad?" is not simply that it's a hymn of "unity" rather than romance—there is no "you" or "I" in "Unity Is Strength"—but also its execution. Faint though the song may be, it is distinctly voiced by many. We do not see the "many" in this scene, but we hear them. It is the same many who are on strike to support the students. It is the same many who would cart away many other bodies later that night, which we do glimpse in the 2001 version.

"How Can You Bear Seeing Me Sad?" is a leitmotif that recurs several times diegetically and nondiegetically in *Lan Yu*. And so is Lan Yu and Handong's embrace, a central image that reappears at many junctures. In fact, if one had to pick a "moment of their commitment," it would be roughly two-thirds into the movie, after Handong's divorce. The reconciliation takes place in Lan Yu's apartment: Handong first asks for a hug. Then he uncontrollably seizes Lan Yu in his arms, overcome with emotion.[14] This sequence parallels the clasps of the earlier reunion, when they met after the crackdown. Both the embrace and "How Can You Bear Seeing Me Sad?" are emblematic of the private displacing of the public after Tiananmen, when state violence dissipated the gatherings on and around the square. Romance did not replace revolt innocuously. The massacre and censorship collaborate in the removal of a mass movement, from the street and from the screen, and in the elevation of intimate unions.

The 2006 version of *Lan Yu*, however, is not simply maimed. It is an alter-production. Penises and Tiananmen are cut out, but differently. The editing of male nudity is smooth: in no way does it disrupt the flow of the narrative. Yet the editing of Tiananmen is abrupt. Daning enters Handong's office, and the next shot is him leaving it, telling Handong on his way out about glimpsing Lan Yu on the square. Something is conspicuously missing from that scene. The same illogic occurs when the film jumps from Handong in a bathrobe outside his bathroom on the night of June 3, presumably thinking about Lan Yu, to Lan Yu and Handong somehow back together in a car. The discontinuity of the narrative indicates that something of consequence was taken out. The splices are different for a reason. Contrary to the hullabaloo, the sex is not consequential. The real crux is Tiananmen. Through its suppression from the mainland Chinese version of *Lan Yu*, we comprehend the significance of the 1989 movement. It is not "just background." To dismiss it is to make not only the film but also China's subsequent trajectory inconsequent, incomprehensible. The alter-production that is *Lan Yu*—the 2001 version in conjunction with the 2006—acts out censorship and its crucial role: in shutting down independent film festivals, which has only worsened in recent years; in disappearing unruly associations, such as protestors rescuing other protestors who are otherwise strangers; in literally leading to "How Can You Bear Seeing Me Sad?" and the preoccupation with the private sphere the song represents. The two versions in their discrepancy make public this censorship and, in preserving sonic reminders of workers on strike for a collective cause and of "Unity Is Strength," constitute a remaking of publics undone.

But Stanley Kwan does not stop there. The post-Tiananmen shift is borne out not just by the couple in place of the crowd, sex in place of solidarity. Rather, the director portrays relations in the postrevolutionary age as dominated by crony capitalism. Crony capitalism, in part, was what prompted the Tiananmen movement in the first place—and what was left unscathed, nay, protected by the massacre. As the scholar Wang Hui remarks, "The creation of today's market society was not the result of a sequence of spontaneous events, but rather of state interference and violence."[15] The massacre quashed the popular protests and safeguarded the continued domination of the state-capital nexus. The couple in *Lan Yu*, therefore, is implicated in the coterie, and one's sex partner is also one's business partner. If people can no longer link arms but instead wrap them around each other, then they also light each other's cigarettes and clink glasses. If rousing anthems like "Unity Is Strength" are drowned out by plaintive refrains, then those plaintive refrains are muffled in turn by hushed conversations.

FROM COMRADES TO CRONIES

Lan Yu is adapted from a novel that was first published on the Chinese-language internet in the late 1990s under the penname *Beijing Comrade*.[16] The term *comrade* (*tongzhi*) has been appropriated for gay identity in the Chinese-speaking world since the end of the 1980s.[17] In the film, however, gay romance is appropriated by crony collusion. This is not to suggest, of course, that there is actually no love or desire between Lan Yu and Handong, that their relationship is founded solely on commerce. As practiced in reform-era China, crony capitalism is built on the time-honored Chinese construct of *guanxi*, commonly translated as "connections."[18] Crony capitalism precisely does not preclude the bonds of kinship, friendship, or love; it derives from them. Yet it renders family more than family, friends more than friends, lovers more than lovers. This "more" is called profit.

I "rack focus" from the two protagonists, Lan Yu and Handong, to two seemingly minor characters, Liu Zheng and Daning. The former is Handong's business associate, the latter his brother-in-law. I examine the relations between Handong and Lan Yu through the lens of Handong's relations with these two other men. I do so not to depreciate the representation of queer sexuality in the film but to show that in Stanley Kwan's post-Tiananmen China, desire—gay or straight—is enmeshed in a network of interests.[19] *Lan Yu* stages the conspiratorial as the ruling form of sociality, contrasting the circle of conspirators with the square of strangers, so to speak. The circle survives and thrives; the square dies. In fact, in sustaining and maintaining the state-capital order, the sociality of the circle is responsible for ravaging the sociality of the square.

First, it is only through Liu Zheng that Handong and Lan Yu meet in the first place. We do not see Lan Yu, however, in the scene in the club where Liu Zheng makes the introduction. Instead, we see Liu Zheng and Handong watching him and talking about him. They begin behind a sliding door, which takes up nearly half of the frame. Then they move to the bar, where again the door conceals more than half of another shot. Finally they proceed back to the door, where they pause before Handong approaches Lan Yu. These stagings suggest that Handong and Liu Zheng are not so much conversing as conspiring, their gaze both libidinal and predatory. The obscuring door encloses a space of secrecy from which both of them spy on their prey.

Meticulous design characterizes Handong's interactions with Daning as well. On Chinese New Year's Eve, Handong brings Lan Yu to his mother's home, where he introduces Lan Yu to his family for the first time (as a college classmate's brother). But the narrative attention is elsewhere: this is also where we first meet Daning. Instead of a New Year's Eve dinner with everyone around the table, the episode concludes with a private talk between Daning and Handong (figure 3.1). Both the length of the shot and the composition emphasize their privacy. Not only do the windows in the back mark out an interior and an exterior—Daning's wife, who is also Handong's sister, Yonghong, is seen passing by the window to the left of Daning's head—the frames in the foreground, too, indicate a peeking into intimate space. This intimacy is again highlighted toward the end of the scene when Yonghong interrupts their conversation by knocking on the window from the outside to call them to dinner.

The two men were talking business. Daning brought up Handong's "contract with the Ministry of Foreign Trade for a 30-million-yuan loan." The pricing of loans by financial institutions based on "connections"

FIGURE 3.1 Handong and Daning, from the film *Lan Yu* (2001), talk privately.

rather than credit risk is one of the hallmarks of crony capitalism.[20] Although never stated outright, Daning evidently works for the government, whether at the municipal or central level. Handong asks him if the loan has been approved. Daning does not know but reassures him: "your connections [*guanxi*] are so strong."[21] In the online novel on which *Lan Yu* is based, Handong's father is a high-ranking cadre whose connections help his son's business prosper. While not as explicit, hints in the film suggest that Handong's privileges result not only from the network he himself has cultivated but also from his father's position. After his father's death, Handong mentions that the funeral was arranged by a party secretary, and that "some ministers" sent wreaths. The 30-million-yuan loan, then, is shorthand for high collusion between the political and economic elite. Public servants like Daning and public institutions like the Ministry of Foreign Trade serve private schemes.

Daning proves himself to be on the government's inside again in the Tiananmen sequence discussed above. He pays Handong a visit on June 3 to "deliver a message in person": "I can't talk about this thing on the phone." The message is that Tiananmen Square will be cleared that night. He also adds that he saw Lan Yu around the square. Just as Liu Zheng brought Handong and Lan Yu together the first time, it is Daning

FIGURE 3.2 Handong lights Daning's cigarette in his office in a scene from the film *Lan Yu*.

who plays the go-between this time. But this scene more than facilitates the reunion of ex-lovers. After Daning enters Handong's office and closes the door, the shot lingers outside. Through the door's window we see their hands touch as Handong lights Daning's cigarette (figure 3.2). What we are about to (over)hear, against the backdrop of a mass movement, is the confidential sharing of valuable information by an insider within his closed, personal circle.

There are two plot twists in the final third of the movie after Handong's divorce and recommitment to Lan Yu. In both cases, either Liu Zheng or Daning is presiding. One morning Handong receives a call, presumably from Liu Zheng, informing him of the arrest of a bank chief. This bank chief must be a member of their coterie because later that night, Handong and Liu Zheng share a drink in the dimly lit office, pondering their own fate. Handong knows what his charges will be—"smuggling, bribery, illegal fundraising"—and he wonders if his arrest warrant is imminent. Liu Zheng is no mere subordinate. Just as in the beginning Handong got to know Lan Yu through his contacts, so now the associate says he can get the warrant delayed for a few days. The boss is not without contacts himself. In a subsequent scene, right before he is arrested, he is able to procure for Lan Yu, who previously wanted to study in the United States, a passport as well as guarantees from domestic and American banks. As for a visa, he hands him the business card of someone who used to handle the matter in the Ministry of Foreign Trade. It is a gesture of love, certainly, made possible only by the deployment of his crony forces. The *guanxi* network subtends all.

In the other plot twist, Daning and Yonghong visit Handong in jail (figure 3.3). The couple may sit equidistantly in front of him, but in the framing the brother-in-law is closer than the sister. Handong is afraid to implicate Daning, who assures him that in his statement to authorities, "we are in-laws, nothing else." This very stressing of "nothing else" proves the opposite, that the two are in cahoots. Yonghong tells her brother that his personal and company assets have been frozen pending investigation. Handong is dispirited: "Without money, Liu Zheng can't smooth things over no matter how hard he runs around." Then Daning the government official whispers the way out: 3 million yuan. Liu Zheng mortgaged his house but that was not enough. Lan Yu, however, heard about the predicament. He sold the villa Handong gave him, Daning says, and along with the rent money he has collected over the years and his savings, he brought over the cash.

FIGURE 3.3 Yonghong, Daning, and Handong in the visiting area of the jail, where Handong is held.

One of the main grievances of the Tiananmen movement was corruption in the form of "official speculation" (*guandao*), whereby government officials and those with ties to them took advantage of China's transition from a completely planned economy to a partial market economy in the early reform period. At the beginning of the 1980s a "dual-track price system" was implemented under which state-owned industries could purchase designated supplies at plan prices and sell their production above the state quota at market prices. "Official speculation" occurs when supplies bought at state-controlled prices are sold on the open market for a lot more. Although Handong does not specifically engage in this form of corruption, it is clear that his business has benefited quite a bit from government connections. The irony lies in the fact that Lan Yu, who once participated in a movement that denounced such collusion, now knowingly abets an offender. The villa, doubtlessly bought with tainted money in the first place, is exchanged back into money—supplemented by the rentier's income and savings—to be used as a bribe for the release—and reinsertion into the cycle—of a man guilty of bribery. Fed up with the state-capital collusion that contributed to extreme social inequities, workers went on strike in the spring of 1989 in solidarity with the students, which at the time prompted Handong to call them "fake fucking altruists." Now he benefits from Lan Yu's "altruism" in getting out of jail.

If Lan Yu acted out of love, then more than love he shall receive. In return for helping Handong, he gains full acceptance into the club. Handong is out—after a few months' stint in jail and a fine for tax evasion, as we later learn—and he, Lan Yu, Yonghong, Daning, and Liu Zheng are celebrating in Lan Yu's apartment. The family dinner, which we missed on New Year's Eve years ago, is belatedly recompensed. Yet this is not your typical family gathering. There is, however, a single association that fits them all: partners in crime. Five is the unit, not the masses collected on Tiananmen, not even the couple entwined in bed. They may not be family, but they are an extension of kinship sociality—"in-laws, nothing else." No matter how many fill the circle, they can never constitute a square.[22]

If the five form an unusual grouping, it is not because Lan Yu, or rather his and Handong's evident relationship, presents a threat to heteronormativity. In fact, Stanley Kwan downplays in this scene the homosexual in favor of the homosocial. Handong, Liu Zheng, and Daning—"the guys"—are shown at the table. Yonghong and Lan Yu—"the girls"—are seen preparing food in the kitchen. Lan Yu has been embraced, to be sure, but more as a sister-in-law than as a gay man. The moment he appears as gay is the same moment he disappears as man. He is rendered one woman next to another while the men, Handong seated between Daning and Liu Zheng, play their drinking games.

Lan Yu nevertheless constitutes a threat, and that is why he has to die. Just as Handong cannot remain bound in prison, so Lan Yu must not hold him captive. Handong has to stay in circulation. The price to be paid for the unfreezing of his capital is the freezing of his lover's head in the morgue. It is no coincidence that Handong receives news of Lan Yu's death—due to a construction site accident—during his first return to the office, while Liu Zheng is with him. His partner, who at the beginning of the film apprised him of Lan Yu, now near its end apprises him of the state of the company's finances. Despite the tax evasion fine, lawyers' fees, and other expenses, there is still enough left to restart the business. In other words, the two of them, Handong and Liu Zheng, will have a second life together. At this exact moment, Handong receives the phone call about Lan Yu's accident. But if the earlier phone call bearing news of a cohort's arrest presaged his own, then this one sets him free.

A construction site is a fitting finish for Lan Yu as well as *Lan Yu*. And so we see Handong pause at the place of Lan Yu's death before speeding away in his car in the film's final shot, blurring through Beijing in the ceaseless flow of another round of creative destruction— the "demolition-construction" that Handong says Beijing is constantly undergoing. Lan Yu was but one of its victims. Others had fallen in 1989, obstructions to the cabal of power and privilege that had to be cleared away so the cabal could continue to grow. This growth can be conceived as a "development" from comradeship, understood both as revolutionary solidarity and as transgressive sexuality, to the crony regime.

Creative destruction also characterizes the censorship of *Lan Yu*. The mainland Chinese version was not simply shortened, the nude and Tiananmen scenes excised. In fact, it was longer and advertised as the "producer's extended version." In addition to the three abridgments discussed, it adds two sequences that lengthen the movie from less than ninety minutes, in its 2001 release, to nearly one hundred minutes, in

2006. One sequence expands on Handong's brief marriage. The other sequence evokes Tiananmen.

The latter sequence occurs toward the end of the film, the last scene before the day that Lan Yu dies. It is winter, and Handong and Lan Yu are outside in the snow. Handong wants to hear Lan Yu sing a song. And what song does Lan Yu start singing but "The Internationale": "Arise, slaves afflicted by hunger and cold . . ." Handong interrupts him, not wanting to hear this song. Lan Yu replies: "Besides this, there's nothing else." After getting prompted by Handong, however, he remembers "How Can You Bear Seeing Me Sad?" He then begins to sing this song, in which Handong joins.

"The Internationale" has been the anthem of the left since the end of the nineteenth century.[23] It was also one of the most popular songs sung en masse on Tiananmen Square in the spring of 1989. Indeed, it was the song sung by the final occupants of the square as they left at gunpoint in the early morning hours of June 4. It resurfaces here, in an alter-production from which the casualties of Tiananmen have been deleted. Lan Yu the picketer has joined the other side. State violence in the forms of the massacre and censorship have demolished the publicness symbolized by the square, constructing in its place edifices of intrigue. But the mainland Chinese *Lan Yu* preserves this song, even if it is quickly eclipsed by another, as a residuum of a movement that sang of an alternative sociality, a community of being together other than the coterie or the couple. As Robert Chi observes, at stake in the singing of "The Internationale" was "the very notion of the past as the origin for a plurality of other possible futures, for roads not taken."[24] This anthem was precisely not national. It refers not just to Chinese uprisings but to the world struggle against economic and political subjugations. It limns a collectivity in contradistinction to romantic love, gay or straight, as well as the crony network. Ringing against the wintry expanse of China's postrevolutionary condition, the song still projects hope. What the lyrics of "The Internationale" and "Unity Is Strength" share is "unity" (*tuanjie*), as the only way to reach a different horizon.

Now Lan Yu is singing alone and to one person. Nevertheless, there are consequences to the obstinacy of his "Besides this, there's nothing else." The entire film, like the novel from which it is adapted, is framed as Handong's flashback. If we interpret the cuts to the mainland version diegetically, then Handong gets to live because he blocks out Tiananmen—from his memory, from his recounting. Lan Yu, however, has violated the taboo. He used to be one of the oppressed, a member of the poor who had to sell his body in order to fund his education. Now he sings "The Internationale" as resistance, as a rebuke of what he himself has become, of what the Chinese Communist Party has devolved into, as a revolutionary remainder from a time when people cared about more than their own interests, when workers went on strike to stick up for the hunger-striking students, when the demand for political democracy—freedom of the press and assembly, rule of law—was allied with the demand for the democratization of economic life: social justice, fairness, and security, and an end to official corruption and crony capitalism. Lan Yu remembers this, and therefore he has to pay the price of his life. But still he sings, just as communist martyrs used to before their own executions.[25] He knew he was going to be killed. Yet with his death he will join the Tiananmen fallen as martyrs of the unfinished revolution.

SEX AND TIANANMEN

Lan Yu was shot in China without approval, with a mostly mainland crew, but Hong Kong director Stanley Kwan described the authorities' attitude as "one eye is closed, one eye is open"; "[w]e made the film in Beijing, and the Film Bureau people knew we were there."[26] Despite this tacit permission, the 2001 film exhibits many of the characteristics of the underground film discussed in chapter 2. Most of the shooting took place indoors or at night, with a dearth of crowd scenes.

That Lou Ye's *Summer Palace* (2006) was made at all—and aboveground—reflects bigger transformations. As with the Chinese economy at large and the publishing industry (to be discussed in the next chapter), the film industry underwent reforms beginning in the 1980s, with decentralization and marketization penetrating production as well as distribution. Starting in 1998, for instance, private companies were allowed to apply for production and distribution permits on a case-by-case basis.[27] But it was not until November 2003 that several filmmakers, among them Lou Ye, met with the Film Bureau to propose changes to film censorship, including giving independent films—that is, films not produced by a state studio—a chance for theatrical release. In the following month the State Administration of Radio, Film, and Television (SARFT), parent agency of the Film Bureau at the time, issued in response a set of regulations that streamlined the process.

Shooting for *Summer Palace* began in September 2004. The timing was no coincidence. Previously, a full movie script had to be submitted to the central film bureau and approved before shooting could begin. Now with the new regulations, only a plot synopsis is required initially, and a regional film bureau then either grants the permission to shoot directly or asks for a full script, with the final cut still needing to pass censorship by the central bureau before exhibition.[28] It is safe to assume, with a title like *Summer Palace*—the vast imperial garden complex near Peking University that is only tangentially related to the story—that a misleading synopsis was sent in.

An actual synopsis would read like this: Yu Hong, a girl from northeastern China, gets into a Beijing university in 1987, where she has a tempestuous romance with fellow student Zhou Wei. On the night of June 3 and 4, 1989, as the military moves in on the capital to suppress the popular demonstrations, Yu Hong learns that Zhou Wei slept with her friend Li Ti. The lovers go their separate ways, Yu Hong back home before venturing south and then inland, Zhou Wei eventually moving with Li Ti to Berlin, where the latter's boyfriend is. Zhou Wei returns to China after Li Ti's suicide, and in 2001 he and Yu Hong see each other once more before parting, presumably, for good.

The events of 1989 take place in the middle of the two-hour film. With a plot that pivots on Tiananmen and a double betrayal—Zhou Wei cheating on Yu Hong and the military killing unarmed citizens—surely some subterfuge was involved in getting the project approved. The filming even made it into the news. An entertainment report from October 2004 states that thirty-seven out of over two hundred extras, on the set that was inside a sports complex in southeastern Beijing, experienced vomiting, diarrhea, and fever due to possible food poisoning. There is no mention of what *Summer Palace* is about or who is its director.[29]

The number of extras indicates how different the production is from that of Wang Guangli's *I Graduated* (1992) and Tang Xiaobai's *Conjugation* (2001), both examined in chapter 2, as well as *Lan Yu*, which were all surreptitiously shot without permission. Authorization literally opened doors for *Summer Palace*. The dorm scenes were shot in the Beijing Film Academy, from which Lou Ye had graduated in 1989. Not only could there be outdoor scenes in the daytime—a making-of featurette on the U.S. DVD documents the cast and crew casually boating on Kunming Lake in the Summer Palace—but also mass spectacles were now possible. The same featurette includes take after take of scores of people running and clambering onto trucks and buses, surrounded by booms. In lieu of handheld cameras capturing clandestine images in the night, dollies on tracks support crane shots that loom over large crowds. Even the chaos and conflagration on the night of June 3 to 4 could be re-created with help from firefighters on-site.

I Graduated and *Conjugation*, both set in the aftermath of Tiananmen, make no attempt to reenact the crackdown, giving instead fly-by glimpses of Tiananmen Square snapped from taxicabs. Lou Ye does not shoot near the square. That his depictions of the movement could be shot in Beijing at all, however, is remarkable. Prodemocratic flyers and posters appear on campus and inside dormitories. As the demonstrations gather momentum, students are shown crowded on the backs of trucks headed for the square (figure 3.4). Even more daring, of course, are the

FIGURE 3.4 Students crowded on the back of a truck headed for Tiananmen Square, in a scene from the film *Summer Palace* (2006).

multitudes and mayhem on the night of the massacre, with the confrontation starkly illustrated, with protestors on one side and the repressive state apparatus on the other. Compared to *I Graduated, Conjugation,* and *Lan Yu, Summer Palace* enacts another kind of alter-production. Produced through censorship as are all the films, *Summer Palace* uses a loophole newly opened in state policy, however, to reenact how publicly expressed was the ferment of 1989.

Just as daring are the film's sex scenes. The first one, with Yu Hong and her hometown boyfriend coupling outdoors, sets the transgressive tone. From that point Yu Hong proceeds through a full-frontal display with Zhou Wei, an affair with a married man, and sex in a public restroom with a coworker. Forming the sidebar are Zhou Wei and Li Ti cheating on their partners with one another, first on the night of June 3 to 4, then in Berlin. All are graphically portrayed. That the sex scenes—not to mention the Tiananmen ones—were shot in China meant that *Summer Palace* could never have been shown there.[30] To obtain the permit to shoot is one thing; to be allowed to exhibit is another.

Here the story gets murky. The Film Bureau refused to review Lou Ye's film, citing only picture and sound quality.[31] *Summer Palace*, without approval, premiered at the Cannes Film Festival in May 2006 anyway. For this act of insubordination, SARFT handed down the punishment in September of that year: Lou Ye and coproducer Nai An could not engage in film work in China for five years. The pronouncement cited the "Regulations on the Administration of Movies" in effect since February 2002, which proscribed entering films in international festivals without prior approval.[32] There was no mention at all of the sensitive content of the film. The decision was seemingly a matter of protocol.

That picture and sound quality were allegedly at issue, not the sights and sounds of the social movement and the sex scenes, appears to have been the Film Bureau's wily way of handling a touchy situation. Yet it turns out the problem might indeed have been technical. Although filming began in September 2004 and lasted a year, *Summer Palace* was still not ready by the time it was officially selected in April 2006 as one of the features in competition at Cannes. According to another coproducer, Fang Li, sound mixing was not finished by then. Even a week before the festival was to begin, postproduction was still ongoing.

The Film Bureau not reviewing it, then, may not have been simply a tactic of obstruction.[33]

Whichever the explanation, the consequence was the same: ban from filmmaking. But this was not the first time a harsh punishment was meted out to a director in post-Tiananmen China, and not even to Lou Ye himself. Well-known filmmakers including Tian Zhuangzhuang, Zhang Yuan, Wang Xiaoshuai, and Wu Wenguang were all at one point forbidden from filmmaking for screening films abroad without official permission.[34] Lou Ye had two previous films banned, the 1995 *Weekend Lover* and the 2000 *Suzhou River*, the latter, as a repeat offense, resulting in a two-year ban on filmmaking.[35] The third time, the sentence was lengthened to five years. He is thus no stranger to sanctions. A film with sex and Tiananmen prominent is no doubt another gauntlet flung in the face of the state administration.

After *Suzhou River* and the attendant punishment, Lou Ye appeared to fall into line. His next film, *Purple Butterfly* (2003), was coproduced by a state studio and enjoyed a wide release in the country. With *Summer Palace*, however, Lou Ye once again went rogue. Despite the five-year filmmaking ban, the following five years were no less fertile for him. *Spring Fever* appeared in 2009, and *Love and Bruises* followed in 2011. Both films, like *Summer Palace*, were French coproductions. Also like *Summer Palace*, both were shot partly in China, in a flagrant affront to the ban. *Spring Fever* is set in Nanjing, while *Love and Bruises* moves between Paris and Beijing. The former premiered in Cannes, the latter in Venice.

With this kind of productivity, one wonders if the official ban were a deterrent at all or rather a catalyst. Indeed, one might suspect the controversy surrounding the censorship review of *Summer Palace* to be a publicity stunt. As stated earlier, there was no way the film could have been exhibited in China: It was not a matter of cutting out or altering discrete problematic scenes. Submitting the film for review dramatized the confrontation between artist and officialdom. The foreordained outcome of this confrontation could then be neatly and literally packaged. Thus, the front cover of the U.S. DVD issued by Palm Pictures is underscored with "Banned by the Chinese Government." Flip to the back and you will find this description: "the film that the Chinese government did not want the world to see!" Included in the DVD itself, along with the making-of featurette, is a segment on "*Summer Palace* and Chinese Censorship." These are selling points to the U.S. viewers/consumers given access to the otherwise unseeable.

A similar charge has been leveled at Chinese filmmakers of the generation prior to Lou Ye's.[36] Zhang Yimou (b. 1950), Chen Kaige (b. 1952), and Tian Zhuangzhuang (b. 1952), all deeply embedded within the Chinese film industry, nevertheless performed in the wake of Tiananmen the role of outsiders and challengers to the industry and to the government for international festival curators, publicists, and critics.[37] They presented sumptuously scandalous images that the Party-state would keep from view, allegedly couching rebukes of the present in historical allegories. Lauded for their audacity overseas, they were able to continue to work in the industry despite run-ins with the authorities because they were in fact insiders of the system. Reprobation at home, therefore, only increased the cachet and circulation of their films abroad. Zhang Yimou set the precedent. His codirected *Ju Dou* (1990) and his *Raise the Red Lantern* (1991) were not released in China until 1992. But the former, coproduced by the Japanese entertainment group Tokuma Enterprises, and the latter, coproduced by the Taiwanese distributor ERA International, were both nominated for an Academy Award for Best Foreign Language Film.

Does the same kind of parlay apply to *Summer Palace*, which not only premiered overseas like Zhang's two films from the early 1990s but also has never been released in China? Could Richard Burt's formulation of the "fetish of censorship" apply here? With Lou Ye's film, of course, it is not a case of capitalizing on the small differences between a "cleansed" Chinese version and a "complete" foreign version that makes the latter an object of desire. As the U.S. DVD reminds U.S. viewers, this product is simply unsupplied in China. If sex sells everywhere, then sex plus Tiananmen plus a Chinese ban sell three times as well in the West. Is Lou Ye pimping for the prurient interests of international consumers rather than domestic ones?

One Chinese commentator, writing online in 2008, answers in the affirmative. Titled "*Summer Palace*: Using Sex and Politics to Get Attention Outside of Art," the piece accuses Lou Ye of rehashing the formula of domestic disobedience and foreign fanfare because it has succeeded before.[38] The director "plays to the gallery" and is "opportunistic." The film has no artistic merit and instead trades in the globally comestible currency of sex and politics. While the sex scenes are castigated vehemently, the commentary can make only oblique reference to "politics." Mixing the two in *Summer Palace*, according to the writer, leads Lou Ye to unwittingly imply that hedonistic people like Yu Hong "are seemingly the real root cause of the '89 scenario." The writer does not explore, however, how this implication would actually align with the party position. While the official line states that the 1989 protests were fomented by "extremely few people" (*jishaoshu ren*) "harboring ulterior motives" (*bieyou yongxin*), it would most welcome the suggestion that participants were youngsters high on hormones and not political ideals.

Such is the incisive criticism by Jason McGrath, who argues that *Summer Palace* "in fact *fully supports the official government narrative of the 1989 protests*."[39] McGrath does not accuse Lou Ye of catering to Western tastes. He also does not opine, like the commentator above, that the film has no artistic merit. Rather, he cites from the art itself, pointing to "the bizarrely complete disconnection between the political events of 1989 depicted in the film on the one hand and its overall mode of narration and characterization on the other." As for the characterization, McGrath contends that it is deeply depoliticized: "the students are depicted as entirely narcissistic and hedonistic, and their joining in the protests appears to be no more profoundly motivated than their decisions to go to rock-and-roll bars or to have sex with each other."[40]

As for the narration, there is audiovisual evidence for McGrath's observations as well. Before the first scene, an epigraph of white text on black screen marks a private entry into *Summer Palace*. It is an entry from Yu Hong's diary, which reads: "There is something, that comes suddenly like a wind on a summer night, that takes you off guard, that leaves you restless, following you like a shadow impossible to shake. I don't know what it is, so I can only call it love." The audience is thus immediately thrust into the intimate, given a voyeuristic peek of Yu Hong's inner world. What is more, the diary constructs an interior realm from whose depths the subsequent images and sounds would seem to flow forth. Other diary entries are interspersed throughout the film, not as on-screen text but as voice-overs spoken aloud by Yu Hong.

The first-person narrative mode, therefore, is accentuated by the monologues overheard.

If the opening of *Summer Palace* announces a subjective point of view, then it concurrently announces "love" as its subject. This would appear to be the double lens through which Lou Ye connects the personal with the political. In fact, in an interview for the making-of featurette, the director expounds upon what he sees as an analogous relationship between love and June Fourth, 1989:

> 1989 was just like a lovemaking between students and the government. It didn't go well, didn't feel very good, and the government slapped the students. The slap was too hard, spilled blood. The government knew the slap was too hard, and it used the next ten years to retrieve this excessive act. If you look at it from this perspective, June Fourth and two people in a love relationship are exactly the same. China used a short amount of time to end the disorder of June Fourth, with severe, military means. But in reality China used the next ten years in striving to move forward unceasingly, developing the economy, becoming more open, more democratic. All this is like a love affair between them.

These remarks are more than flippant. They trivialize the killing of hundreds of lives into a slap that drew some blood. June Fourth and lovemaking become June Fourth as lovemaking. A scene in the film even enacts this simile. When students rush and climb onto trucks heading to Tiananmen Square, the song "Lovemaking," from the play *Rhinoceros in Love*, begins to play.[41] The song reaches its climax as the students, including Yu Hong and Zhou Wei, crowd against one another in the back of the truck (see figure 3.4). The scene is one of euphoria: bodies pressed together, swaying in unison to the motion of the truck, bouncing up and down in jubilation. Layered with "Lovemaking" are squeals of rapture and the collective singing of Cui Jian's "Nothing to My Name," the rock anthem of Tiananmen. Participation in the protests is depicted as an orgiastic experience.

This scene references the real because it cuts immediately to actual footage from Tiananmen—taken from Carma Hinton and Richard Gordon's documentary *Gate of Heavenly Peace* (1995)—that shows students packed atop trucks, holding banners.[42] The music does not cut. "Lovemaking" continues, reaching its climax again over archival footage of students pouring out of trains from all over the country into Beijing, forests of banners, and multitudes of demonstrators filling avenues and Tiananmen Square. Only as the song ends is the audience brought back to the diegetic world of *Summer Palace*.

How to interpret the editing, this juxtaposition of the fictional against the historical? Not as the latter and the apparent transparency of its political message belying the former's depoliticized reenactment, or as the former subverting the latter's gravitas with "party" spirit, but instead, I would argue, as the music straddling both calling into question any one-way reading of the politics of 1989. As in the film *Conjugation* and the novel *Death Fugue*, discussed in chapter 2, the main characters in *Summer Palace* evince no commitment to the movement. Does that mean, however, that these three works are politically compromised? Do Yu Hong and Zhou Wei have to be ardent activists whose passions for each other and for democracy are inseparable? What other forms of politics are possible? And what forms of politics, in the aftermath of the massacre and the retightening of state censorship, are rendered impossible?

In the modern Chinese literary tradition, the so-called revolution-plus-love narrative formula first became popular in the late 1920s. Seeking romantic liberation from traditional constraints (such as the arranged marriage), protagonists in this formula wed their individual longings to revolutionary ones of national salvation and construction.[43] In such fiction, especially from the Maoist period, erotic desire is subsumed under a more collective project. *Summer Palace*, on the other hand, unfolds a variation on the "revolution plus love" mode, as the next section shows. The revolution is crushed, while "love" is allowed to run rampant. Collective action, in Lou Ye's representation, has indeed been repressed. But who is responsible?

POSTREVOLUTION PLUS LOVE

Missing from the criticism on *Summer Palace* is an accounting for repression. Repression in relation to the film takes at least two forms. First, there is the reenactment of the military repression on the night of June 3 to 4, 1989. Even though soldiers are pictured only with their weapons pointed skyward, gunfire crackles in the soundtrack. This initial detonation sends the heretofore peaceful and orderly demonstration, consisting of sit-ins and mass singing, into chaos. Only in the ensuing panic do we see protestors chucking bricks and bottles at a burning military vehicle, with armed soldiers advancing. Thus civilian "violence" is framed as a response to preemptive shooting by the military. Bullets scattered the alternative collective formations of Tiananmen.

Second, there are the conditions in which *Summer Palace* itself was produced. It did not have to be filmed on the fly like *I Graduated* and *Conjugation*. But in spite of—and because of—the authorization to shoot, it could not cross certain red lines. The soldiers' guns are aimed skyward, as mentioned above, in keeping with the official narrative seen in *Songs of the Republic's Guardians* (discussed in chapter 1) that all shots were "warning shots fired into the sky." Not just the main characters are unscathed. No dead are depicted, not even any wounded. As audacious as the film may be, only in the context of producing in China through censorship—conceived as repressive as well as authorizing—can one evaluate Lou Ye's minimization of state brutality, both in the film and in his remarks cited above. State brutality is missing but not absent, displaced affectively into the rage on display. Besides the rocks and bottles thrown at the advancing army, a classmate of Zhou Wei's returns to their dorm room the morning after and bursts into tears of fury. He has to be restrained and ultimately bawls in Zhou Wei's arms. His reaction—similar to Lan Yu's crying in Handong's arms—is an indictment of what took place the night before.

How to account for the maximization of sex? The second half of *Summer Palace*, set after Tiananmen, shows no slackening in this area. Yu Hong, who has broken up with Zhou Wei, goes on to have sex with a married man and a coworker. Zhou Wei and Li Ti subsequently immigrate to post-Wall Berlin, where they cheat on the latter's boyfriend. Yet carnal satiation brings none of them satisfaction. There is a connection between the nude bodies of dead soldiers shown in government documentaries like *Flutter, Flag of the Republic* (discussed in chapter 1) and the nude bodies of Yu Hong, Zhou Wei, and Li Ti shown in *Summer Palace* as well as Lan Yu and Chen Handong in *Lan Yu*. The former is hallmarked by political passion, the latter by sexual passion—because the dead, desecrated bodies of civilian martyrs are unable to be exhibited. Their apotheosis is foreclosed. This is the bigger taboo, not bare bodies entwined in bed but the naked truth of corpses strewn in the streets of Beijing.

Narratives in the revolution-plus-love mode frequently culminate in a double fulfillment, the public along with the private. *Summer Palace* unravels in a double failure, however: the revolution is scattered, and so are the lovers. Zhou Wei and Li Ti in due time move to Berlin. Yu Hong moves back home to the Northeast and then goes south to Shenzhen before heading inland to Wuhan. Just as the crowds were driven from Tiananmen Square, so does she drift hither and thither like a lost soul.

The original design of the narrative, according to Lou Ye, was to follow a north-south trajectory. The opening setting is the town of Tumen on the border with the Democratic People's Republic of Korea (North Korea). A picture of Kim Il-Sung even hangs in Yu Hong's home. Her boyfriend works in a post office with all the drab trappings of the socialist-era workplace. After Yu Hong returns to Tumen from Beijing in the wake of Tiananmen, she was to sojourn in Wuhan before winding up in Shenzhen, this north-south route in parallel with China's movement from the socialist to the postsocialist era (the fishing-village-turned-metropolis of Shenzhen, bordering Hong Kong, was one of the first Special Economic Zones [SEZs] where a market economy was implemented at the beginning of the 1980s).

As the movie turned out, however, Shenzhen is essentially skipped, reduced to a subtitle mention without actually being pictured. Rather than a southward, "capitalist" path, the film traces a movement inward and eventually backward. Instead of serving as an allegory for national transformation, therefore, Yu Hong journeys into the interior, revolutionary in the sense of circling back. She is a revolutionary in postrevolutionary times. Barred a political outlet for her passions like others of her generation, she nevertheless does not redirect them toward the economic. She is not close to being the ideal capitalist subject. Despite the incessant exchange of her sex partners, one can never accuse her of prostituting herself. Love for her is never a commodity. What is remarkable about all her relationships, juxtaposed against those in *Lan Yu*, is the utter absence of the money factor. When Yu Hong makes love outdoors with her hometown boyfriend for the first time, the scene is shot with glaring white light, capturing the couple as in a criminal act. Transgression, and not consumption, characterizes her motive.

Yu Hong's love is decidedly not quotidian but carries a residual yearning for the beyond. It permanently seeks change, never content with the present, always striving after an ideal. Zhou Wei is but a figure for that ideal without telos. In addition to the opening diary entry on-screen, *Summer Palace* contains many voice-overs by Yu Hong, brief monologues that could represent other entries from her diary. This is the first one: "If my life were not under inspection by an ideal, then life's ordinariness would pain me unbearably." She cannot stand the everyday and the commonplace. What is this ideal that propels her? It consists in a kind of existential vehemence. Referring to her relationship with Zhou Wei, she continues: "It cannot be thought of in terms of happiness or unhappiness. I only want to live a little more intensely." This yearning is utterly alien to the bourgeois aspiration of romantic fulfillment.

Even at the peak of her relationship with Zhou Wei, an incapacity for stasis gnaws at her. This penchant is evinced in a postcoital exchange when she says that she wants to break up with him "because I cannot live without you." After an episode of separation and brief reconciliation, she again intones from her diary: "The most unfortunate part is that I know this kind of thing will happen to me again later." She is caught in a cycle of permanent revolution from which she cannot break free. The following perhaps best captures her mode of life: "In wartime you can give your all; in peacetime you are at an utter loss." Yu Hong thrives in the extraordinary and withers in the ordinary. These voice-overs, drawn from fragments of her diary, certainly suggest a private mode of narration. Yet they should be viewed not solely diegetically, within the film world that opens in the late 1980s, but also nondiegetically, emblematic of the film's making in the wake of the violent scattering that took place on June 4, 1989, of the fragmentation that the massacre foisted on what was once together and whole, the breaking of collectivities into solitary individuals.

In the end, the revolution comes to a close. Zhou Wei, back in Chongqing from Berlin, learns that Yu Hong has been married for two years. He reaches out to her via email, and they meet a final time, at a highway service station in Hebei province near Beidaihe. The location could not be less settling and more opportune. After finding themselves in a hotel room and kissing and fondling, they ask each other: "What then?" They have seemingly come full circle, in that other meaning of revolution. Yet they can no longer go back to what, when, and where they were before. Yu Hong eventually walks out and does not return; Zhou Wei drives away.

At the end of the film, captions reveal the various fates of the four main characters, over images of their dancing at their first rendezvous in a bar. Yu Hong worked in the service area until winter 2003; what happened to her afterward is not revealed. Zhou Wei continued to work in Chongqing. Li Ti's boyfriend lost contact with everyone, his whereabouts unknown. All that remains for Li Ti is an epitaph. The four friends, like the main characters of *Conjugation* (discussed in chapter 2), have dispersed, disappeared, or died. The images of them together, dancing, however, presents a sharp contrast with the text on-screen. Given this juxtaposition, the "partying" in the film cannot be construed as mere hedonism, apolitical self-indulgence that provides insufficient motive for the political protests of 1989. Rather, on display is the joy of collective life, the ferment both physical and spiritual of the late 1980s. *Summer Palace* portrays college students not simply as horny. There are numerous scenes of young people gathered together, including in bars, to engage in intellectual discussion and debate as well as to recite and listen to poetry. In dorm rooms they bunch together to dance, read, and play music. Off campus they attend movie screenings. The time prior to the crackdown is pictured as one of cultural vibrancy and exuberance, and always of a crowd.

The scene of the four main characters dancing in the bar is not the only flashback at the end. After the closing credits begin to roll, three series of images replace the black in the background. The first series is of students jumping onto trucks to go from their campus to Tiananmen Square. The second is of students undergoing military training in the wake of Tiananmen, shown in military garb and carrying rucksacks while trying to board moving public buses. The third and final series, before the background returns to black underneath the credits, is of a demonstration in Berlin that Zhou Wei, Li Ti, and Li Ti's boyfriend happen upon one day, which they traverse and walk with in part.

Compared to *Lan Yu*, where the entire narrative as flashback issues from the point of view of Handong, these flashbacks in *Summer Palace* are fleeting yet omniscient, representative not of personal narration but of the "third-person plural," a generation.

All three flashback sequences are of collectives but each highlights a different moment. The first one is characterized by spontaneity and exhilaration, the rush of joining in a protest movement. As portrayed by Lou Ye, political and nonpolitical sociality flourished in the 1980s both before and during Tiananmen. It was a time of both the private, symbolized by the diary entries, and the communal, as testified by all the group activities and the songs sung in unison, from Cui Jian's "Nothing to My Name" on the back of the truck to the Communist "Unity Is Strength" on the night before the bloodbath. The bar scenes do not signify only sex and indulgence. Far from glorifying hedonism or romantic love as the summit of existence, *Summer Palace* suggests that people cannot find happiness and fulfillment solely in the personal. Celebrated is not the desublimation of politics into sex but Eros as the urge for unities, a Marcusian understanding in which Eros, as simultaneously a sexual as well as revolutionary drive, finds expression not just in coupling but also in congregating—poetry readings, marches, movie screenings, debates, dancing, donations of blankets for those staying overnight on the square—all of which are depicted in the film. This Eros could never pass Chinese state censorship.

The second sequence of images, on the other hand, is characterized by the triumph of "surplus repression," to continue with Marcuse's conceptualization, here understood as both the violent repression of the protests and the repression since then that clamps down on political possibilities. In contrast to the first sequence, the scene of military training evinces coercion, with the student participants forced to take part in drills and exercises that sought to inculcate in them not so much martial qualities as identification with soldiers. Visually the shots of students boarding moving public buses recall the earlier ones of students climbing aboard trucks headed to Tiananmen Square. Yet the latter are a travesty of the former. Absent is any jubilation or exultation. Instead, the students, including Zhou Wei, scramble around as if lost, and even after they successfully board the bus, there is no excitement on their faces, only resignation. Military training is but another instantiation of the productive dimension of censorship. It was precisely in the immediate wake of Tiananmen that two of the most prestigious universities in China, Peking University in Beijing and Fudan University in Shanghai, instituted year-long programs of military training that lasted until 1993. The Chinese state does not just cut down bodies in the street. It also molds bodies and their movements, enforcing obedience.

The third sequence is foreign, part of a side trip to Berlin taken by the film. Zhou Wei and Li Ti may meet up with friends and sleep together, but they cannot find community there. They are outsiders to the demonstration they come across, mere observers if not trespassers. Li Ti commits suicide later on the same day, and Zhou Wei eventually moves back to China. Along with the three previous flashbacks—dancing in a bar, clambering onto trucks, and military training—the final images of marching in Berlin end not on a note of the personal and the libidinal but on alternate forms of togetherness. The first and second link up social and political conviviality. The third rules out spontaneous forms of the latter, with the irony of the fourth being that a rally for communism—the demonstrators carry banners for Marx, Lenin, and Mao—is allowed in a postsocialist city like Berlin and not in a nominally socialist country led by a communist party. Thus are Zhou Wei and Li Ti alienated from an activist ethos of solidarity squelched by the massacre and its aftermath. Yet the yearning for more still stirs. These final flashbacks, and not the documentary footage interpolated in the middle of the film, are the real return of the repressed.

As portrayed in *Summer Palace*, the dominant form of sociality after Tiananmen is the one-on-one interaction: Yu Hong and her hometown boyfriend, Yu Hong and a married man, Yu Hong and a coworker. The collective singing of "Nothing to My Name" or "Unity Is Strength" is replaced by Yu Hong singing solo karaoke. This sonic shift should not be taken for granted because we heard the gunshots, and we saw the soldiers with guns. The crowd that had gathered on Tiananmen Square was brutally dispersed. Multitudes are reduced to individuals, and the film illustrates how unsatisfying such isolation is. Love may often be sublimated into politics in Maoist culture, and politics desublimated into love in the immediate post-Mao period.[44] But in Lou Ye's film, the dynamic between sex and politics is not one of sublimation or desublimation. The director does not pit the self against the masses, romance against revolution. Rather, the self can be realized only through mass activity, and romance and revolution are indissolubly entwined. With the crushing of the 1989 movement and the scattering of the collective huddled on Tiananmen Square, the personal is doomed to devastation, as epitomized by Li Ti's suicide.[45] No amount of sex could save her.

In March 2012, Lou Ye experienced another case of censorship, this time not in filmmaking. As he explains on his microblog on Sina Weibo, he was recently interviewed by a mainland Chinese publication, but when the interview was published, he noticed many parts were left out, especially those concerning film censorship. He says that such elision is a kind of infringement: at first, you become angry; after ten or twenty years, you'll no longer feel anything; thirty years later, you'll wonder how come you haven't been infringed upon. To be censored becomes a habit. "Before I try to get habituated," Lou Ye writes, "I still hope to let people see the deleted portion." The reporter asked him whether he must have known that *Summer Palace* would not pass censorship. His response, absent from the published interview, was that he thought it was possible: "Because not a single person has said 'June Fourth' cannot be filmed. I also haven't seen any rule or regulation to that effect, just like how no one has told me that the Cultural Revolution can't be filmed. This is an invisible censorship. In actuality those who are censored are complicitous. The existence of censorship is completed by censors and the censored together. Do you want to play a role in it?" The reporter's question implied that Lou Ye knew *Summer Palace*, with its sex and Tiananmen scenes, was never going to pass censorship. But he made it anyway in order to make a scene, thereby profiting from the publicity of the ban to circulate the film worldwide and taking advantage of the "fetish of censorship" in the global capitalist market to entice viewers to peep at the forbidden in China. In such a view, Lou Ye's response to the reporter's question is itself a faux show of naïveté.

Another view of Lou Ye's response is this: he is precisely making a scene, both with *Summer Palace* and with this microblog entry, making public the secret that is the Tiananmen movement; making public the fact that it cannot be filmed, cannot be mentioned; making public what was omitted from the published interview; making public the invisible work of censorship itself. Censorship makes, but it is also made, and not only by censors. It is a collaborative production, an unspoken deal undersigned by all those who uphold its tacit terms. Lou Ye breaks the deal, and it is his "naïveté" that saves him. In the words of Judith Butler, "A subject who speaks at the border of the speakable risks redrawing the distinction between what is speakable and what is unspeakable."[46] Lou Ye speaks at this border or, rather, he transgresses this border. By speaking the impermissible, he pushes the border outward or at the very least ascertains the location of that invisible border so that others after him can cross it again, knowing there is a beyond.

As mentioned earlier, Lou Ye did not stay idle during the five years of his ban from filmmaking. He made two films, *Spring Fever* in 2009 and *Love and Bruises* in 2011, both of which involved shooting in China. When the ban officially ended in 2011, the director did not miss a beat. He began filming *Mystery*. He did not avoid controversy this time either.

In 2012 Lou Ye publicly disclosed, again on Sina Weibo, his back-and-forth with censorship authorities regarding *Mystery*. The film was scheduled for nationwide release in mid-October, but Lou announced on his microblog in early September that, despite *Mystery* having received exhibition approval, the censorship review had run into difficulties. The Beijing branch of the SARFT's Film Bureau asked for two emendations.[47] Lou Ye agreed to only one of them, arguing that the film had already undergone revision after a first round of inspection in order to premier at the Cannes Film Festival earlier that May. In subsequent posts, Lou Ye continued to share with his over 200,000 followers the ongoing negotiations. Ultimately the director had to fade to black the end of an objectionable scene. In protest, he also removed his name from the film's opening and closing credits.

As with his sanitized interview, Lou Ye refuses to become habituated to infringement. If he has no choice but to play a part in it, he will at least clear his name from the roster of the complicitous. He purposely reveals to the public the secretive processes of censorship. Those who do so are always open to the charge that they are selling the scandal of Chinese repression to an eager audience in the West. But Lou Ye, with *Summer Palace* and his Weibo, and *Lan Yu*, in both Stanley Kwan's and Zhang Yongning's cuts, make a scene out of censorship, exposing what has been cut not only from a film or an interview but also from China's past, present, and potential futures.

The two films depict not so much a failed revolution as a revolution crushed, with the couple and the coterie left unscathed to absorb the scattered crowd. They are not depoliticized portrayals of Tiananmen that glorify materialism and hedonism. They do not picture the protests as a mass orgy or a mere background to the timeless theme of love's supremacy. Gunshots on the night of June 3 to 4, 1989, in both *Lan Yu* and *Summer Palace*, were what shattered the social and political movement, fragmented into the sex partner and the business partner. Neither film celebrates the transactional relationship.

Instead, both films revive the sights and sounds of the alternative social worlds violently dispersed in 1989. Whether shooting without permission in the dark of night or shooting openly with a large cast and crew, they attest to the challenges and possibilities of visualizing and auralizing Tiananmen in China. *Lan Yu* contrasts the embrace of lovers with the rescuing of the wounded by ordinary people. It also leaves in place the gashes to the filmic body in the "inconsequential" cutting of the Tiananmen sequence, thereby marking the event as a moment of rupture that the regime tries to suture away. *Summer Palace* shows characters out of step with the postrevolutionary times, after political fervor has been mown down and redirected to the carnal. Both films, in juxtaposing the pop bathos after 1989 with the mass singing of revolutionary anthems during the demonstrations, reanimate the multiple yet collective voices of the movement.

CHAPTER FOUR

The Orthography of Censorship

Participatory Reading from Print to the Internet

In 2016 a professor in China asked permission to translate an article of mine. The article, "Blanks to Be Filled: Public-Making and the Censorship of Jia Pingwa's *Decadent Capital*," had appeared in an issue of the journal *China Perspectives* the previous year. Now the professor told me that an editor at the mainland journal *Contemporary Writers Review* (*Dangdai zuojia pinglun*)—likewise a professor—wanted to publish this article in translation.

I happily agreed: the journal was an esteemed publication I always followed. In the ensuing email exchange, my translator informed me that, as the topic of the article is "still sensitive," some of its contents may have to be "omitted or purified in the translation." I expressed my appreciation for his and the editor's undertaking of the project despite the sensitivity. I also asked to see the translation before publication.

When I later received the draft, I saw that there were indeed omissions. What was deemed "impure" in the original? Predictably, missing were all references to Tiananmen. Less predictably, references to repression were themselves repressed: not only the military repression on the night of June 3 to 4, 1989, but also the voiding of the past. For example, gone was my discussion of the performance of amnesia in Jia Pingwa's novel as well as the forced nature of this forgetting.

Not just my article, however, but my hands, too, were not entirely clean. How did I respond to this bowdlerized version? I complied. I did not push for more of the original to be translated. I did not ask the absent portions to be marked with blank squares, as is the case in Jia's novel, examined below. I did not negotiate for a "here was deletion" to be inserted wherever there was an occurrence. That the citation of the article in English and "the translation has been slightly abridged" were included in the first footnote of the Chinese version was hardly any consolation.[1]

The irony of an article on censorship getting censored was not lost on me. If I were harsh on myself, I would say that I kowtowed because I was an early-career scholar keen on an extra line in my CV. If I were less harsh, I would say that I wanted my research to be more accessible to Chinese readers. For the curious, they could follow the trail of the citation to the "unabridged."

It might not have mattered in the end. The published Chinese version was further foreshortened from the translator's preemptive truncation—and not due to space constraints. No one individual is to blame, not the editors, the translator, or me. It was a collaborative effort, each of us playing a part in the reproduction of state censorship. What is more, it was collegial, perpetrated by fellow academics.

Writing now several years later, I have a chance to change the reproduction into an alter-production. And for inspiration, I turn to another text and its editorial intervention. The writer Hu Fayun finished *Such Is This World@sars.come*, a novel set around the 2002–2003 severe acute respiratory syndrome (SARS) epidemic in China, in 2004. He could not find a book publisher for it, so he published it on a website. That website was then shut down. In 2006, however, the novel appeared as a book. But a reader noticed the discrepancy between the book and online editions and in turn posted the differences online, marking within parentheses what was removed in print from the internet version.

What you will find below in the first half of this chapter is a revised version of my article that appeared in *China Perspectives*, revised not least in the sense that I, too, have inserted parentheses, so to speak, into the text, bracketing all that was left out of the Chinese version. You can see for yourself—within braces {}—what the translator omitted and what was additionally removed in publication. Censorship reduces *and* produces, as I have argued in this book. It brought forth a curtailed copy of my writing. It also induced me to issue an "updated" edition that makes public all that was supposed to be hidden, including the work of censorship itself.

This parenthetical praxis is part of the larger analysis in this chapter of what I call the orthography of censorship. The orthography of censorship contains, among other symbols, the parenthesis, the ellipsis, and the blank square—☐—sometimes seen in Chinese texts that traditionally designates an undecipherable character in manuscript and in modern times can also signal excision. These symbols perform censorship: they enact it and display it. They constitute both a system of signification as well as ruptures in this system. Collectively they represent the continuum from the "correct writing" (*orthographia*) of censorship to heterodox practices of interventionist reading that open up the writing to communal resignification.[2]

Jia Pingwa's 1993 novel—now published in English translation as *Ruined City*—narrates the downfall of a celebrated writer who is embroiled in a series of extramarital affairs and a protracted lawsuit, and who ultimately never finishes the novel he is working on. Infamously, the text contains blank squares—"☐☐☐☐☐☐"—representing parts of the manuscript that were allegedly deleted before publication. *Ruined City* was banned in 1994 but unbanned in 2009, although with the blank squares removed and replaced with ellipses in the reissued edition. Hu Fayun's *Such Is This World@sars.come* concerns a middle-aged woman's entry into Chinese cyberspace, where she begins to read and write, against the background of SARS. As mentioned above, a netizen compiled a list of the discrepancies between the version first posted online and the later print version. He then published it in an internet forum, where it prompted further discussion and commentary.

Both novels, across their multiple editions, entice readerly participation. The little squares in *Ruined City* inserted by Jia Pingwa are symbols of extradiegetic intervention. Because of their very blankness, they not only mark the place of deletion but also keep alive a space for remembrance and reimagination. Through these blanks waiting to be filled, I as a reader can enter into a dialogue in writing, reconstructing the removed squares back into the novel as a gesture of refilling the Square, which was cleared in 1989. By alerting readers, in the afterword of *Such Is This World*, to censorship, Hu Fayun sends them on the trail of comparative analysis. One reader's legwork, shared publicly, in turn transforms other readers into investigators in a burgeoning public that cuts across reading and writing.

These two case studies represent two moments in post-Tiananmen literary history. The chapter begins with the sensation surrounding the publication of *Ruined City* and the commentary surrounding the blank squares in its text. With reference to modern Chinese critical discourse, I argue for their significance as placeholders for a past that cannot be broached; at the same time, I point to their possibilities for engagement that reenact the open space of Tiananmen Square. I next explore the narrative in *Such Is This World* through my concept of the "workshop," in which reading and writing are collaborative and creative. Then I follow the novel into cyberspace where production is characterized by public-making: the communal unmasking of the SARS outbreak as well as of censorship. My analysis shuttles back to the novel and its portrayal of Tiananmen, which reveals the role that violence has played in shaping China's course since 1989. In instrumentalizing the orthography of censorship in print and online, both novels save a space where Tiananmen can be reinserted into the always-already censored text. They may be displaced—to the pirate underground and to the Chinese blogosphere and internet forums—but they unfailingly make a comeback, assisted by the contribution of many.

* * *

THE LITERARY MARKETPLACE

The reforms that began at the end of the 1970s in agriculture soon spread to all sectors of the economy. With decentralization and marketization as guiding principles, the Chinese government started to reduce its role in the early 1980s in what was a lackluster publishing industry. Although it lifted controls on book prices and paper allocation and allowed publishing houses to engage in direct marketing, it withdrew subsidies, forcing these state-owned enterprises to be financially self-sustaining and responsible for their employees' benefits.[3] Publishers also could no longer count on the government to purchase their books, like grain. The hydra-headed market thus made its first appearance, with its dauntingly limitless potential of readers whose tastes, demands, and desires now had to be taken into account.

In this newly competitive environment, Jia Pingwa's *Ruined City* was conceived. The novel was *the* literary event of the 1990s. First published amid a veritable furor in the summer of 1993, it signaled, perhaps more than any other work since the economic reforms, the transformation of China's publishing industry. Over a dozen publishers vied for the manuscript before it was even completed. There were rumors, promotional ploy or not, of bidding wars and a million-yuan advance. The Beijing Publishing House eventually won the book contract.[4] Demand for the novel was so high that the publishing house sold its printing rights to six other presses. Cultural consumption had arrived.[5]

Then in January 1994, the General Administration of Press and Publication (GAPP) handed down the ban. Speculated on for months before it came—perhaps another ruse to drive up sales—the ban cited that *Ruined City* was "low in character, mixed with pornographic descriptions."[6] Printing and distribution were stopped, copies were recalled. Not only were the publisher's profits confiscated, it was assessed twice the amount in fines.[7] {Then editor at the Beijing Publishing House Tian Zhenying, a Shaanxi-native like Jia who had professedly read the manuscript of *Ruined City* nine times in a row and so moved the author that he gave her the rights, was forced into early retirement.[8]}

That a state-owned publishing house and editor were punished, and not the author, is indicative of a certain loosening of literary control in reform-era China, to be sure, but also of the devolution of prepublication censorship from central authorities to in-house gatekeepers. Jia Pingwa nevertheless did not escape entirely unscathed. While publicists and favorable critics drew immediate comparisons to *The Plum in the Golden Vase*, the erotic novel of manners of the late Ming, many others registered disappointment if not outright disdain.[9] Born in 1952 in Shaanxi province, Jia had been previously acclaimed for his series of writings, both fictional and nonfictional, set in the rural region of Shangzhou in the province's southeast, works that paint the simple and peaceful lives of villagers in the early reform years.[10] Now, not only has he abandoned the countryside for the "ruined city," he has been allegedly coopted by the latter's hedonism and commercialism, peddling (soft) pornography.[11] *Ruined City* contains a healthy dose of implicit sex, as in this description featuring the protagonist, the celebrated writer Zhuang Zhidie, and one of his mistresses: "He watched her squirm through drunken eyes; his lips twitched, his eyes rolled back, and he cried out. □□□□□□ [The author has deleted 50 words]" (91).[12]

This citation is remarkable as well for another feature of the text: blank boxes followed by "[The author has deleted x number of words.]" This feature, in fact, drew just as much criticism as the sex, prompting fulmination in some quarters (not to mention titillation in others). One commentator from 1993, for example, took the high road of finger wagging: "Jia Pingwa wants adolescents to imagine things when they come across '□□.' He should suffer the rebuke of conscience."[13] Instead of guarding against the imagination of the young, another commentator summons nationalist outrage, deeming Jia's squares "a false challenge of the censorship of publications intended to curry favor with readers in Hong Kong, Taiwan, and the West who are antipathetic to the institution of publishing in mainland China."[14] The following respondent, however, saw in the squares not a pandering to outsiders but a relaxation of policy: "compared to the deletion method of 'cutting but not letting it be known whether it was cut or where it was cut,' this is certainly more open and respectful of the author and can be considered a kind of progress."[15] Most trenchant perhaps is the critique below, which argues that the squares, far from designating transparency, are like walls that ultimately prevent readers from entering, ruling out any input:

> Jia Pingwa uses this method to suppress the author's authority even as he reconstitutes that authority another way. For no reader's imagination can ever solve the riddles; no reader can discuss equally these abstruse deletions with the author. Thus, the fabricated deletions become the token and code of this style, the most enticing in the story of Zhuang Zhidie. This is also a token and code moving towards consumption and the market.[16]

Far from symbols of censorial obtrusion or authorial compromise, Jia's squares, so the argument goes, toy with the public. They function as an interface oriented toward readers/consumers, whom they do not merely entice. Rather, they are a tease, the consummate commodity that beckons but never satisfies.

The charge of selling out is frequently found in the commentary on *Ruined City*. Yet it is surely ironic that the businessman of letters—the very figure of lamentation and deprecation in criticisms of Jia Pingwa—is variously incarnated in the novel. Besides Zhuang Zhidie are three other eminent cultural figures in the fictional city of Xijing, where the story is set. One is an artist who forges famous paintings and then spends the gains on women. Another is a calligrapher who sells his brushwork to fund a gambling habit. And this is how a friend of Zhuang's describes the song-and-dance troupe of the third, a former Shaanxi-opera performer: "Singing tunes that others steered clear of and sporting costumes that rivals dared not wear, they toured the country for five years, playing to packed houses wherever they went; the money fell like snowflakes" (17). For the troupe leader—as for the creator of this character, Jia Pingwa—the breaking of taboos is what brings in the cash. The venerable arts of ages past, whether it be Chinese painting, calligraphy, Shaanxi opera, or—to further extend the comparison to Jia himself—the classic Chinese novel are not so much given up as retooled for more profitable purposes in the market age. An associate of Zhuang Zhidie's who helps Zhuang's wife run a bookstore advises Zhuang on the secret to success in the cultural arena:

> In this day and age, there's nothing wrong with a writer owning a business. Fame is wealth, and you shouldn't squander it. You can't get rich from writing alone . . . Writing books is not as good as selling them, and editing books is better than both. Many bookstores now edit their own books, either by buying a book number from a publishing house or by printing books illegally.[17] Chapbooks are all about sex and violence, and there's no need for proofreading. With print runs in the millions, those people are getting rich. (78–79; translation modified)

The commercialization of literature, capitalizing on sex—parodic reflexivity is indeed characteristic of *Ruined City* as a whole. But to what extent is Jia complicit in the very things he pokes fun at? Is he lampooning the man of letters who opts for lucre, or is he profiting from the very portrayal? I will return to these questions later. Suffice it to say here that one can hardly find a more disheartening portrait in contemporary Chinese literature of the state of the culture industry.

The opening sentence in *Ruined City* identifies the setting as the fictional city of Xijing in the 1980s, but the cynicism that drips from the entire novel is more in line with its composition in China in the 1990s. Nowhere in the narrative is the idealism associated with the {decade that bridges the introduction of economic reforms at the end of the 1970s and the crushing of the 1989 Tiananmen Square protests to be glimpsed.}[18] Instead, intrigues, affairs, swindling, and bickering dominate the plotline. Corruption is prevalent from the press to the judicial system: newspaper articles are all paid for, and judges are open to influence. Behind their public façades, these institutions are driven by private dealings. The government is no different. Zhuang Zhidie seeks to win favor for a court case of his by marrying his pretty housemaid to the mayor of Xijing's handicapped son. Although politics at the national level is not depicted, Jia does imply that it simply replicates the local: "A few people talk something over at someone's house, and national policy is formulated" (284). Residents of Xijing know each other only too well. They are inextricably entangled in a bog of relationships, unable to put aside their personal interests, mutual or conflictual, for any broader horizon. Given a cast of characters filled with the cultural elite, the total absence of discussions of aesthetics, current events, or social issues among them is revealing.

{Just as the Chinese state, ever since the 1989 protests that centered on a public square, has aimed to close alternative publics, so too} does *Ruined City* seemingly represent no alternatives. Although Jia cannot be accused of glorifying the venal characters in his novel, as testified by their deplorable outcomes, Zhuang Zhidie's failed escape from Xijing and ultimate demise—not to mention his inability to finish the novel he is working on—might simply mirror the impasse facing an author writing in {post-Tiananmen} China. This is the threat. The narrative as well as the blank squares themselves reenact the impairment and perversion of the public. And herein lies the danger of Jia Pingwa's performance of censorship. Are those squares another instance of Jia's self-referentiality, and if so, to what extent do they point to his complicity? Is his playing a mere reproduction of the effects of censorship without offering a way out?

{As seen earlier, many commentators aired their stances on those squares when the novel was published in 1993, as if to compensate for not being able to stand on another square that had been cleared four years previously. In part through the *Ruined City* controversy, Chinese intellectuals, quieted after the 1989 military crackdown on public demonstrations and the general clampdown on public discussions afterward, found their voices again.[19] Riding on the industry in the book was another, albeit much smaller, industry in its commentary, evidenced by many titles, all from 1993.[20] The novel may not have portrayed any publics but it did bring them about, reading publics both popular and critical. These publics were shut down, or driven underground, upon the 1994 ban. Although the pirate economy kept *Ruined City* alive, reception became technically an illicit undertaking.[21] Gone were public debates on the novel.

With the novel's republication in 2009, the critical public could resurface as well. And so, on the occasion of *Ruined City*'s unbanning, the author Ma Yuan remarked upon its foresight: "Thirty years ago Chinese intellectuals would be ashamed to talk about money, but by now I've seen so many writers bow and kneel down before power and money. More and more I see certain people around me becoming more and more like the Zhuang Zhidie type in *Ruined City*."[22] A tale that supposedly takes place in the 1980s and was written in the 1990s rings no less true in the new millennium. As the logic of the market penetrates further into China's "creative industries," the novel seems only to gain in prescience, no more so than when it is repackaged for sale fifteen years after the ban. But in his comments above, Ma Yuan slips in an element, "power" or "authority" (*quanli*), that is not readily apparent in the force field through which Zhuang Zhidie and other characters move. The addition—power plus money—suggests that the book's rerelease, aside from considerations of artistic vindication, has to be viewed in light of these twin vectors.

THE SQUARES IN QUESTION

Perhaps to distance itself from the media circus surrounding the 1993 publication, the 2009 publisher, Writers Publishing House, did not hype the unbanning. In fact, *Ruined City* was reissued as part of a trio of new editions, safe in the middle, flanked by two untainted works, the 1987 *Turbulence* and the 2005 *Shaanxi Opera*. One can surmise various reasons for the "rehabilitation": the sex was no longer so shocking, or Jia Pingwa had in the meantime won the prestigious Mao Dun Literary Prize for *Shaanxi Opera*, or those at GAPP who had handed down the ban were no longer there. In terms of the editions themselves, however, there are some concrete differences. The 1993 book features a cover with the title in typescript over an image of a crumbled sheet of paper, with a purplish cloud in the background. The color design of the 2009 book, on the other hand, can be described only as hot pink. In lieu of the mechanical title of sixteen years ago, Jia's own dashing calligraphy runs down the cover. One is reminded that even the state-owned Writers Publishing House, run by the China Writers Association (CWA), now has a division devoted to market assessment.[23]

Preceding each of the three novels in the new edition are three introductory essays by three literary critics.[24] These essays serve to legitimize the republication of a novel that was "low in character, mixed with pornographic descriptions." Fifteen years after the ban, the "pornographic descriptions" have remained intact. Not one character from the original has been removed, as the media liked to report. But the text was changed. What Jia Pingwa had "self-censored" in 1993 was censored a second time, this time for good. In the 2009 edition, the blank squares— □□□□□□—were replaced by ellipses: . . . . . . Replaced, too, was the count of deleted words by "[Here the author has made deletions.]" In some instances, the evidence of deletion was deleted altogether.[25]

The editor at *People's Literature* Li Jingze, author of the first prefatory essay in the new edition, "On Zhuang Zhidie," proposed the change.[26] This is how Li, referring to Jia, justifies in part the decision: "By drawing the blanks, he exhibited prohibition and at the same time transgressed the exhibited prohibition. Because of this, he incurred— and it served him right to incur—censure."[27] The words that jump out are the overbearing "served him right." Li traces the provenance of the blanks to the edited clean editions of Ming and Qing erotic fiction. He does not, like commentators before him, accuse Jia of arousing his readers' carnal fantasies, or even of commercialism. Rather, Li finds him guilty of shirking authorial responsibility: "I believe that the essential immorality of those "□□□" is this kind of sneaking away by Zhuang Zhidie, this kind of irresponsibility. Jia Pingwa strongly felt that he was powerless to touch, imagine, and describe certain things inside this character's mind and body; he could not make Zhuang Zhidie bear definite personal responsibility for his actions, including moral and ethical responsibility."[28] Li Jingze wants Zhuang Zhidie to stay in place, to suffer lifelong imprisonment in the diegesis for his immoral behavior. Zhuang might pay with his life at the end, but death is an insufficient finality. That is why Li, in the reauthorized edition, assumes the responsibility to remove those blank squares, closing the doors through which Zhuang—and Jia Pingwa—can abscond. And this time, the intervention comes not from GAPP, as in 1993, but from within, as it were, from an editor, a critic, a colleague.

At the time of the 1993 publication, rumors of an original, unexpurgated edition circulated—as well as pirated "unexpurgated editions" themselves with the blanks filled in, so to speak. Since then, Jia Pingwa has revealed in interviews the story behind those blanks followed by "[The author has deleted x number of words.]" He did not write out the sex scenes completely, knowing they would never see the light of day. Then in revision, he made some further deletions. The editor also made some more, and Jia added the blanks and the final number of deleted words. The "x," therefore, does not correspond to the actual number of words taken out.[29] It is a collaborative fabrication by author and editor.

May one then conclude that Li Jingze's production constitutes a rectification? The story of *Ruined City*, from 1993 to 2009, has not changed in the slightest, as the publisher and reviewers are fain to point out. After causing so much controversy, after provoking so much rebuke, have the blank squares—tiny price tags on our lecherous thoughts, little escape hatches for our weaker selves—been finally, legitimately effaced? After all, the novel has now been proofread for the erroneous and the extraneous: the count was a sham, and the blanks had nothing there.

A historical precedent sheds some light on this question. For this is not the first time that blank squares have appeared in modern Chinese critical discourse. In May 1934, in "More on '.....' '□□□□,'" the writer Lu Xun humorously remarked that ".....' are foreign and imported, while blank squares are homegrown. He had in mind ancient writings on bamboo strips whose missing or indecipherable characters are transcribed as □s. He was responding to a piece called "On '.............' '□□□□,'" published earlier in the month in the bimonthly journal *In the World of Men* by one of its editors, Xu Xu.[30] As Xu declares in his piece, "The fact that '□□□□' '. . . . .' are commonly found in the news in newspapers and the telegrams of important personages is already a problem encountered by everyone."[31] For Xu, the blank squares evince a reluctance or inability to say—due to mental laziness or cowardice—what ought to be said. It is a problem affecting all of society, and he lauds scientists like Darwin, for example, for daring to say—that we come from apes—what others dare not, and writers who are able to describe what readers cannot find words for.

In his response Lu Xun follows Xu in deploring the appearance of the blank squares in contemporary publications. But the reasons he gives are quite different. It is a phenomenon, he says, that makes two sets of people happy: the government censor, who sees that his work is done for him, and the reader, who is aroused by the fill-in-the-blank squares. He believes it to be a kind of commercial deception, the selling of something not there: "Nowadays all things have to be bought with money, and so naturally all things can be sold for money. But the fact that even 'nothing' can be sold for money is rather beyond expectations."[32]

The encroachment of capitalist ethics into the cultural and intellectual domains, especially in Shanghai where Lu Xun lived at the time, certainly perturbed him.[33] A mere six months after the response above, however, Lu Xun was assessing the blank squares differently. In "The Demons of the Chinese Literary Scene" of November 1934, he observed that the Kuomintang government censors no longer allowed authors to leave blanks in place of words struck out. He also referred to the system of prepublication censorship instituted that June after a meeting in Shanghai between authorities and publishers.[34] Blanks were touched on again a year later in "Preface to *Decorative Literature*" of December 1935, when he cheered the fact that "newspapers could keep blank what was deleted (the technical term is 'open a skylight')."[35] It was becoming clear that blank squares resisted rather than assisted the work of censorship.[36]

Perhaps he remembered a blank square in his own writing. It appears in the short story "Medicine," published in *New Youth* in May 1919. Old Shuan, believing it will cure his consumptive son, buys a steamed bun soaked in blood that—the reader later learns—was spilled from a revolutionary just executed. Near where Old Shuan makes the purchase is a place called Ancient Blank Ting Kou. This is an allusion to the famed revolutionary Qiu Jin, who was killed by Qing troops in July 1907 at a place called Xuan Ting Kou, in Lu Xun's hometown of Shaoxing. In the text, the character *xuan* is replaced by a blank square.

Who was responsible for this square? Did Lu Xun himself sketch it in the manuscript? Or did an editor insert it before printing? Either way, the little square serves as a kind of Post-it Note to remind readers of someone no longer there, or—to use another metaphor—a blank memorial tablet erected right there on the page for a past event that still could not be written about directly.[37] In "Medicine" as in *Ruined City*, the blank square performs censorship, revealing it as a force that does not merely come down at the end to cut or cross out but one that is present from the beginning, constitutive of the writing. Like Lu Xun before him, Jia Pingwa writes through censorship, his work not so much marred by it as formed with it.

What separates Jia's novel is its 1994 ban. In his case, therefore, the target was not only certain contents of the book but the book in its entirety. With the 2009 unbanning and the novel's readers being allowed once again to assemble openly, what is needed is a reassessment of the blank squares. Their banishment from the new edition confirms that they were and have always been the most offensive aspect of *Ruined City*. It is in the new edition that one finds the barefaced reassertion of authority, intoned from the intellectual high ground of a backward-gazing prefatory essay, along with the shedding of all accountability. Both the squares and the count of deleted words have been removed, nullifying any ability on the part of readers to "discuss equally." Order has been restored as the roles of not just author and expurgator but also producer and consumer are once again fixed. Whether one regards the editorial change as a distortion or a revision, it calls for a critical retort, by which I do not intend a return. I have no office to restore the squares or to carry out a recount of the "deleted words." Yet rereading the text is a gesture I fully own as a reader who can only figuratively replace the replaced.

{For every blank in *Ruined City* is an *ou-topos*, a not-place inserted to say no to the engulfing dystopia that appears all but ineluctable. This *ou-topos* is not also an *ou-chronos*. It is not beyond time but precisely a threshold for time to flow over and wash over the seeming permanence of a demoralized and disillusioned post-Tiananmen present.} Herein lies

Jia's telling treatment of time. In no way can one attribute it to short-sightedness. Much as "Beiping" in Sheng Keyi's *Death Fugue*—discussed in chapter 2—is a stand-in for Beijing, Xijing, or "western capital," is a portmanteau for Beijing and Xi'an, the latter the capital of many ancient dynasties (and the current capital of Shaanxi province, where Jia continues to live and write). The novel resonates with innumerable echoes from the distant past, and vestiges of the glory days of a now "ruined city" litter the diegetic décor: pieces of the crumbling city wall, rusted copper cash, centuries-old ink stones.[38] The odor of decay is heavy. It is thus far from the case that the narrative lacks a historical frame of reference. The disintegration of the present is etched against a backdrop of former grandeur. The fate of the capital is mirrored in the fate of the characters, especially of the protagonist, all of whose relationships break down and who at the end tries to flee the city, only to die at the train station. There is no way out. Because of the parallel with Xijing/Xi'an's trajectory, the social, moral, and physical decline and degradation that unfold in the story seem inevitable, inescapable, immutable.[39]

The novel's temporality is also astonishing for another reason: it makes few references to the socialist era, all of which are brief and glancing. Remnants of the era are reduced to artifacts, as from an archaeological dig. A fan bearing the calligraphy of Kang Sheng{, that Cultural Revolution hatchet man, as well as a scroll of Mao Zedong's own calligraphy} turn up. Yet they function precisely as antiques, objects to be treasured or traded and no longer as talismans. Needless to say, the legacies of the socialist experiment persist in the People's Republic to this day. But within a framework that is decidedly postsocialist, *Ruined City* makes no mention of the former nationalization of industry, collectivization of agriculture, and communalization of daily life. No specter {of Marx or Mao} hovers over Xijing.[40] {It is as if that previous chapter of Chinese history that spanned approximately thirty years existed in some remote, curious past. Curiously enough, the novel also contains an admonition against humankind's historical amnesia—coming from the rumination of a cow (from whose teats Zhuang Zhidie drinks milk directly, by the way): "The cow wanted to explain the past to humans, but unfortunately was unable to use human speech. Oftentimes humans forget what happened in the past, and after something has taken place, they open their thread-bound books to read 'How can there be such astonishing similarities in history!' They sigh. The cow had to laugh at the pitiable humans" (146; translation modified). The story is set ostensibly in the 1980s, which makes the socialist epoch its immediate past. The novel was written in the early 1990s, which makes the 1989 movement *its* immediate past. Both of these immediate pasts are glaringly missing. Jia Pingwa's "forgetting" of them enacts his characters' as well as his contemporaries' short-term memory loss in their headlong rush for riches and turn-ons. But it is more than a forgetting. The blank squares are emblems of enforced omission. They stand in, then, for the recurring *ou-topos*—the not-place and not-motif—that is Tiananmen Square. In this way does a graphic hiatus—□□□□□□—represent a historiographic one.

Objections will no doubt be raised that I am twisting Jia's blanks, which we all know signify sex too hot to print, without the "philosophy."[41] *Ruined City* may have been written four years after Tiananmen, but there is precisely not the least hint of it, or of national events and debates on social ills. If politics occupy the narrative, then it is the politics of one-upmanship: the calculation of interests, the exchange of favors, and the jockeying for advantage in the web of desire.} In keeping with the self-reflexivity of the novel, however, a little piece of writing within the writing casts a different light on the relationship between literature and politics:

> First-rate writers enter politics
>> ink up with officials and become their aides.
> Second-rate writers switch fields
>> they write ads as their trade.
> Third-rate writers join the underworld
>> reprinting porn to be paid. (442; translation modified)

This doggerel, which goes on a bit longer, is uttered by a junkman who recurs periodically throughout the novel. He was not always a junkman. He was once a teacher whose petitions to provincial authorities about unjust treatment at work fell on deaf ears. He was physically removed from Xijing by police at the behest of government officials. When he returned to the city, he became a junkman, wandering the streets and shouting out his services as well as biting ditties. The one above classifies the literary scene limned in *Ruined City*. The reader is familiar with depictions of scribblers who churn out smut or copy. But the first group, those who enter politics, presents a category alien to the novel. What it reveals is the cooptation of writers by power, that other element, in addition to money, that the author Ma Yuan identified in his interview as the forces underlying present-day Chinese literary production. The only possible politics for this literature is either to aid the official narrative or to reduce the very meaning of "politics" to intrigue and maneuvering.

The junkman had in fact been kicked out of Xijing for another verse: "*If I say you're all right, you're all right, whether you are or not. / If I say you're not all right, you're not all right, even if you are*" (7). "You" may refer to the mayor of Xijing, whose project of urban revitalization consisted of commercializing the city's past, remaking avenues into a postmodern pastiche of architectural styles of various dynasties, all selling "local" culture. But this couplet calls up another mapping. The entire country is in disarray, with not the intellectual or cultural elite but a junkman voicing its conscience. Only the seemingly deranged are capable of speaking truth to power, power that enforces the truth of its speech.

But allegorical reading should not be restricted to Xijing for China and Zhuang Zhidie for intellectuals. The blank squares constitute an orthography of censorship, not just of deletion but also of productiveness. With their removal in 2009, {20 years after Tiananmen,} what has become clear is that the challenge they pose lies in their politics of possibility. {The blank squares open not only into an elided past but also onto a future unforeclosed.} To substitute ellipses for squares is to blot out the former's receptivity. Those little squares, measuring no more than a few square millimeters on the page, are windows to worlds of meanings as well as yearnings. And they were closed, shrunken to the true void—as opposed to the blank—that is the black dot, neither because they were some "token and code moving towards consumption and the market"—{the state-mandated direction for decades}—nor because they let the author shirk responsibility for what he wrote, but because they called on the reading public for a reengagement and response not predetermined. They pointed forward to the myriad potential ways of filling them{, and backward too, designating the open space of a public square on which people had collected one late spring, functioning as visual cues or bookmarks holding the place in the pages of history}. That is why the 2009 rerelease is not so much a loosening of censorship, or even industry trumping ideology, as a repackaging of strategy to shape the public realm. {The blank squares could not be allowed to rest in peace underground. The banned book had to be brought back to life, only to be subjected to another violence, the clearing of its squares a reenactment of what happened on a June night, those ellipses without count like so many bullets echoing in the dark.}

* * *

THE ADVENT OF THE INTERNET

A mere ten years separate the banning of *Ruined City* in 1994 and Hu Fayun's completion of *Such Is This World@sars.come* in 2004. Yet a sea change washed over China during that period, leaving nothing unaltered in its wake. That change was the internet.[42]

In fact, 1994 was the year China first connected to the World Wide Web.[43] So when Hu finished writing the novel in 2004, China had been online for exactly ten years. By then there were some 94 million users—a large number, to be sure, but only 7 percent of the total population.[44] The Chinese internet's youth at the time explains the trajectory of *Such Is This World*, which traces a coming of age, except the protagonist, Ru Yan, is a middle-aged widow, and the age is digital.

At first Ru Yan uses the internet only to stay in touch with her son, who introduced it to her before he left for graduate school in France. With the handle "Such Is This World," she then joins an online community of parents with kids studying abroad. Soon, however, she is exploring the vast world of the Chinese Web, which for her is a land of revelation and daring:

> Her biggest shock was reading a great many works that had never made it into print. These writings had a point of view, with respect to their theoretical foundations, political doctrine, and conceptual framework, which at first was somewhat troubling to her. Ru Yan was the kind of person who had never concerned herself with

politics and theory, and her indifference implied a certain skepticism and disapproval. But these articles, novel and incisive, with their recklessly bold judgments, mesmerized her even as they frightened her. They also gave her access to raw facts—the true facts of historical events that had been neglected or buried or repackaged, so that this history now began to reveal a disconcerting face. (153; translation slightly modified)[45]

The world of print and the World Wide Web appear in juxtaposition. If the former is equated with restriction and distortion, then the latter equals freedom and truth. The internet is portrayed as an altogether new medium, in fact an *im*medium, providing its public with direct access to "raw facts" that bypass any "repackaging," not just by censorship but even, it is implied, by the narrative and commodity form.

If Ru Yan is unaccustomed to this rawness, then it is relished by Damo, the novel's other main character, a lay intellectual who works as an electrician. With a website of his own and highly active online, he is the master craftsman to her apprentice. He later tells Ru Yan why he no longer publishes in print journals: "[T]hey don't offer the freedom you get online, where you can write whatever you think. After that, writing for the standard periodicals is like putting a halter on a wild horse" (191). The internet is where one can both read more widely and publish with more ease. Ru Yan, only a browser at first, begins to write, posting personal pieces—about her son, the weather—that draw praise from members of the online forum to which she belongs.

But her honeymoon is brief. It turns out there are online halters after all. Not long after Damo's paean is the novel's first depiction of internet censorship, regarding a "strange disease" that will later be diagnosed as SARS. Ru Yan has in the meantime become the moderator of the forum, and when posts mentioning this strange disease disappear, members think she is the one deleting them. When Ru Yan tries to spread the word herself, she receives this seemingly automatic response: "SERVER ERROR: Your message is temporarily unable to be posted" (201). Thus is censorship masked behind technical difficulties. But netizens soon sense foul play. The passage below shows that they invent an abundance of alternative names for SARS in order to elude filtering:

The odd thing was that both *"feidian"* and "SARS," as soon as they came into use, became proscribed vocabulary on the forum. Any post containing them would be detected and automatically blocked by a software monitoring system. Users found ways to camouflage their messages. The disease came to be denoted as "FD," "'lying point," "boiling point," "using a lot of electricity," "worn-out mattress;" or as "murder," "scatter to death," "incredibly stupid" . . . all that mattered was that people could figure it out. The surveillance of the Internet has honed people's ability, untaught, to decipher the intended meaning of muddled Chinese compounds. This trick doesn't work, however, against censorship operated by hand. (326–27; translation slightly modified)

When one thinks of Chinese censorship and the internet, one most likely conjures the Great Firewall that keeps websites like YouTube, Facebook, and Twitter out. Or the automatic filtering of sensitive terms, as depicted above. Or the vast army of web monitors that scrub domestic pages clean of anything untoward. Ever since China connected to the World Wide Web in 1994, writings, both academic and journalistic, abound on Chinese internet censorship and its verso, resistance: their forms and contents, their challenges, and their prospects.[46] What is lacking, however, is their conceptualization as a distinctive kind of production, including alter-production.

I take a different approach. Instead of looking at what censorship wipes out and how it does so, I examine what the combination of Chinese censorship and the internet produces. The focus here is not on the techniques of resistance—the Roman alphabet, puns, and so on—but on the kind of production. Netizens persist in publicizing SARS, coming up with ever-creative ways to do so. Their coding may not work against individual censors, yet it precisely forces censorship's production to become, at least in part, manual. We begin to realize how much human input, in this age of algorithmic generation, is demanded from both sides. The scanner cannot supersede the eye. What is more, neither the eye of the netizen nor the eye of the censor is "untaught," unschooled in the ways of decryption. Coding and decoding are experienced communally. They may not be taught directly, but they presuppose a public intelligibility of writing and reading practices handed down the ages. The collaboration is therefore synchronic and diachronic in nature, relying on both the sharing of the present and the sharing of the past. The ends differ but the means are the same, everyone—censors included—teaching and learning from one another throughout the production process.

This process can be conceived in terms of a "workshop." There are at least three attributes of the workshop: participation, creative labor, and experience. First, production may begin with an individual, but quickly it takes on an open character, involving readers (and viewers) in a way that blurs the boundaries between creator and audience. Second, despite occurring online, what is produced is not just a product of algorithms, bots, and machine learning. Human beings are actively behind each act, deploying their ingenuity and creativity. Third and finally, production is predicated on experience, action not only honed by past knowledge passed down communally but also pointing the way forward for participants to follow.

These three attributes derive from both censorship and the internet. Thanks to the latter, "barriers to entry" into public discourse have never been lower in China. With increasing online access, more and more people are "publishing" (texts, images, videos) and participating publicly (commenting, forwarding, "liking") and, in consequence, potentially forming publics. This unprecedented popularization of public-making gives rise to the unprecedented popularization of the experience of censorship. This is not to claim that censorship has become more totalizing than ever. Precisely because it is much less so than during the high socialist period, it is all the more open to experience. In the postsocialist period and before the digital age, not getting published could be ascribed to the "natural" barriers of merit and market. Now, however, when one's online publication is taken down, censorship (and not economics or aesthetics) is pointed out as the culprit. A public grows: the censored public.

Such is the apprenticeship of Ru Yan. As mentioned above, she goes from a reader to a writer, sharing within a small community only personal and poetic musings in the beginning. But after undergoing the censorship of posts about the strange disease, not only is she undeterred from subsequently making public her brother-in-law—a doctor in southern China—getting infected, she also enlists Damo's help in dissemination. She herself is more practiced this time around, hiding the public concern of her article, which her partner in crime immediately reposts elsewhere, under the innocuously private title "My brother-in-law . . ." (269). We could say this is her first workshop product.

Ru Yan was not previously interested in politics. She is contrasted with her deceased husband, who "cared a lot about affairs of state" (92). She becomes politicized, however, in the sense not of protesting in the street but of engaging in another kind of manifestation: making public discourse and making discourse public. Her forum's former moderator warns her that they are renting webspace from a commercial site, "with clear regulations that we can't publish news articles of a political nature." One can infer that Chinese commercial websites that sublet space to fora like theirs are themselves subject to another landlord's terms of lease, the ultimate landlord in town. Ru Yan asks to see the regulations, to which the former moderator replies: "This kind of regulation is itself top-secret: no way are you going to read about it" (270; translation slightly modified). Not only is SARS kept under wraps but the wraps themselves are shrouded in obscurity.

It is evident that *Such Is This World* dramatizes censorship: of the internet, of news of SARS, and of Tiananmen, as we will later see. If it is the antagonist, then Ru Yan and Damo are certainly the protagonists. The two of them are joined in the agon by unnamed netizens who propagate Ru Yan's piece (with an addendum by Damo):

> This post began to spread at once from one website to another, like that staple of horror films, the self-replicating monster. And in its wake, on each website, there followed a swirl of intense commentary. Hard on its heels followed a tidal wave of deletions. But as the post was deleted in each place, it was speedily re-posted. The wave crashed on the shore, obliterating the footsteps which the monster had left in the sand; but as soon as the wave receded, the invisible monster left another line of footprints. (242–43)

In *Ruined City*, the same milk cow that suckles Zhuang Zhidie and laments humankind's forgetfulness compares, in another passage, the urban populace to a handful of sand that can never coalesce.[47] Here in *Such Is This World*, footprints on the sand are synecdochical for a portion of the online populace. These footprints indicate neither identity nor replication. What they have in common are not the same ridges on a toe-tip but the direction in which they tread. They may be washed by wind and wave, but posting, reposting, and commenting are the steps they take together toward the public realm.

Hu Fayun's narration of censorship stands in sharp contrast to *Ruined City*, where the writer Zhuang Zhidie, much more of a public figure than either Ru Yan or Damo, confronts no apparent censorship: It is the other writer—the extradiegetic "author"—who both encounters and performs it. Perhaps it comes as no surprise that nondiegetic performances of censorship appear in *Such Is This World* as well, not just by the author and not just in one edition. The novel has a publishing history no less eventful than that of Jia Pingwa's.

THE WORKSHOP OF THE WORLD

Hu Fayun completed *Such Is This World@sars.come* in March 2004. He originally wanted to publish it in print, but plans to do so fell through because of the banning of two other 2004 books.[48] This is how Hu relates what happened next with the novel:

> In the summer of 2005 an old classmate Xiao Yuan forwarded it to a friend's website. Not long afterwards, the website was shuttered. Thereafter *Such Is This World@sars.come* circulated as an electronic text among friends acquainted and unacquainted. Between fall and winter it reached the hands of the incoming editor-in-chief of *Jiangnan*, Yuan Min. She immediately asked a friend Ding Dong to tell me that she really liked it and hoped to publish it in the first issue of her literary journal's revised edition. And so at the start of spring 2006, *Such Is This World* entered the world as intactly as possible.

Half a year later it came out as a book as well. The above bibliographical sketch appears in the afterword of the edition published by the China Radio International Publishing House in October 2006. The following January, however, in a closed-door meeting with publishers, a senior official of GAPP, the same state agency that had banned *Ruined City* in

1994, identified a "list of illegal publications." *Such Is This World* was one of the eight works named. Although there was never an official ban, Hu's novel could no longer be advertised.[49] The closed-door meeting was an attempt to minimize the éclat of censorship, with mixed results.[50]

But the story of its publication does not end there. Sina, one of the largest online media companies in China, operates both blogging and microblogging platforms. In March 2009, in the comments section of Hu's first Sina blog entry, which is the 2006 afterword quoted verbatim from above, a blogger named Shi Yan Wu Tian shared his project of comparing the book version with the version that had first appeared online: "I spent two days collating the two versions of *Such Is This World* and 'caught' all the deleted text, which I offer blog buddies to read. The abridged version of *Such Is This World* cut approximately 8,000 characters (including punctuation)." He then proceeded to post the differences right in the comments section. In April, however, he related the removal of his posts and directed readers to another website: "Oftentimes I would post and get deleted, post and get deleted, so I'm no longer going to post here. Interested blog buddies can go to 'Hu Fayun Bar' to see the complete text."[51] "Hu Fayun Bar" is an online fan forum, where under the topic "*Such Is This World@sars.come* cut parts," Shi Yan Wu Tian has indicated not only the deletions within parentheses but also where each deletion occurs in the book edition and how many characters are deleted each time.[52]

Before we examine Shi Yan Wu Tian's alter-production, we can perhaps posit that it took its initial cue from Hu himself. In the afterword of the 2006 book, the author makes two references to censorship, first the shuttering of the website on which the novel initially appeared, then its appearing in the journal *Jiangnan* "as intactly as possible." Elsewhere Hu is much more graphic. In an online post, he speaks of his original version being altered in different ways by the journal and the book, describing the latter thus: "Though its core is not hurt, it is nevertheless an injured edition, like a girl walking out of a growth of thorns whose face, legs, and arms are streaked with blood."[53] Traces of injury, although not preserved within the text like Jia Pingwa's blank squares, are nevertheless hinted *around* the text, tracks that may indeed have sent Shi Yan Wu Tian on his hunt: the figure of bodily wholeness lost beseeches recovery and restitution. It matters little that even the original is constituted through censorship, as will be shown below. What we have here is not merely an exhibition of censorship but its enactment. The novel both narrates it and lives it.

Shi Yan Wu Tian can also infer from Hu's afterword that an "intact" version exists online. This version is an alter-production: denied printing and distribution at first, *Such Is This World* circulated alternatively. We will remember that an old classmate of Hu's submitted it to another friend's website. "Friend," in fact, appears three times in that short excerpt cited above, a testament to the collaborative, manual effort that sustained the novel while it was in limbo. In an interview on Phoenix Satellite TV-US, Hu remarked that the novel had first made a splash overseas. The video of the interview did not pass Sina's censorship, but its transcript was provided by another "net friend."[54] Transmission was never automatic, passing through hands both named—Xiao Yuan, Yuan Min, Ding Dong—and unnamed, all those who ushered *Such Is This World*'s publication. That the internet kept it alive is not an argument for technological determinism. It is the human being who breathes life into the novel.

It took Shi Yan Wu Tian two days to catch the differences between the online version and the 2006 book. When he publicized them, he went from a reader to a writer, similar to Ru Yan, for which he himself was repeatedly censored. Thus is the reenactment of censorship propagated and proliferated from the author to his public. Hu Fayun gave a series of lectures on the Cultural Revolution at Wuhan University, the transcripts of which he posted on his blog. The text of the eleventh and last lecture, however, was repeatedly deleted despite Hu's various efforts. Other bloggers suggested posting it elsewhere, but Shi Yan Wu Tian's attempt was likewise censored: "I just reposted on my own blog your deleted essay (the 11th) and incurred the same deletion. Evidently this is not a place for speaking."[55]

As in every workshop, learning is hands-on and handed down. Hu Fayun's sharing of his experience enables Shi Yan Wu Tian's own experience, which the latter in turn shares with other netizens. And he gains an audience as well. Many bloggers thank him for the collation, including one Lao Jiao who raves about the work's potential: "What can be gleaned from the deleted parts and what can be derived by comparing them to the authorized edition extend far beyond the words themselves. Years later, there may be the birth of a new field called 'comparative editions,' and at that time people will remember brother Wu Tian's pioneering work."[56] Lao Jiao follows Shi Yan Wu Tian to *"Such Is This World@sars. come deleted parts"* at "Hu Fayun Bar," where he continues: "I've always thought that finding the differences between a book's 'abridged edition' and 'intact edition' and then comparatively analyzing every section and sentence is a unique and even highly effective method to understand the current 'climate.' "[57] The restoration of the repressed facilitates this task of political meteorology. To test what he has suspected all along, he launches a topic in the forum called "Recreational analysis of *Such Is This World@sars.come* cuts (1)."[58]

I will not delve into Lao Jiao's hermeneutics. What his "publication" reveals—as do Shi Yan Wu Tian's and Hu Fayun's—is the (alter-)productiveness of censorship, especially in the internet age. On the path from the plural *Such Is This World@sars.come* to *"Such Is This World@sars. come* deleted parts" to "Recreational analysis of *Such Is This World@ sars.come* cuts (1)," roadblocks resulted neither in dead-ends nor so much in detours as in diffusion. Not only did the novel stay alive but multiple lives were engendered. It bears emphasizing that this productiveness is not of the mass or recursive kind but of the workshop variety. It is characterized by mutual instruction and the forming of alternative publics. Nowhere is this dynamic more on display than on Hu Fayun's Sina blog, which the next section surveys.

FROM BOOK TO BLOG

In a comment to his own first blog entry, which, as noted before, is *Such Is This World* the book's afterword, Hu complains of the opacity of censorship: "I originally wanted to post some pieces, but there are always sensitive terms or other problems, but they don't give a 'list of bad terms' either, so it often takes a lot of effort."[59] The "effort" is the manual trial and error required to avoid automatic filtering.

The writer and activist Liu Xiaobo had been taken into custody in December 2008 for coauthoring Charter 08, a manifesto circulated online that called for democratic reforms in China. In December 2009 he was sentenced to eleven years in prison. A week after Liu's winning of the Nobel Peace Prize on October 8, 2010, Hu derides its cover-up: "An event known the world over, an event on which the leaders and governments of all countries voice their views, an event destined to go down in the annals of history—to conceal it in the internet age betrays an ignorance and madness that belong to an end-time fairytale."[60] These words are followed by an image of various titles of entries deleted, so we see why Hu cannot be more explicit about the Nobel Prize: his current text is already the product of much "effort."[61] In case readers are unaware of the context, an unsigned poster offers an explanation that can only be encrypted: "Talking about no bell peas price one buy L I U X I A O B O."[62]

These hieroglyphics, decipherable or not, nevertheless render one thing transparent: instead of initiating talk about Liu and the prize, they direct it to censorship itself. Other bloggers begin to share their own stories, such as: "I once wrote a commentary that contained Mr. Hu and Zhang Yihe's names as well as the titles of their two banned books, which got deleted." Proscription of one form—a book, for instance—entails proscription of others by association, including the name of the same book. The experience of proscription widens from the writer of the book to writers of the name of the book, an illustration of what Carlos Rojas calls the "dialectics of censorship and dissemination."[63] A public grows: the censored public.

By the middle of the following year, Hu is castigating the imposed silence on another world event: "Yeemen, Yeegypt, Twonisia, Libbya, Cyria . . . these nations not often within our purview—within a single night, they made this big country of ours appear this wretched, made a certain power this terrified, to the point that it cannot say their names."[64] He is referring to the Arab Spring, the series of revolutionary protests and civil wars that erupted in the Arab world beginning in December 2010. The wordplay Hu resorts to presents the visual testimony to what he is attesting. A month earlier, he was already commenting in code in the entry "lby."[65] When one visitor asks what "lby" means, someone gives a more decodable answer: "Li%by%a%." Another blogger, on the other hand, offers a reflection on this back and forth: "One can tell between the lines of Mr. Hu that this text (only so many words) underwent numerous rounds of 'protection'—incessant changes and combinations—in order to remain here, and so it is secretive and abstruse, like a riddle for people to guess at." The blogger recognizes that the writing on display is only the result of a laborious experiment. Yet the result risks becoming "secretive and abstruse" to the point of incomprehension and incommunicability. This danger, ever present, asks for a communal response that unites elucidation with ingenuity.

The other side is a collective too, composed of Party-state censors as well as "in-house" web administrators who monitor their own sites. Hu prefaces his comments on the Libyan revolution in the entry above with a challenge to the latter: "Sina's web admins, you've worked hard; I've already made you work for a long time. Here's another one; keep on working. History will remember you."[66] They must have put in overtime the previous Christmas: the entry "The beautiful Christmas present given to me by Sina web admins" contains an image of the deletion of an essay posted two years earlier.[67] An anonymous blogger rejoins: "Happy new year, web admins! Wish you earn more and work less in the new year. Be smart: when someone is checking, block some stuff; when that person leaves, restore everything. In the future we will certainly recognize you heroes on the 'invisible front.'" The remark may be in jest, but unlike Hu Fayun's, this direct address does make an appeal. The message generated automatically after every deletion is "Dear Sina blog buddy: Your piece '—' has been deleted by the administrator. We deeply regret the inconvenience caused you." In the comments section of another entry, another anonymous poster even shows empathy: "The web admins' conduct is understandable, because it is their job. Their apology means that they too know what they do is wrong, but they can only obey the command from above."[68] It is a point Hu well appreciates. Back in an August 2008 entry, he did not fault any individual after his interview was distorted in a newspaper.

> Fundamentally speaking, this is not the problem of a particular journalist, or even that of the decision-making editor or chief editor, but the problem of our institution of the press. For many years now, our news does not report on newsworthy reality but rather carries out the propagandistic aims handed down by certain ministries or certain persons. Under this institution of the press our many journalists who loved and respected journalism are ultimately "forced into prostitution."[69]

Three years later, in "No anger, only pity," he reiterates that his anger is not aimed at the web administrators themselves: "I am not referring to some specific person, but to the system that they serve and live off parasitically."[70] It is clear he feels more than pity for these brokers of censorship.

Under the same entry, someone shares with the blog community his experience both of censorship and in maneuvering around it: "I also always get 'Deared' by Sina's admins, so I set up a blog at Blog China, where there's censorship too, but every piece goes through. I link what Sina deletes to there." Instead of outflanking, another advocates a more confrontational tactic, with the help of Sina's microblogging service, Sina Weibo: "Mr. Hu, make your essay into a long Weibo and post it, open multiple Weibo accounts and post it simultaneously. There are many avenues in the information age—work those SOBs to death." Hu asks how it can be done, to which the same blogger replies: "The search tools of those SOBs work only on text; they are powerless against images." In true workshop spirit he goes on to explain how to combine small images (of text) into a long one.

Hu learns about long Weibos, but he must have already known, whether through his own experience or from somebody else, that images elude automated detection. For a day earlier, an hour after the removal of the text of "That night of affliction"—an account of his wife resolving to go to a long-planned meeting in Beijing on June 4, 1989, despite seeing on television the bloodshed of the night before—Hu posted the essay as an image.[71] In fact, visual plus textual production is a common feature of Tiananmen-related entries. In "June 4, 2010," named after the date of the post, Hu is pictured standing beside a replica of the Goddess of Democracy statue on the University of British Columbia (UBC) campus. He writes, "On a little square I saw that beautiful goddess. I know some things have not disappeared." Someone else echoes the sentiment: "Yesterday I and a few net friends went to the square. As we were about to leave, we agreed to come back next year, come back every year, making it an inextinguishable agreement." Hu responds: "As long as the square is there, the memory will be." The entry on the same day the following year, "Untitled," is simply a picture of a gardenia with drops of water on it. Communion in this community is nearly telepathic. A reader comments: "Thinking alike"; another: "Do not forget this day!"[72] When Hu's Sina Weibo account was frozen on June 4, 2013, one blogger wrote, "The web admin is reminding you that today is a special day, reminding you not to forget this day," while a second quipped, "64 is too sensitive. I don't even plan on celebrating my 64 birthday."[73]

These elliptic messages and images act out both the remembrance of the Tiananmen movement as well as its enforced forgetting. We will find a corresponding performance in *Such Is This World*. Just as no impenetrable wall seals off the virtual world from the real world, and vice versa—Hu Fayun sharing his visit to the UBC campus and the Goddess of Democracy with the online community, a group of "net friends" gathering offline to observe an anniversary—so the fictional world of the novel is interconnected with these two worlds. We now return to this world while at the same time weaving through the other two.

IN PARENTHESES

Lu Xun, in collecting his miscellaneous essays into independently published volumes, used to add a black dot beneath every character—the Chinese equivalent of underline—that had been taken out by editors or Kuomintang censors upon initial publication in the Republican-era press. In our digital era, Shi Yan Wu Tian has done something similar to Hu Fayun's text, reinserting as well as marking out (with parentheses) what was cut (from the 2006 book). Both gestures constitute an orthography of censorship: Lu Xun's punctuates the writer's defiance, while Shi Yan Wu Tian's can be viewed as a figure for gashes, the unhealed and unhealable wounds of an "injured edition." The parentheses also perform the grammar of censorship. To parenthesize is to judge extraneous and expendable. The removal of the parenthesized, as my own sentence earlier in this paragraph demonstrates, would not cause any structural damage. Nothing essential, you could say, would be lost: my paragraph would still read smoothly.

Shi Yan Wu Tian puts the parentheses back in place, revealing just how much of *Such Is This World* was deemed dispensable. Not all excisions were censorial in nature.[74] But mere editing cannot account for the repeated elision of references to inglorious events in the history of the People's Republic of China (PRC), including the campaign against the so-called Hu Feng clique of 1955, the Anti-Rightist movement of 1957, the Great Leap Forward of 1958–1961, and the Cultural Revolution of 1966–1976.[75] These events have all, in the post-Mao period, been officially reevaluated, so their censorship targets further reevaluations that venture beyond the verdicts pronounced once and for all. The Tiananmen movement, on the other hand, has received a different treatment: a near total blanketing. Thus their mentions are rigorously deleted from the 2006 book.[76]

Tiananmen nevertheless occupies a central position in *Such Is This World*. In this seventy-chapter novel, an extended sequence spanning chapters 36 to 38 recounts the transformation of the character Maozi, Damo's longtime friend, from a free-thinking intellectual who supported the 1989 protests to a defender of the regime whose writings adulate its leaders. One can tell from Shi Yan Wu Tian's restorations that even the online version is constituted through censorship. The protests are alluded to as "that public disturbance" at the "start of spring," and in Tiananmen's aftermath—"early June of that year"—Maozi sobs in his room: "It's too frightening, it's just too fucking frightening" (223–25). These oblique references are in the original and not the result of editorial alteration.

But Shi Yan Wu Tian's parentheses disclose what was, including Maozi's involvement in the movement: "Maozi had been active, even making two trips to Beijing, (signing petitions, marching, writing essays, speaking at colleges). He had been in the limelight."[77] Following Shi Yan Wu Tian, I have inserted parentheses into A. E. Clark's translation. They enclose Maozi's past participation, retroactively struck out so that it could never have been part of the past. In a way they also perform Maozi's own stifling of the memory. His colleagues thought that "Mao N. N. had gone mad (at the sound of gunfire in Beijing)," and indeed he was diagnosed with "temporary insanity with amnesia."[78] The diagnosis is spot-on because his insanity is temporary and his amnesia is not. Maozi soon recovers and ascends the academic ladder, now penning encomiums of government policies instead of essays for the movement. He is both thanked and thankful: "A fine position, a good income, a nice car and a beautiful home, a lovely wife and a promising son . . . he had it all. (In candid moments he often said that Deng was The Man, and Maozi gave him unqualified support. Without old Mr. Deng, Maozi would never have had this good life. A man must show gratitude to his benefactor. Not long after that public disturbance, when Maozi changed direction, this was a major reason why.)"[79]

It is enough to know that Maozi is living swimmingly in post-Tiananmen China. That this life is the reward of a conscious volte-face, his reverencing of the man who ordered the crackdown on the demonstrations in which he took part, is unimportant: it can be forgotten without harm. So the writing between the curved lines is negated without a trace until Shi Yan Wu Tian retraces both the writing and the lines. By interpolating them, he not only qualifies our understanding of Maozi's course of development—which the original online version would provide—but also reenacts the role that censorship has played in China's course of development since Tiananmen. Like the writer Zhuang Zhidie and his artist friends in *Ruined City*, Maozi is a member of the intellectual and cultural elite. Whereas the former are ostensibly motivated only by greed and lust, violence and the fear of that violence—and not houses and cars—set in motion the latter's change in course. The parentheses not only resuscitate "the sound of gunfire" but also make public how another form of violence, censorship, has shaped the Chinese public. To read them in conjunction with Jia Pingwa's blank squares is to view Zhuang Zhidie in a different light. His dissipated and turbulent way of life, and not censorship, may appear to have obstructed his writing. But the blank squares that his author draws are not just extradiegetic after all: they are his as well.

There are hazards involved in exhibiting prohibition. But Jia Pingwa was not deterred. Neither was Hu Fayun. And neither was Shi Yan Wu Tian. Neither were all the bloggers who partook in the alter-production. And neither were Ru Yan and Damo. In the face of a sensitive administration, they all refuse to desensitize themselves. All three worlds—fictional, real, virtual—are interlinked and not ranked. That Shi Yan Wu Tian is only an online identity, that Ru Yan and Damo are characters in a novel, do not diminish their productiveness. Near the end of *Such Is This World*, a conference is organized for Wei Liwen, an old intellectual—in fact, an alleged member of the Hu Feng clique—who was Damo and Maozi's mentor and who died of SARS. When the conference is forced to be cancelled at the last minute, Damo does not desist:

(Damo wrote a piece: "A conference devoted to one man's life and work, convened in the mind." At the conclusion of the essay he quoted from the song which Teacher Wei had sung as he lay dying:

Unity is strength. Unity is strength,
A strength like that of iron and steel.
Open fire on the fascists, let the whole undemocratic system be wiped out!
Facing the sun, moving toward freedom and a New China,
Glory to the ends of the earth!

Damo had this piece serve as a preface to the dozens of essays he'd received as tributes to be shared at the conference, and he posted them all to his website, *Word and Thought*. Two days later, the site was shut down and deleted. Damo was prepared: he had already made a zipfile suitable for download, for he knew that these voices would be propagated, even as the light from a star continues to spread out through the universe for thousands of years. Other websites were quick to pick this up, for they saw it as an act of love and memorialization for the old man as well as a kind of intellectual torch relay.)[80]

As one can see, the entire citation is parenthesized, meaning that a fictional passage removed from a real book is restored in a virtual copy. This censored fictional passage also narrates censorship—precisely of a commemorative, congregative act—in the real and virtual worlds. It is about an aborted real-world event that, nevertheless, in its virtual incarnations achieves an even greater public thanks to the expertise, contribution, and collaboration of many.

"Unity Is Strength," as noted in chapter 3, where the song appears in *Lan Yu* and *Summer Palace*, is a People's Liberation Army song from the early 1940s, that is, before the establishment of "New China," the People's Republic. "Unity" (*tuanjie*) here is not univocality. It bespeaks community and commonality of purpose, pointing to the contestation of censorship as always a work in progress—"toward freedom and a New China"—not only carried on hand in hand among interconnected worlds but handed on, as light continues to shine after the star itself is gone.

That the entire passage above is parenthesized, that is, disappeared from the print edition of *Such Is This World*, is not an indictment of Hu Fayun's editor at the China Radio International Publishing House. Nor are the ellipses that replace the blank squares in the reissued edition of

Jia Pingwa's *Ruined City* an indictment of the literary critic and editor Li Jingze. The authors themselves are not mere victims either. Both Jia and Hu must have complied with the changes made to their texts before publication, just as I did when presented with the draft Chinese translation of my article on Jia's novel. The translator is not to blame. And neither is the editor at *Contemporary Writers Review* who cut some more from the draft. We all are complicitous.

Yet not all of us are complacent. As compromised as the Chinese version of my article is, it preserves in translation this line: "a blank memorial tablet erected right there on the page for a past event that still could not be written about directly." The blank memorial tablet refers to the blank square in Lu Xun's "Medicine," published in May 1919. Exactly seventy years later, there occurred an event that even today cannot be written about directly. The Chinese translation of my article reinserts the blank squares taken out of the reauthorized *Ruined City*, not simply back into the novel but into the Chinese public realm, opening a skylight right there on the page through which to espy Tiananmen Square in 1989.

The Chinese translation appeared in 2016. In the same year, the Jiangsu Phoenix Art Publishing House issued a seven-volume *Collected Writings of Ah Cheng*, an author who came to prominence in the mid-1980s. This collection uses blank squares in place of words cut out from the text. In the book *Venice Diary*, for instance, the entry for June 4, 1992, is but a single line: "□□□□, it's been three years." The four missing words, based on editions published in Hong Kong and Taiwan, are "Today is June 4." Blank squares, however, appear only in the 2016 printing of the mainland edition. In subsequent printings, from 2018 to the year of this chapter's writing in 2021, all the squares have disappeared, replaced by a parenthesized notice at the end of each piece: "(This text has been abridged.)" Not even ellipses mark the place of deletion. This sleight of hand transpires not between different editions but between different printings of supposedly the same edition.

You could say that "nothing" was lost: not one word was altered. Yet the elimination of blank squares from the 2009 edition of *Ruined City* and recent printings of the *Collected Writings of Ah Cheng* demonstrates what is at stake. "Nothing" has to be removed. For this "nothing" could refer to the Tiananmen movement, to the Great Leap Famine, to SARS, to everything and everywhere the regime wants you to move along: nothing to see here. Each open square has to be patrolled, monitored, or best of all, closed, because every open square poses infinite danger, its blankness begging to be filled, to be repopulated with aberrant meanings, representing the endless possibility for participation and intervention.

At the end of December 2019—seventeen years after the SARS outbreak—an ophthalmologist named Li Wenliang in the city of Wuhan—where *Such Is This World@sars.come* is set—began to notice strange flulike symptoms in his patients. In a group chat on the social media service WeChat, he alerted his friends to the occurrence. His warning was then shared beyond this circle, despite his request to the contrary. In early January 2020, Li was officially reprimanded by local police and forced to sign a document admitting the falseness of what he spread.

Li would return to work in the hospital and get infected by a novel strain of SARS coronavirus, later dubbed COVID-19. One could say he was thus vindicated, no longer a "rumor-monger" but an inadvertent whistleblower of what subsequently became a global pandemic. From his hospital bed, he stated in an interview that "there should be more than one voice in a healthy society."[81] Li died from the disease on February 7, 2020.

Others picked up the whistle. A colleague at the same hospital, Ai Fen, gave an interview in which she revealed how hospital authorities tried to quash her early warnings as well. The interview, titled "The Whistler-Giver," was immediately disappeared upon publication online.[82] Before long, however, like that indestructible monster described by Hu Fayun, it reappeared, at first simply as repostings by netizens. But when they were in turn swept clean, the creative bug bit. Netizens began sharing the piece in a multitude of forms, from rendering the text backward and sideways to translating it into pinyin, calligraphy, and emojis as well as oracle bone, bronze, and seal scripts. In so doing, they became not mere readers or even translators but re-creators, partaking in what could be viewed as "an act of love and memorialization" for Li Wenliang, "as well as a kind of intellectual torch relay." They retooled the orthography of censorship with an interventionist praxis that, more than transmitting what was blocked, built communities of understanding and resignification.

Conclusion

The Other Side of Censorship

The story of the Wuhan doctor Li Wenliang with which the previous chapter concluded is not simply one of repression: a whistleblower whose silencing by authorities led not only to his death from COVID-19 on February 7, 2020, but also to the early, unchecked spread of the disease that eventually became a global pandemic. His story is also one of propagation. The Chinese government, after Dr. Li's death, declared him a martyr. It quickly mobilized censorship's productive forces to spin a preventable tragedy into tried-and-true tales of heroism and sacrifice, into narratives of the superiority of the "socialist system" in dealing with emergencies, into the dissemination of "positive energy" (*zheng nengliang*) in lyrics of triumph and songs of praise for the regime's response. Already by mid-February, for instance, a "positive energy training" of internet writers from Hubei Province—whose capital is Wuhan—was organized with instructions from the Hubei Publicity Department. The keynote speech, delivered by a member of the Hubei Writers Association, was followed by discussions on how, among other things, to lend "literary strength" to the fight against the novel coronavirus.[1]

Already in the January 31 entry of her lockdown diary, the Wuhan author Fang Fang remarked: "I really want to remind my Hubei colleagues: later on you will most likely be requested to write prose and poetry of praise, but please, before you write, reflect for a moment on whom you should praise."[2] This kind of foresight was previously voiced by Sheng Keyi in her 2011 novel *Death Fugue*, examined in chapter 2, where the protagonist Yuan Mengliu was variously pressured to write a poem of praise for the false utopia where he found himself. It is also a theme elaborated upon by the acclaimed author Yan Lianke.

On February 21, 2020, Yan delivered an online lecture to graduate students at Renmin University of China, in Beijing, and the Hong Kong University of Science and Technology.[3] In his lecture, titled "After the pandemic, let us become human beings with memory," Yan urges his audience to have memory, by which he means the capacity to remember. Memory in this sense serves as the soil for memories in the plural. Like Fang Fang earlier, Yan observes a trend: because the number of COVID-19 cases in China are decreasing, the "gongs and drums of celebration" have already begun to sound, as well as songs of victory in homage to greatness and wisdom, elicited from on high. Yet he counters this current, instead posing the question: Why do humanmade disasters time and again befall the Chinese people? Because individual memories, Yan asserts, are programmed, replaced, and wiped out. People not only forget what they are told to forget, but they also remember what they are told to remember. They not only fall silent when told to be silent, but they also sing when told to sing. In short, they are enjoined, in the dual senses of the word.

The prohibitive is tethered to the propagative. In place of individual memories is national memory, which Yan conceives as not something that organically binds a people but a manicured account that ruthlessly weeds out alternative remembrances of things past. That is why, seventeen years after the 2002–2003 severe acute respiratory syndrome (SARS) epidemic in southern China (depicted in Hu Fayun's novel *Such Is This World@sars.come* and discussed in chapter 4), the tragedy is replayed in the form of a novel coronavirus. If this tragedy is replayed, then who is its director? What are the conditions of this production? Yan explicitly states that one must not interrogate who the director is. Instead, he probes the players, those who "employ pure, lyrical tones of the nation in reading, reciting, and repeating." We are familiar with this tone because, in Sheng's *Death Fugue*, we encountered such a speaker, Jiawan, who in the aftermath of the so-called Tower Incident—an allegory for Tiananmen—penned "lyrics praising the political apparatus" and thereby reaped fame and fortune.[4]

In contradistinction to these approved voices, Yan brings up the example of Fang Fang. However well-known her online diary is, Yan does not glorify her case but observes that it is but one out of many. Even if one cannot publicize one's voice like Fang Fang, one can nevertheless keep the voice alive in one's heart. And what should this voice say? "It is not like this!" Each person has an obligation to remember, in the midst of the "gongs and drums of celebration," the howls and sobs of people who have suffered and who have lost.

Yan Lianke concludes his address by advocating for a resilient approach to recalcitrance. Echoing the words of Adorno—which Sheng Keyi also echoes in her novel—Yan contends that to write poetry after Auschwitz may be barbaric but not to write, not to remember, is even more so. If you cannot be a whistleblower, then be a whistler-hearer. If you cannot speak aloud, then whisper. If you cannot whisper, then stay silent. But maintain your memory so that, even if your memories cannot be openly shared at present, they are preserved and one day passed on to posterity.

Compared to COVID-19 as well as SARS, the memories of the Tiananmen movement have been handled in an inverse fashion by the Chinese government. For the two viral outbreaks, the initial response was hushing up, followed by media campaigns extolling administrative effectiveness combined with the quashing of inharmonious plaints. The aftermath of Tiananmen, on the other hand, witnessed the state-sponsored production and distribution of a mass of materials intended to fix once and for all the final word on the protests as "counterrevolutionary riot" (as detailed in chapter 1), replaced a couple of years later by the policy of more or less total silencing ever since. In all three cases, dissemination and suppression are inextricable from one another.

But the regime's policy is changing. In May 2015, on the occasion of the twenty-sixth anniversary of the Tiananmen movement, a group of overseas Chinese students published online an open letter in Chinese.[5] The stated aim of the letter, which spread via email groups and social media, was to present to students in China the "truth" of the movement that the writers learned from resources outside China.

The party's tabloid newspaper *Global Times* responded a week later.[6] The language of the editorial's title, "Overseas forces attempt to incite post-80s, 90s generation," should be familiar to readers of this book. Government propaganda produced in the wake of Tiananmen, surveyed in chapter 1, frequently ascribed "incitement" (*shandong*) to the words of the 1989 protestors. The editorial lumps together the letter writers, Chinese studying abroad, with foreigners. To write openly about the movement outside China—the only place where this is possible—is to be in cahoots with the external enemy. The students' open letter is accused of distorting the truth of Tiananmen, referenced here as the "political turbulence of '89." Its writers have been brainwashed and constitute an alien minority. What is more, they are "an extreme minority within a minority."

The main argument of the *Global Times* editorial is that those who were at Tiananmen Square in 1989, now around fifty years of age, are the ones who should have the right to pass judgment on that event. The editorial admits that those who were involved were "not a few." And what is the verdict that they have settled on, having "reflected" (*fansi*)—another recurring theme examined in chapter 1—over the past few decades on the "turbulence"? The opposite of the one in the open letter, the editorial claims, speaking on behalf of the "majority."

Whence comes this supposedly unanimous attitude toward Tiananmen? From society itself, according to the editorial, which no longer wants to "contend" over it, "letting that page be flipped over"—as if it were as natural as the changing of the seasons, and not coerced with bloodshed. The Chinese people have reached a "consensus," "understanding with sympathy" (*lijie*) how Tiananmen has been "downplayed." In conclusion, the editorial commends them for their "cooperation," which it attributes to the choice of "looking forward" (*xiangqiankan*).

Was it a choice? Or did the cudgel come down, leaving people with no choice but to disperse and "look forward/look toward money," the double entendre of *xiangqiankan*? The editorial disputes the truth of the letter writers, "young people who did not witness historical factuality," who were not present on the scene in Tiananmen Square in the spring of 1989. But the regime pins its hopes precisely on this generation and all subsequent generations, on the fact that they were not witnesses, that the witnesses will die out, forget, be forced to move on, and that the generations to come will have no memory of what happened, no ability to discern what actually took place, other than abiding by the official government account.

The editorial itself is proof that "contention" over Tiananmen is not over, that its page in history refuses to be ripped out. The editorial also brought the open letter more attention, and so the Chinese version of the editorial was removed from the *Global Times* website. But its appearance and disappearance may be more complex, as another *Global Times* editorial a year later indicates.

In May 2016, the tabloid again published an editorial pertaining to Tiananmen, this time in response to Western media coverage of the scheduled release for later in the year of the last prisoner incarcerated in relation to the protests, Miao Deshun.[7] Tiananmen here is again referred to as the "political turbulence of '89," but also, in quotation marks, as the "democracy movement." This time around, the editorial waxes more lyrical: "The time that Miao spent in prison is a note hitherto hardly heard in the 'democracy movement elegy.' " Time has shown him to have stood on the "opposite side of history." As with the piece from a year ago, this editorial portrays the eclipse of contentious voices—"extremely few" (*jishaoshu*)—as a natural process: "They are quietly washed away by the waves of history." Also like the previous editorial, it was taken down from the *Global Times* website. But this piece persists elsewhere on the Chinese internet, from the official news agency Xinhua to the online portal Sina, to the nationalist guancha.cn, where there are over one hundred comments on it.

What are we to glean from these two cases? That the Chinese regime is not a monolith: here we have the speech of one party organ, *Global Times*, suppressed by another. Or that government authorities know well that the taboo on Tiananmen is something the rest of the world knows well. Thus, the publication of the two editorials can be a way to demonstrate that, contrary to what the West may think, we do mention Tiananmen in China!

Most significantly, however, these two cases may not represent a slipup, the regime losing its grip on the uniformity of policy, a well-meaning but injudicious editor violating the taboo. They may instead represent a controlled experiment, the two *Global Times* editorials testing the official Tiananmen narrative on the Chinese public decades after 1989. On the one hand, the regime does not want to "play up" Tiananmen, and so the editorials were withdrawn from the official website. On the other hand, they can be used to mold and gauge public opinion, by which I do not mean the comments on the guancha.cn website, for instance, where what appears has doubtlessly been filtered to reflect only "correct" opinions. But the editorials remind readers of the party line, and at the same time their reception on social media can be analyzed to evaluate the extent to which that line has gained traction and among which segments of the population.

It is not out of the question that one day, Tiananmen may be unfrozen. Quietly, without much fanfare, it will be referenced in a leader's remark, reappear in student textbooks, or make a cameo in a TV series—not as a movement for social justice and democracy in which millions across the country participated, but as it was framed in the immediate aftermath: an anti-China "counterrevolutionary riot" "incited" by "extremely few people" funded by the U.S. government to subvert party rule. It got disorderly and violent and had to be put down by the military, which did not use deadly force. The newly smug state might even showcase voices from "the people" regurgitating this "stance."

Many factors would have contributed to such a scenario, not least of which is the changed and changing historical moment. Since Tiananmen, the Chinese state has seemingly only increased its authority. Far from bringing about a shattering of regime legitimacy, the massacre on the night of June 3 and 4, 1989, ushered in an era of superlatives. China now touts the world's second largest economy. Instead of providing only cheap labor in the global sweatshop, Chinese are buying up lands as well as brands all over the world. Urban students today partake of a lifestyle rivaling that of students in the United States. In fact, many of the former, as a result of the rapid rise in wealth, have joined the latter in American classrooms, enjoying a freedom of travel and consumption that their college counterparts who congregated on Tiananmen Square three decades ago could hardly dream of.

They and the rest of their compatriots have the right to ditch the memories of 1989 as their country continues its forward march down what commentators have dubbed the "China century." But this right to forget is a sham when the right, nay, the obligation to remember is vitiated. One cannot overlook the state's strenuous suppression of efforts to bring the contentious meanings of the past into the public. Not only did the Tiananmen movement occupy the heart of the nation, it also projected onto the most public of spaces, a public square, alternative visions of what China and its people could become. It is the political dimension of these visions that the current regime, no matter its economic successes, cannot countenance.

But the scenario sketched above, with the thawing of Tiananmen, would not spell the end of its censorship. Rather, it would bring to the fore what this book has foregrounded all along: that censorship makes as much as it breaks. *Made in Censorship* reveals the public scope of the making. On the one hand, the regime, in the wake of the crackdown, unleashed a torrent of textual and audiovisual propaganda such as *Songs of the Republic's Guardians* and *Flutter, Flag of the Republic* to realign the reading and viewing public back with the party, as detailed in chapter 1. On the other hand, a plethora of productions continue to contest the authorized narrative—from the center of attention to the periphery, from film to fiction, from online to off. Chapter 2 highlights *I Graduated* and *Conjugation*, shot without permission, and *Death Fugue*, published only in a literary journal, in illuminating their perilous perches on the margins of the public realm. Chapter 3 analyzes the relationship among censorship, productiveness, and commercialism through the scandalous *Lan Yu* and *Summer Palace*. Chapter 4 examines the role that readers of *Ruined City* and *Such Is This World* play in the recollection of the disappeared. All four chapters show not only the significance of the Tiananmen movement thirty years later but also that the public-making of censorship is always a work in progress.

Made in Censorship has focused on the public realm of mainland China. Yet I would be remiss not to point out the extraterritorial ambitions of censorship. Publishers in China, for instance, are no longer the only ones who have to comply with demands from Chinese authorities. Foreign publishers, too, are answering the call. In 2017, Cambridge University Press agreed to block access in China to over three hundred articles in the academic journal *The China Quarterly* related to topics that included Taiwan, Tibet, and, of course, Tiananmen.[8] Only after a public outcry did the publisher backtrack and reinstate access to Chinese users. This incident may be the most infamous, but it is far from the only one. Complicity is the uncuttable cost for any "global business" wanting to maintain presence in the Chinese market.[9]

The Cambridge University Press incident elicited another editorial response from the *Global Times*.[10] The Chinese side was not trying to influence *The China Quarterly*'s editorial decisions, so goes the explanation. The only area affected is China, where the government has full authority to determine and enforce laws and regulations. At stake is the defense of sovereignty, not an "offensive against the outside world."

One may add that the same reasoning applies to the regime's push for "internet sovereignty." The internet should not be a borderless free-for-all. Just like geopolitical space, cyberspace should be defined by jurisdictions. Such is the justification for the blocking of YouTube, Twitter, and the *New York Times*. China is merely asserting its rights as a self-determining nation.

The reasoning is disingenuous. The Chinese state seeks very much to expand its discursive regime beyond its borders. With an embarrassment of riches at its disposal, it is always launching new ventures targeting not just domestic audiences but also (social) media consumers of the world. The purported aim is to "tell China's stories well." But this drive cannot be construed as mere "soft power." Not far from the persuasive is the coercive edge of the sword. As the state projects its censorship abroad, the compromised circumstances in which Chinese writers and filmmakers create will be experienced by those outside its jurisdiction proper. The case studies in *Made in Censorship* may treat artworks produced inside this jurisdiction, but their example might soon be illustrative of the global condition.

Even in my own case, the extraterritoriality of censorship is evident. When I started in grad school, senior scholars cautioned me—with the best of intentions—against writing about Chinese censorship, much less censorship pertaining to Tiananmen, at so early a stage in my career. Why? Because doors in China would shut on me that otherwise might be open. No invitations to conferences. No awarding of fellowships. Whatever their personal convictions, scholars would be reluctant to collaborate with me. I may even get my visa denied, which for a junior scholar would deal a severe blow to research. These repercussions should not be understood solely in the repressive sense. They are a formative force, determinative of the research agendas of junior scholars, steering them toward topics that are "apolitical," or of a politics amenable or indifferent to the regime, away from subjects not because they are unimportant or shopworn but precisely because they are still "sensitive."

These are the real effects of state censorship, which not only shapes the Chinese public realm but encroaches upon the American academy.

At the same time, I am cognizant that Oriental censorship is a popular product in the West, where I am. Tales of Chinese repression, the literary genre to which this book appears to belong, find a receptive audience here, especially in times of geopolitical tension. What is more, critiquing Chinese censorship is doubly productive for me as a U.S.-based scholar. First, like the figure of the opportunistic artist discussed in chapter 3, I, too, am capitalizing on the fetish of censorship professionally. Second, I am a beneficiary of mainland Chinese colleagues not being able to write on this subject, leaving a gap in the scholarship that I can then fill.

Such is my position. On the one hand, pressured by the consequences of my research decision, on the other hand, open to criticism of academic hucksterism. This very position, however, allows me to undertake the enterprise in the first place. And thus I am bound by obligation not to represent or speak for my Chinese colleagues but to avoid passing the buck. If they cannot tackle this project, and I put it off too, then are we resigning ourselves to the censorship regime, which involves not just articles taken down, paragraphs removed, or the banning of books and films, but also the redaction of history, the tailoring of memory, the molding of the public?

I am far away. But the publics I endeavor to assemble are precisely not predicated on physical presence. The literature and film I have focused on in this book map the terrain of contention temporally and spatially. They point toward a future when the Tiananmen movement can be reconfigured in the where of China. Despite emerging from contexts of censorship, they show that public-making is ongoing, changing with the passing of time, complicated by multiple media. They dispute the not-here and the never. Borders are porous in both directions. Just as Chinese state censorship may be exported, so do I forward my research to addresses in China. The people there and I share at least one hope in common: to reclaim a public square for the public. This fellowship binds us in a circle that, growing outward, traces a spiral oriented toward a new horizon.

Glossary

baogao wenxue	报告文学	reportage literature
baoluan	暴乱	riot
baotu	暴徒	thug
bieyou yongxin	别有用心	harboring ulterior motives
buming zhenxiang de qunzhong	不明真相的群众	crowds ignorant of the truth
dongci bianwei	動詞變位	conjugation
dongluan	动乱	turmoil
duotai	堕胎	abortion
gong	公	public
guandao	官倒	official speculation
guanxi	关系	connections
hukou	户口	residency status
jingshen	精神	spirit, spiritual
jingying	精英	intellectual elite
jishaoshu ren	极少数人	extremely few people
lijie	理解	understand with sympathy
mangliu	盲流	drifters

qizhi xianming	旗帜鲜明	to take a clear-cut stance
quanli	权力	power, authority
qunzhong yanyuan	群众演员	extras
renmin	人民	the people
shandong	煽动	incite
shanghen wenxue	伤痕文学	scar literature
shencha	审查	censorship
tifa	提法	formulation
tizhi	体制	regime
tongzhi	同志	comrade
tuanjie	团结	unity
xianchang shilu	现场实录	recordings on location
Xinwen lianbo	新闻联播	*National News Bulletin*
xuechao	学潮	student movement
yiqie xiangqiankan	一切向前/钱看	all look forward/toward money
zhengnengliang	正能量	positive energy
zhenya	镇压	suppression
zhuanti pian	专题片	special topic program
zhu xuanlü	主旋律	main melody
zuzhi	组织	organization

Notes

INTRODUCTION: MAKING THE CENSORED PUBLIC

1. Jonathan Watts, "Chinese Newspaper Editors Fired Over Tiananmen Square Ad," *The Guardian*, June 7, 2007, https://www.theguardian.com/media/2007/jun/07/pressandpublishing.china.

2. "We must cease once and for all to describe the effects of power in negative terms: it 'excludes,' it 'represses,' it 'censors,' it 'abstracts,' it 'masks,' it 'conceals.' In fact, power produces; it produces reality; it produces domains of objects and rituals of truth. The individual and the knowledge that may be gained of him belong to this production." Michel Foucault, *Discipline and Punish: The Birth of the Prison*, trans. Alan Sheridan (New York: Vintage, 1995), 194.

3. Michel Foucault, *History of Sexuality, Volume 1: An Introduction*, trans. Robert Hurley (New York: Vintage, 1990), 88–89.

4. Michael Holquist, "Corrupt Originals: The Paradox of Censorship," *PMLA* 109, no. 1 (1994): 16; italics in the original.

5. Frederick Schauer, "The Ontology of Censorship," in *Censorship and Silencing: Practices of Cultural Regulation*, ed. Robert C. Post (Los Angeles: Getty Research Institute, 1998), 149; italics in the original.

6. See Raymond Williams, *Marxism and Literature* (Oxford: Oxford University Press, 1977), 121–27.

7. Sophia Rosenfeld, "Writing the History of Censorship in the Age of Enlightenment," in *Postmodernism and the Enlightenment: New Perspectives in Eighteenth-*

Century French Intellectual History, ed. Daniel Gordon (New York: Routledge, 2001), 127–28.

8. Michael Dutton, *Policing Chinese Politics: A History* (Durham, NC: Duke University Press, 2005), 12.

9. "Notwithstanding the apparent continuity signaled by the 'reform era' appellation, however, it was not until the early 1990s that the fundamental *cultural* logic of the People's Republic of China underwent a basic market-driven rupture." See Jason McGrath, *Postsocialist Modernity: Chinese Cinema, Literature, and Criticism in the Market Age* (Stanford, CA: Stanford University Press, 2008), 2; italics in the original.

10. Tiananmen poetry deserves a special study onto itself. One major volume is Jiang Pinchao, ed., *Liusi shiji* (Monterey Park, CA: Liusi wenhua chuanbo xiehui, 2007). Many poems by the writer and Nobel Peace Prize laureate Liu Xiaobo are gathered in *June Fourth Elegies*, trans. Jeffrey Yang (Minneapolis, MN: Graywolf Press, 2012).

11. A salient example of recent scholarship that also does not dismiss Party-state discourse but reads it seriously is Christian P. Sorace, *Shaken Authority: China's Communist Party and the 2008 Sichuan Earthquake* (Ithaca, NY: Cornell University Press, 2017).

12. For a history of the development of propaganda in the PRC and an overview of its institutional structure, see Anne-Marie Brady, *Marketing Dictatorship: Propaganda and Thought Work in Contemporary China* (Lanham, MD: Rowman & Littlefield, 2008).

13. Cyberspace Administration of China, "Wangluo xinxi neirong shengtai zhili guiding," December 20, 2019, http://www.cac.gov.cn/2019-12/20/c_1578375159509309 .htm.

14. In the immediate wake of June Fourth, during a campaign ostensibly against pornography, books by writers and intellectuals who had supported the demonstrations were also banned. See Yi Chen, "Publishing in China in the Post-Mao Era: The Case of *Lady Chatterley's Lover*," *Asian Survey* 32, no. 6 (1992): 569 and 581; Richard Curt Kraus, *The Party and the Arty in China: The New Politics of Culture* (Lanham, MD: Rowman & Littlefield, 2004), 93; and Geremie R. Barmé, *In the Red: On Contemporary Chinese Culture* (New York: Columbia University Press, 1999), 20–21.

15. "Xi Jinping Asks for 'Absolute Loyalty' from Chinese State Media," *The Guardian*, February 19, 2016, https://www.theguardian.com/world/2016/feb/19/xi-jinping -tours-chinas-top-state-media-outlets-to-boost-loyalty.

16. Wu Hung, *Remaking Beijing: Tiananmen Square and the Creation of a Political Space* (Chicago: University of Chicago Press, 2005), 10.

17. Wu, *Remaking Beijing*, 36.

18. Wu, *Remaking Beijing*, 16.

19. Michael Warner, *Publics and Counterpublics* (New York: Zone, 2005), 14.

20. Wang Hui, Leo Ou-fan Lee, and Michael M. J. Fischer, "Is the Public Sphere Unspeakable in Chinese? Can Public Spaces (*gonggong kongjian*) Lead to Public Spheres?," *Public Culture* 6, no. 3 (1994): 601–602. In an earlier reading of Habermas, Miriam Hansen observes the public sphere's "dual function as a *historical* category," which "offers a model for analyzing fundamental changes in relations among economy, society, and state, and in the conditions and relations of cultural production and reception." See Miriam Hansen, *Babel and Babylon: Spectatorship in American Silent Film* (Cambridge, MA: Harvard University Press, 1991), 9; italics in the original. Although the "cultural" layer may be missing from his own account, Rowe does not miss it in Habermas's, as he relates: "the bourgeoisie gradually came, through its new media for articulation and discussion, to postulate the existence of a 'public,' or 'public opinion,' as 'the abstract counterpart of public authority.' " See William Rowe, "The Public Sphere in Modern China," *Modern China* 16, no. 3 (1990): 312.

21. Wang, Lee, and Fischer, "Is the Public Sphere Unspeakable," 605.

22. Magisterial works of Tiananmen historiography include Timothy Brook, *Quelling the People: The Military Suppression of the Beijing Democracy Movement* (Stanford, CA: Stanford University Press, 1999), and Jeremy Brown, *June Fourth: The Tiananmen Protests and Beijing Massacre of 1989* (Cambridge: Cambridge University Press, 2021), in English, and Wu Renhua, *Liusi shijian quancheng shilu* (Taipei: Yunchen wenhua, 2019), in Chinese. Tiananmen memoirs abound. Fang Lizhi, *The Most Wanted Man in China: My Journey from Scientist to Enemy of the State*, trans. Perry Link (New York: Henry Holt, 2016); Shen Tong, with Marianne Yen, *Almost a Revolution* (Boston: Houghton Mifflin, 1990); and Michael S. Duke, *The Iron House: A Memoir of the Chinese Democracy Movement and the Tiananmen Massacre* (Layton, UT: Peregrine Smith, 1990) are but a few.

23. See Margaret E. Roberts, *Censored: Distraction and Diversion Inside China's Great Firewall* (Princeton, NJ: Princeton University Press, 2018).

24. Rowe, "The Public Sphere," 316–17.

25. Chien-hsin Tsai, "In Sickness or in Health: Yan Lianke and the Writing of Autoimmunity," *Modern Chinese Literature and Culture* 23, no. 2 (2011): 78.

26. Xiaobing Tang, "Why Should 2009 Make a Difference? Reflections on a Chinese Blockbuster," MCLC Resource Center, December 2009, https://u.osu.edu/mclc/online-series/tangxb/#fnb1.

27. Kirk Denton, *Exhibiting the Past: Historical Memory and the Politics of Museums in Postsocialist China* (Honolulu: University of Hawai'i Press, 2014), 3. His monograph examines Chinese museums as well as exhibitionary culture more broadly in evaluating the state's (re)constructions of the past.

28. Rui Hou, "The Commercialisation of Internet-Opinion Management: How the Market is Engaged in State Control in China," *New Media & Society* 22, no. 12 (2020): 2238–56.

29. Maria Repnikova and Kecheng Fang, "Authoritarian Participatory Persuasion 2.0: Netizens as Thought Work Collaborators in China," *Journal of Contemporary China* 27 (2018): 763–79.

30. For a study of proregime, nationalist voices online and an accounting for "authoritarian resilience," see Rongbin Han, *Contesting Cyberspace in China: Online Expression and Authoritarian Resilience* (New York: Columbia University Press, 2018).

31. Margaret Hillenbrand, *Negative Exposures: Knowing What Not to Know in Contemporary China* (Durham, NC: Duke University Press, 2020), 2.

32. Warner, *Publics and Counterpublics*, 67.

33. Miriam Hansen, "Early Cinema, Late Cinema: Permutations of the Public Sphere," *Screen* 34, no. 3 (1993): 201.

1. REBUILDING THE REPUBLIC: STATE PROPAGANDA IN THE WAKE OF TIANANMEN

1. Louisa Lim, *The People's Republic of Amnesia: Tiananmen Revisited* (New York: Oxford University Press, 2014), 85–88.

2. For a critique of Western codings of the events at Tiananmen Square as a different form of Orientalism—China not as essentially other but as generally same— see Daniel Vukovich, "Uncivil Society, or Orientalism and Tiananmen, 1989," *Cultural Logic: A Journal of Marxist Theory & Practice* 16 (2009): 1–37, https://doi.org/10.14288/clogic.v16i0.191558.

3. For an overview of the PLA's propaganda work, see Wang Juntao and Anne-Marie Brady, "Sword and Pen: The Propaganda System of the People's Liberation Army," in *China's Thought Management*, ed. Anne-Marie Brady (New York: Routledge, 2012), 122–45. *Quotations from Chairman Mao*, also known as the *Little Red Book*, originated in the PLA in 1964.

4. The historian Jeffrey Wasserstrom, in analyzing the mythmaking around June Fourth from all quarters—government propagandists, students, and Western reporters and commentators alike—heuristically reads all accounts as "fictions" in order to tease out characterizations and plotlines shared across them. See Wasserstrom, "History, Myth, and the Tales of Tiananmen," in *Popular Protest and Political Culture in Modern China*, ed. Jeffrey N. Wasserstrom and Elizabeth J. Perry (Boulder, CO: Westview Press, 1994), 273–308, where Wasserstrom employs Northrop Frye's distinction, in *Anatomy of Criticism: Four Essays* (Princeton, NJ: Princeton University Press, 2020), between tragedy and romance.

5. An example is Sichuan ribao bianjibu, ed., *Chengdu saoluan shijian shimo* (Chengdu: Sichuan renmin chubanshe, 1989). For a corrective of what took place in this city, see Lim, *The People's Republic of Amnesia*, 182–205.

6. Qiao Youxuan, ed., *Beijing chunxia fengbo shilu* (n.p.: Haihua chubanshe, 1989). A simplified Chinese script was instituted in mainland China beginning in the late 1950s.

7. Che Muqi, *Beijing Turmoil: More Than Meets the Eye* (Beijing: Foreign Languages Press, 1990), is an English translation of Che Muqi, *Beijing fengbo de qianqian houhou: Yige zhishifenzi de guancha, sikao* (Beijing: Renmin Zhongguo chubanshe, 1990).

8. Scholars have indeed drawn parallels between the Cultural Revolution and the 1989 Tiananmen movement, not because the latter is another instance of "turmoil" but because of the shared repertoires of collective action, such as posting on walls handwritten posters (so-called "big-character posters") and "linking up"—traveling the country to establish contacts and networks. See Craig Calhoun and Jeffrey N. Wasserstrom, "Legacies of Radicalism: China's Cultural Revolution and the Democracy Movement of 1989," *Thesis Eleven* 57 (1999): 33–52.

9. Examples include Zhonggong zhongyang xuanchuanbu, ed., *Jianjue yonghu Dangzhongyang juece jianjue pingxi fangeming baoluan* (Beijing: Renmin chubanshe, 1989); Zongzhengzhibu xuanchuanbu and Jiefangjunbao bianjibu, eds., *Hanwei shehuizhuyi gongheguo* (Beijing: Changzheng chubanshe, 1989); and Gonganbu zhengzhibu xuanchuanbu, ed., *Shizhongbuyu di jianchi renmin minzhu zhuanzheng* (Beijing: Qunzhong chubanshe, 1990), promulgated by the propaganda departments of the Central Committee of the CCP, the PLA General Political Department, and the Ministry of Public Security's Political Department, respectively.

10. From Gongqingtuan Beijing shiwei, ed., *70 tian dashiji: Hu Yaobang bingshi dao Zhao Ziyang jiezhi* (Beijing: Beijing chubanshe, 1990), and Zhongguo jiaoyu baoshe and Beijing jieyan budui, eds., *Gongheguo weishi yinglie ji* (Beijing: Zhongguo zhuoyue chubanshe, 1989), 3–4, respectively.

11. Guojia jiaowei sixiang zhengzhi gongzuosi and Zhongguo jiaoyu baoshe, eds., *"Jingying" yu dongluan* (Beijing: Renmin jiaoyu chubanshe, 1989), and *Pantao "jingying" haiwai yanxing lu* (Beijing: Jiaoyu kexue chubanshe, 1990).

12. Zhonggong Beijing shiwei xuanchuanbu, ed., *Pingxi fangeming baoluan: Xuexi cailiao huibian* (Beijing: Beijing qingnian chubanshe, 1989); Zhonggong Beijing shiwei xuanchuanbu, ed., *Xuechao, dongluan, fangeming baoluan zhenxiang: Ziliao xuanbian* (Beijing: Zhongguo qingnian chubanshe, 1989); Zhonggong Hubei shengwei xuanchuanbu, ed., *Pingbao "beiwanglu": Xuexi cailiao xuanbian* (Wuhan: Hubei renmin chubanshe, 1989).

13. James Lull, *China Turned On: Television, Reform, and Resistance* (London: Routledge, 1991), 202.

14. Beijingshi sifaju fazhi jiaoyu jiaocai bianxiezu, ed., *Zhizhi dongluan pingxi fangeming baoluan falü wenti jieda* (Beijing: Beijing chubanshe, 1989); Wu Song-nian, ed., *Shishi yu sikao: Zhongxuesheng shishi zhengzhixue wenda (1989 nian 5 yue–1990 nian 3 yue)* (Beijing: Xinhua chubanshe, 1990); Zhonggong Beijing shiwei xuanchuanbu lilunchu, ed., *Xuexi Deng Xiaoping zhongyao jianghua chedi pingxi fangeming baoluan wenti jieda* (Beijing: Beijing chubanshe, 1989); Zhong-gong Liaoning shengwei gongchandangyuan zazhishe, ed., *Pingxi fangeming baoluan 500 ti* (Shenyang: Liaoning daxue chubanshe, 1989).

15. Li Jinkun, ed., *1989: Dongluan hou de huigu yu sikao* (Tianjin: Tianjin renmin chubanshe, 1989).

16. Robert Chi, "*The Red Detachment of Women*: Resenting, Regendering, Remembering," in *Chinese Films in Focus: 25 New Takes*, ed. Chris Berry (London: BFI, 2003), 156.

17. Joseph W. Esherick and Jeffrey N. Wasserstrom, "Acting Out Democracy: Political Theater in Modern China," *Journal of Asian Studies* 49, no. 4 (1990): 839.

18. Chuan Fu, *Shinian xuechao jishi (1979–1989)* (Beijing: Beijing chubanshe, 1990), and Hua Yuan, *Tongshi mingjian: Zichanjieji ziyouhua de fanlan jiqi jiaoxun* (Beijing: Beijing chubanshe, 1991).

19. Gongqingtuan Beijing shiwei and Beijingshi xuesheng lianhehui, eds., *Zuguo mama qingting woshuo: Shoudu daxuesheng zai fengbo hou de sikao* (Chongqing: Chongqing chubanshe, 1990).

20. Among the many are Beijing gonganju zhengzhibu, ed., *Shoudu gongan ganjing pingbao jishi* (Beijing: Zhongguo shehui chubanshe, 1989); Zhonggong Beijing shiwei bangongting, ed., *Beijing zhizhi dongluan pingxi fangeming baoluan jishi* (Beijing: Beijing ribao chubanshe, 1989); and Jiangxi renmin chubanshe, ed., *Fangeming baoluan muduji* (Nanchang: Jiangxi renmin chubanshe, 1989).

21. Zhonghua renmin gongheguo sifabu xuanchuansi, ed., *Chedi jielu fangeming baoluan de zhenxiang* (Beijing: Falü chubanshe, 1989), and Zhongyang dangxiao de jiben luxian yanjiu ketizu, ed., *Beijing fengbo zhenxiang he shizhi* (Beijing: Dadi chubanshe, 1989).

22. See Perry Link's dissection of the political "language game" in his *Anatomy of Chinese: Rhythm, Metaphor, Politics* (Cambridge, MA: Harvard University Press, 2013), 278–348.

23. Guangming ribao chubanshe bianjibu, ed., *Pingbao yingxiong pu: Pingxi Beijing fangeming baoluan yingmo shiji baogaoji* (Beijing: Guangming ribao chubanshe, 1989), and Chen Shenggeng, ed., *Lishi de beiwen: 1989 wujing budui zhizhi dong-luan pingxi fangeming baoluan jishi* (Beijing: Jingji guanli chubanshe, 1989).

24. Zheng Nianqun, *Zai jieyan de rizi li* (Beijing: Jiefangjun wenyi chubanshe, 1989); Ye Xuan, ed., *Pingbao jishi* (Taiyuan: Beiyue wenyi chubanshe, 1990); and

Zhongguo renmin jiefangjun zonghouqinbu chechuanbu, ed., *Tiema chicheng wei Jinghua* (Beijing: Jiefangjun wenyi chubanshe, 1990).

25. For a collection of nearly 200 pieces by members of the PLA, military police, and public security, see Zongzheng wenhuabu zhengwen bangongshi, ed., *Jieyan yiri* [*One day of martial law*], 2 vols. (Beijing: Jiefangjun wenyi chubanshe, 1989). The title comes from a seminal work of reportage from 1936, *One Day in China*, ed. Mao Dun, which previously spawned 1938's *One Day in Shanghai*, 1949's *One Day Crossing the Yangtze* (on the last decisive victory of the Communists over the Nationalists), and 1956's *One Day in the Volunteer Army* (on the Korean War of 1950–1953). Zhong Bu, ed., *Xinshiqi zuikeai de ren: Beijing jieyan budui yingxiong lu* [Those most worthy of our love in the new era: record of Beijing martial law troops' heroic achievements] (Beijing: Guangming ribao chubanshe, 1989), responds to another well-known piece of reportage, from the Korean War: "Who Is the Most Worthy of Our Love?" (1951).

26. Both Wang Zongren, coauthor of "Symphony of Fire and Blood," and Mu Jing, who contributed two pieces (one using a pseudonym), worked in the PLA's General Logistics Department's Political Department.

27. Both Shi Xiang, author of "Phoenix in the Fire," and Zhang Weimin, author of "Road of Fire, Song of Blood," belonged to the Office of Literary and Artistic Creation in the PLA's Beijing Military Region Political Department. Su Fangxue, author of "A Star in the Solar System," was in the Office of Literary and Artistic Creation of the PLA's General Armaments Department's Political Department.

28. The CWA, composed of a national-level organization and provincial branches, was founded in 1953 and modeled after the Soviet literary administration. For a study of the production, dissemination, and reception of Chinese literature from the 1950s to the mid-1980s, see Perry Link, *The Uses of Literature: Life in the Socialist Chinese Literary System* (Princeton, NJ: Princeton University Press, 2000).

29. *Songs of the Republic's Guardians*, 160–62. Unless otherwise indicated, all citations of *Songs of the Republic's Guardians* are from *Gongheguo weishi zhige: Shoudu jieyan budui yingmo shiji baogao wenxueji* (Beijing: Jiefangjun chubanshe, 1989). The translations are mine.

30. For the thesis that formulations play a larger role in standardizing political language than does ideology, see Michael Schoenhals, *Doing Things with Words in Chinese Politics: Five Studies* (Berkeley: Institute of East Asian Studies, University of California, Berkeley, 1992).

31. For a detailed look at the origins of reportage literature, especially the role played therein by the Czech writer Egon Erwin Kisch, see Rudolf Wagner, *Inside a Service Trade: Studies in Contemporary Chinese Prose* (Cambridge, MA: Council on East Asian Studies, Harvard University, 1992), 325–57. In China, *baogao*

wenxue was first used and promoted by the Chinese League of Left-Wing Writers in 1930. The form gradually underwent canonization and institutionalization from the 1930s onward, though only after the Cultural Revolution did the idea of reportage as an independent literary genre take hold. See Charles Laughlin, *Chinese Reportage: The Aesthetics of Historical Experience* (Durham, NC: Duke University Press, 2002), 1–2, 19–20.

32. First proposed by Zhou Enlai, Deng Xiaoping enacted them at the Third Plenum of the 11th Central Committee in 1978.

33. Yomi Braester, "Photography at Tiananmen: Pictorial Frames, Spatial Borders, and Ideological Matrixes," *positions: east asia cultures critique* 18, no. 3 (2010): 636.

34. Haun Saussy, "Crowds, Number, and Mass in China," in *Crowds*, ed. Jeffery T. Schnapp and Matthew Tiews (Stanford, CA: Stanford University Press, 2006), 251, traces crowd portrayals to the Western-Han *Shiji*, or *The Grand Scribe's Records*.

35. Haiyan Lee, *Revolution of the Heart: A Genealogy of Love in China, 1900–1950* (Stanford, CA: Stanford University Press, 2007), 235.

36. Marston Anderson, *The Limits of Realism: Chinese Fiction in the Revolutionary Period* (Berkeley: University of California Press, 1990), 201. Not all conceptions of the crowd were negative in the 1920s. For an examination of Zhu Qianzhi's celebration of the irrational crowd in his 1921 *Philosophy of Revolution*—and a study of the transformation of the crowd trope in both intellectual and artistic works in the first half of the twentieth century—see Tie Xiao, *Revolutionary Waves: The Crowd in Modern China* (Cambridge, MA: Harvard University Press, 2017).

37. The "Beijing Students' Autonomous Federation" and the "Beijing Workers' Autonomous Federation," both formed during the protests, are mentioned always in scare quotes, as if they were organizations in name only, their autonomy from party control a proof of their fraudulence.

38. The student communications center at Tiananmen Square, which had started at Peking University, contained amplifiers, speakers, microphones, loudspeakers, mimeograph machines, and typewriters. See Craig Calhoun, *Neither Gods nor Emperors: Students and the Struggle for Democracy in China* (Berkeley: University of California Press, 1994), 45.

39. "Cultural memory works by reconstructing, that is, it always relates its knowledge to an actual and contemporary situation": Jan Assmann, "Collective Memory and Cultural Identity," trans. John Czaplicka, *New German Critique* 65 (1995): 130.

40. According to Andrea Worden, over half a million copies of Lei Feng's diary were reissued before the first anniversary of June Fourth, with a preface in which the then director of the PLA General Political Department, Yang Baibing, wrote: "In

this blood-and-fire, life-and-death struggle there emerged many Lei Feng-type soldiers" (quoted in "Missing Lei Feng," China Channel, March 5, 2021, https://chinachannel.org/2021/03/05/missing-lei-feng/).

41. Such is the case in "Deep Feelings at a Critical Moment: Major General Zhang Kun and Female Worker Ma Zhanqin."

42. Lin Daojing, once a suicidal woman, ultimately joins the movement to resist Japanese incursions in Yang Mo's 1958 novel *The Song of Youth*, trans. Nan Ying (Beijing: Foreign Languages Press, 1964). The abused servant girl Wu Qionghua eventually fights in *The Red Detachment of Women*, Xie Jin's 1961 film.

43. Liu would win the Nobel Peace Prize in 2010 while serving an eleven-year jail term for state subversion. He died in July 2017 shortly after being granted medical parole.

44. Jin Zhong, "Wentan 'heima' Liu Xiaobo," *Jiefang yuebao* 12 (1988), http://www.open.com.hk/old_version/1011p68.html.

45. Hong Kong was a British colony from 1841, the time of the First Opium War between the British Empire and the Qing dynasty of China, to 1997, when sovereignty reverted to the PRC.

46. For a classic account from the different angles of history, experience, and myth, see Paul A. Cohen, *History in Three Keys: The Boxers as Event, Experience, and Myth* (New York: Columbia University Press, 1998).

47. According to Craig Calhoun, arrests began before June 4, 1989, not with students but with workers. After June 4, the target of repression was again not students but workers and residents. See Calhoun, *Neither Gods nor Emperors*, 113, 148.

48. "Social problem reportage literature," as opposed to reportage on particular events, became prominent in the 1980s. See Yingjin Zhang, "Narrative, Ideology, Subjectivity: Defining a Subversive Discourse in Chinese Reportage," in *Politics, Ideology and Literary Discourse in Modern China: Theoretical Interventions and Cultural Critique*, ed. Kang Liu and Xiaobing Tang (Durham, NC: Duke University Press, 1993), 211–42.

49. Michael Berry's *A History of Pain: Trauma in Modern Chinese Literature and Film* (New York: Columbia University Press, 2008) expands upon trauma as a central theme in modern Chinese literary and cultural studies, tackling six traumatic events in modern Chinese history, one of which is June Fourth. Other notable monographs that reckon with trauma in the Chinese twentieth century, stemming from national catastrophes, foreign incursions, as well as transnational capitalism, include David Der-wei Wang's *The Monster That Is History: History, Violence, and Fictional Writing in Twentieth-Century China* (Berkeley: University of California Press, 2004), and Ban Wang's *Illuminations from the Past: Trauma, Memory, and History in Modern China* (Stanford, CA: Stanford University Press, 2004).

50. Haiyan Lee, "The Charisma of Power and the Military Sublime in Tiananmen Square," *Journal of Asian Studies* 70, no. 2 (2011): 409.

51. Ying Zhu, *Two Billion Eyes: The Story of China Central Television* (New York: New Press, 2012), 76.

52. *A Record of the June Turbulence in Beijing*, in English, is but one exception. Lull's *China Turned On* contains illustrations from this hour-long documentary.

53. I make these conjectures based on time stamps and captions that occasionally run on the bottom of the frame in a recording of *Xue yu huo de kaoyan* (Trial by blood and fire), an approximately two-and-a-half-hour program consisting of four episodes made by CCTV in July 1989.

54. One of the two *National News Bulletin* anchors on that night, Du Xian, wore black while speaking in a ponderous and solemn manner. She was removed from her position afterward.

55. The shuttering was ordered by then Shanghai party secretary and soon-to-be CCP general secretary Jiang Zemin.

56. Some of Fang Lizhi's essays are collected in *Bringing Down the Great Wall: Writings on Science, Culture, and Democracy in China*, ed. and trans. James H. Williams (New York: Norton, 1990).

57. One such program is *One Hundred Mistakes of* River Elegy; see Lull, *China Turned On*, 214.

58. Long Xinmin, "Dianshi yu yulun daoxiang," *Qianxian* 10 (1989): 43.

59. Long, "Dianshi," 45–46.

60. Paola Voci, "From the Center to the Periphery: Chinese Documentary's Visual Conjectures," *Modern Chinese Literature and Culture* 16, no. 1 (2004): 76.

61. *Flutter, Flag of the Republic*—as well as *Songs of the Republic's Guardians*—can thus be understood as simultaneously bearing witness for and against history. On this dialectical relationship, see Yomi Braester, *Witness Against History: Literature, Film, and Public Discourse in Twentieth-Century China* (Stanford, CA: Stanford University Press, 2003).

62. Yaxue Cao, "The Historian of the Tiananmen Movement and the June Fourth Massacre—An Interview with Wu Renhua (Part Two of Two)," *China Change*, June 4, 2016, https://chinachange.org/2016/06/04/the-historian-of-the-tiananmen-movement-and-the-june-fourth-massacre-an-interview-with-wu-renhua-part-two-of-two/.

63. They are *A Hair-Raising 56 Days* and *One Day of Martial Law*, respectively. See Wasserstrom, "History, Myth, and the Tales of Tiananmen," 297–98.

64. Rui Zhang, *The Cinema of Feng Xiaogang: Commercialization and Censorship in Chinese Cinema After 1989* (Hong Kong: Hong Kong University Press, 2008), 35–36. Claire Conceison locates the origin of the term in theater also in 1987. She

likewise dates the official promotion of main melody theater to the wake of June Fourth, with the campaign peaking in 1990 and 1991. See Conceison, "The Main Melody Campaign in Chinese Spoken Drama," *Asian Theatre Journal* 11, no. 2 (1994): 190–92.

65. See Hongmei Yu, "Visual Spectacular, Revolutionary Epic, and Personal Voice: The Narration of History in Chinese Main Melody Films," *Modern Chinese Literature and Culture* 25, no. 2 (2013): 166–218.

66. Paul Pickowicz, "Velvet Prisons and the Political Economy of Chinese Filmmaking," in *Urban Spaces in Contemporary China: The Potential for Autonomy and Community in Post-Mao China*, ed. Deborah S. Davis, Richard Kraus, Barry Naughton, and Elizabeth J. Perry (Cambridge: Cambridge University Press, 1995), 211.

67. Quoted in Zheng Wang, *Never Forget National Humiliation: Historical Memory in Chinese Politics and Foreign Relations* (New York: Columbia University Press, 2012), 96.

68. When the new History of the Chinese Revolution exhibit opened on July 1, 1990, in the Museum of the Chinese Revolution, Jiang Zemin, who had replaced Zhao Ziyang as the CCP general secretary, spoke of "the duty to strengthen education about the nation, strengthen patriotic education, strengthen socialist education, especially for our young people;" quoted in Kirk A. Denton, *Exhibiting the Past: Historical Memory and the Politics of Museums in Postsocialist China* (Honolulu: University of Hawai'i Press, 2014), 62.

69. Lee, "The Charisma of Power," 411.

70. Xue Weirui, "Tiananmen shengqi shi: cong yigeren de shidai dao jiushiliu ren de yishi," *Fengmian*, January 8, 2018, https://xw.qq.com/cmsid/20180108A04R9I00.

71. A recording of *Flutter, Flag of the Republic: A Record of the Quelling of the Beijing Counterrevolutionary Riot* held in the collections of Columbia University contains the Tank Man scene.

2. SONGS FROM AFAR: CONTESTING THE OFFICIAL NARRATIVE FROM THE PERIPHERY

1. *Death Fugue* did come out as a book in both Hong Kong and Taiwan in 2013, in a version different from that of the literary journal *Jiangnan*.

2. Leo Strauss, *Persecution and the Art of Writing* (Illinois: The Free Press, 1952), 24–25.

3. Belinda Kong, *Tiananmen Fictions Outside the Square: The Chinese Literary Diaspora and the Politics of Global Culture* (Philadelphia: Temple University Press, 2012), 27.

4. Luke Robinson, *Independent Chinese Documentary: From the Studio to the Street* (London: Palgrave Macmillan, 2013), 1.

5. For a detailed look at how the editing of *Bumming in Beijing* constructs a reading of personal crisis as political trauma, see Paola Iovene, "A Madwoman in the Art Gallery? Gender, Mediation, and the Relation Between Life and Art in Post-1989 Chinese Independent Film," *Journal of Chinese Cinemas* 8, no. 3 (2014): 173–87.

6. Robinson, *Independent Chinese Documentary*, 45–49.

7. Elizabeth Perry, "Moving the Masses: Emotion Work in the Chinese Revolution," *Mobilization* 7, no. 2 (2002): 111–28.

8. "Until the late 1980s, the state took responsibility for assigning every university student a job upon graduation. Under this system, students with poor marks, a bad political profile, or uneasy relations with school authorities often got poor jobs." See Dingxin Zhao, *The Power of Tiananmen: State-Society Relations and the 1989 Beijing Student Movement* (Chicago: University of Chicago Press, 2004), 106.

9. Qi Wang, *Memory, Subjectivity and Independent Chinese Cinema* (Edinburgh: Edinburgh University Press, 2014), 144–45.

10. For a reading of *Conjugation* as a "sinofrench" film, see Michelle Bloom, "Transnational Chinese Cinema with a French Twist: Emily Tang Xiaobai's 'Conjugation' and Jia Zhangke's 'The World' as Sinofrench Films," *Modern Chinese Literature and Culture* 21, no. 2 (2009): 198–245.

11. Bloom, "Transnational Chinese Cinema," 208.

12. From the perspective of the 2001 film, this countdown recalls the thirty-foot-high Hong Kong Clock erected on Tiananmen Square in 1994, which can be viewed as China's response to political developments in Hong Kong after June Fourth. The placing of the clock on a square of monumental buildings is a spatiotemporal insertion of the "micro narrative" of the British return of sovereignty over Hong Kong to China in 1997 "into the grand narrative of revolutionary history." See Wu Hung, *Remaking Beijing: Tiananmen Square and the Creation of a Political Space* (Chicago: University of Chicago Press, 2005), 336.

13. Huang Jiguang was in turn inspired by the martyrdom of a Soviet soldier whose movie he had seen. For the connection between Huang and Alexander Matrusov—or rather, *Private Aleksandr Matrosov* (1947)—see Thomas Chen, "An Italian Bicycle in the People's Republic: Minor Transnationalism and the Chinese Translation of *Ladri di biciclette/Bicycle Thieves*," *Journal of Italian Cinema & Media Studies* 2, no. 1 (2014): 95–96.

14. See Bao Pu, ed., *Zuihou de mimi: Zhongguo shisanjie sizhong quanhui "liusi" jielun wendang* (Hong Kong: New Century Press, 2019), for a record of a meeting called by Deng Xiaoping half a month after the massacre in which party elders and senior leaders retroactively supported the decision to use force.

15. Joseph W. Esherick and Jeffrey N. Wasserstrom, "Acting Out Democracy: Political Theater in Modern China," *Journal of Asian Studies* 49, no. 4 (1990): 843.

16. Linda Hershkovitz, "Tiananmen Square and the Politics of Space," *Political Geography* 12, no. 5 (1993): 413.

17. "Foot Finger" is the translation that the film's subtitles give. A literal translation of the Chinese name would simply be "toe."

18. Ying Bao, "Remembering the Invisible: Soundscape and the Memory of 1989," *Journal of Chinese Cinemas* 7, no. 3 (2013): 219.

19. One cannot tell from Tian Yu's spoken reply, when Guo Song asks him where he got the capital to open his café, that he used some of the donation money. Yet the English subtitle—"I . . . I still have some money on hand"—implies otherwise.

20. Thus, this broadcast acquires the powers of what Michel Chion calls an "acousmêtre:" "the ability to be everywhere, to see all, to know all, and to have complete power. In other words: ubiquity, panopticism, omniscience, and omnipresence." See Michel Chion, *The Voice in Cinema*, trans. Claudia Gorbman (New York: Columbia University Press, 1999), 24.

21. Tang Xiaobai's mother, Zhang Yihe, tells a variant of these stories in *Liu shi nü* [*The Woman Liu*] (Guilin: Guangxi shifan daxue chubanshe, 2011). Liu Yueying murders her epileptic husband, dismembers the corpse, and keeps it in a preserved-vegetable vat under the bed. When the husband's older sister visits two years later, Liu's son—a year old at the time of the murder—asks whether it is time to eat dad's meat. Zhang's novella is based on her experience with an inmate in prison during the Cultural Revolution. See the fourth and fifth chapters of *Liu shi nü*.

22. Michael Berry, *A History of Pain: Trauma in Modern Chinese Literature and Film* (New York: Columbia University Press, 2008), 339.

23. Translation modified. All citations (those including location numbers) of Sheng Keyi's *Death Fugue*, trans. Shelly Bryant (Artarmon: Giramondo, 2014), are from the Amazon Kindle edition because this is the most accessible edition.

24. Sheng Keyi, *Siwang fuge, Jiangnan* 5 (2011).

25. The statue, made by students at the Central Academy of Fine Arts, is less indebted to the neoclassical Statue of Liberty of Frédéric Auguste Bartholdi than to the Soviet sculptor Vera Mukhina and socialist realism. For an eyewitness account of the transformation of the statue from an already made practice work featuring a man grasping a pole with two hands, see Tsing-yuan Tsao, "The Birth of the Goddess of Democracy," in *Popular Protest and Political Culture in Modern China*, ed. Jeffrey N. Wasserstrom and Elizabeth J. Perry (Boulder, CO: Westview Press, 1994): 140–47.

26. My translation. See location 1855.

27. The exchange between Baiqiu and Mengliu's father aligns Baiqiu with the poet Haizi, who was once similarly turned down in a Changping restaurant. See Maghiel van Crevel, *Chinese Poetry in Times of Mind, Mayhem and Money* (Leiden: Brill, 2008), 119. Haizi also committed suicide in 1989.

28. My translation (see location 317) and location 290, respectively.

29. Lu Xun, "Preface to *Outcry* (1923)," in *Jottings Under Lamplight: Lu Xun*, ed. Eileen J. Cheng and Kirk A. Denton (Cambridge, MA: Harvard University Press, 2017), 23.

30. Yan Bin, "Sheng Keyi fangtanlu," *Fenghuang dushu*, May 12, 2014, http://www .xinhuanet.com//book/2014-05/12/c_126490827.htm.

31. My translations. See locations 5473 and 5476.

32. For a response to the intellectual criticisms of Spielberg's film, see Miriam Hansen's "*Schindler's List* Is Not *Shoah*: The Second Commandment, Popular Modernism, and Public Memory," *Critical Inquiry* 22, no. 2 (1996): 292–312.

33. Jane Perlez, "Chinese Writer, Tackling Tiananmen, Wields 'Power to Offend,'" *New York Times*, October 10, 2014.

3. TRANSGRESSIVE CUTS: MAKING A SCENE IN THE POSTREVOLUTIONARY AGE

1. Richard Burt, "(Un)Censoring in Detail: The Fetish of Censorship in the Early Modern Past and the Postmodern Present," in *Censorship and Silencing: Practices of Cultural Regulation*, ed. Robert C. Post (Los Angeles: Getty Research Institute, 1998), 28–29.

2. Pierre Bourdieu, "Censorship and the Imposition of Form," in *Language and Symbolic Power*, ed. John B. Thompson, trans. Gino Raymond and Matthew Adamson (Cambridge, MA: Harvard University Press, 1991), 138.

3. Liu Xiaobo's "The Erotic Carnival in Recent Chinese History," trans. Nick Admussen, in *No Enemies, No Hatred: Selected Essays and Poems*, ed. Perry Link, Tienchi Martin-Liao, and Liu Xia (Cambridge, MA: Belknap Press of Harvard University Press, 2012), 150–74, delineates the replacement of political passion by a craze for money and sex starting in the 1990s but misses the state's role in promoting this shift.

4. "Sundance Channel interview," *Lan Yu*, directed by Stanley Kwan (Culver City, CA: Strand Releasing, 2003), DVD. In a later interview, he again calls June Fourth "the moment that Chen Handong commits to Lan Yu." See Michael Berry, ed., *Speaking in Images: Interviews with Contemporary Chinese Filmmakers* (New York: Columbia University Press, 2005), 454.

5. Several scholars have argued for the importance of the Beijing Workers' Autonomous Union in the protests, especially after the declaration of martial law on May 19. See, for example, Andrew G. Walder and Xiaoxia Gong, "Workers in the Tiananmen Protests: The Politics of the Beijing Workers' Autonomous Federation," *Australian Journal of Chinese Affairs* 29 (1993): 1–29. Dingxin Zhao, on the other hand, contends that "if we examine the role of the Beijing Workers'

Autonomous Union through such criteria as leadership, sources of material resources, and major activities and participants, it becomes obvious that the union was basically only an appendage of the student movement." See Dingxin Zhao, *The Power of Tiananmen: State-Society Relations and the 1989 Beijing Student Movement* (Chicago: University of Chicago Press, 2004), 176.

6. The first one, in 2001, occurred in the same year as the first grassroots film festival in the PRC, the Unrestricted New Image Festival. The second China Queer Film Festival took place only in 2004, with no disruptions. See Ran Ma, "Regarding the Grassroots Chinese Independent Film Festivals: Modes of Multiplicity and Abnormal Film Networking," in *China's iGeneration: Cinema and Moving Image Culture for the Twenty-First Century*, ed. Matthew D. Johnson, Keith B. Wagner, Tianqi Yu, and Luke Vulpiani (New York: Bloomsbury, 2014), 238.

7. Remy Cristini, "Gay Literature from China: In Search of a Happy Ending," *IIAS Newsletter* 31 (2003): 27.

8. They included the Xinhua News Agency, *Beijing Evening News*, and *Beijing Youth Daily*. See Zhen Xiaofei, "Shishi feifei tongxinglian yingzhan," *Nanfang zhoumo*, January 11, 2007, http://www.southcn.com/weekend/culture/200701110032.htm.

9. See, for instance, Zeng Wobu, "Guan Jinpeng tan dongqing zhizuo *Lan Yu*: Wo bushi pai seqingpian," *Nanfang dushibao*, December 10, 2001, http://ent.sina .com.cn/m/c/2001-12-10/66499.html.

10. Chu Tian, "*Lan Yu* fangying xianchang ceji: Yiban chenggong yiban shibai," Sohu, January 2, 2002, https://web.archive.org/web/20020129105550/http://news.sohu .com/37/81/news147568137.shtml.

11. Zhen, "Shishi feifei."

12. Steve Friess, "Testing China's Censors with a Gay Love Story," *New York Times*, January 12, 2002.

13. Different government institutions controlled different media. Back then, the SARFT controlled film exhibition, while the General Administration of Press and Publication (GAPP) controlled DVDs. For more on this dual-track system, see Yuxing Zhou, "Producing Soft Power Through Cinema: Censorship and Double Standards in Mainland China," *Journal of Chinese Cinemas* 9, no. 3 (2015): 239–52. Pirated VCDs of the film had first surfaced on the mainland around the time of the Gay Film Festival. A *New York Times* article from January 2002 reports such disks being sold on the street in China; see Friess, "Testing China's Censors." In 2001, nearly 40 million pirated audiovisual materials were confiscated. By 2006, that number reached nearly 50 million. See Jinying Li, "From D-Buffs to the D-Generation: Piracy, Cinema, and an Alternative Public Sphere in Urban China," *International Journal of Communication* 6 (2012): 545. This article is a rich account of piracy facilitating an underground realm for cultural circulation and consumption in the context of a repressive regime.

14. The shot of Handong clasping Lan Yu is replayed in black and white just before the closing credits.

15. Wang Hui, *China's New Order: Society, Politics, and Economy in Transition*, ed. Theodore Huters, trans. Theodore Huters and Rebecca E. Karl (Cambridge, MA: Harvard University Press, 2006), 65.

16. The novel was first serialized in September 1998 on the mainland website Chinese Men's and Boys' Paradise under the title *Mainland Story*. See Hugh Ryan, "The Controversial Chinese Gay Erotic Novel You Can Finally Read in English," *Vice*, March 16, 2016, https://broadly.vice.com/en_us/article/beijing-comrades-china -gay-erotica-online. It was later reposted on Yifan, which started in 1997 and is one of the first Chinese literary websites. The English translation of the novel came out in 2016. See Bei Tong, *Beijing Comrades*, trans. Scott E. Myers (New York: The Feminist Press, 2016). "Beijing Comrade" turned out to be a Chinese woman living in New York.

17. Song Hwee Lim traces this usage to film festivals, specifically Hong Kong's inaugural lesbian and gay film festival in 1989 and the 1992 Golden Horse Film Festival in Taiwan, which featured a special section on gay films. See Song Hwee Lim, "Celluloid Comrades: Male Homosexuality in Chinese Cinemas of the 1990s," *China Information* 16, no. 1 (2002): 70.

18. For a distinction between cronyism and *guanxi*, see Naresh Khatri, Eric W. K. Tsang, and Thomas M. Begley, "Cronyism: A Cross-Cultural Analysis," *Journal of International Business Studies* 37, no. 1 (2006): 63–64.

19. A sophisticated reading of queer desire in *Lan Yu* is found in David L. Eng, "The Queer Space of China: Expressive Desire in Stanley Kwan's *Lan Yu*," *positions: east asia cultures critique* 18, no. 2 (2010): 459–87.

20. Many analysts believe that bad debts contributed critically to the Asian Financial Crisis of 1997, although China came away largely unscathed. See Helen Hughes, "Crony Capitalism and the East Asian Currency and Financial 'Crises,' " *Policy* 15, no. 3 (1999): 3–9, and Michael S. Pagano, "Crises, Cronyism, and Credit," *The Financial Review* 37, no. 2 (2002): 227–56.

21. *Guanxi* is mentioned in the next scene as well. An athletic guy whom Handong picked up is posing—in underwear that Handong gave him—in front of the bathroom mirror in Handong's place. He wants to enter the modeling world: "But I can't get in without connections [*guanxi*]."

22. For an exegesis of the dialectic between kinship and stranger sociality in modern Chinese literary and popular culture, see Haiyan Lee's *The Stranger and the Chinese Moral Imagination* (Stanford, CA: Stanford University Press, 2014).

23. This French song by Eugène Pottier was first translated into Chinese from the Russian in the early 1920s by Qu Qiubai, a Communist leader at the time.

24. Robert Chi, "'The March of the Volunteers': From Movie Theme Song to National Anthem," in *Re-envisioning the Chinese Revolution: The Politics and Poetics of Collective Memories in Reform China*, ed. Ching Kwan Lee and Guobin Yang (Stanford, CA: Stanford University Press, 2007), 241.

25. See Xiaomei Chen's extensive catalog of the song's appearances in film and theater in "Singing 'The Internationale': From the 'Red Silk Road' to the Red Classics," in *The Oxford Handbook of Modern Chinese Literatures*, ed. Carlos Rojas and Andrea Bachner (Oxford: Oxford University Press, 2016), 193–215.

26. Dave Kehr, "At the Movies," *New York Times*, July 26, 2002.

27. Ying Zhu, *Chinese Cinema During the Era of Reform: The Ingenuity of the System* (Westport, CT: Praeger, 2003), 149.

28. Seio Nakajima, "Film as Cultural Politics," in *Reclaiming Chinese Society: The New Social Activism*, ed. You-tien Hsing and Ching Kwan Lee (New York: Routledge, 2009), 173.

29. Liu Jing, "*Yiheyuan* qunzhong yanyuan jiti fuxie 37 ren bei songzhi yiyuan," Sohu, October 24, 2004, http://yule.sohu.com/20041024/n222651549.shtml.

30. The case of an Ang Lee film furnishes a useful comparison. Coming a year after *Summer Palace*, Lee's *Lust, Caution* (2007) also features several explicit sex scenes. In order for it to be eventually released on the mainland, these scenes were shot elsewhere—in this case, in a Hong Kong film studio—while much of the rest of the film was shot in Shanghai. Therefore, it could be screened on the mainland, albeit in a truncated version. See Robert Chi, "Exhibitionism: *Lust, Caution*," *Journal of Chinese Cinemas* 3, no. 2 (2009): 184.

31. Michael Berry, *A History of Pain: Trauma in Modern Chinese Literature and Film* (New York: Columbia University Press, 2008), 348.

32. An English translation of the regulations can be found at World Intellectual Property Organization, "China: Regulations on the Administration of Movies," last modified December 11, 2001, https://wipolex.wipo.int/en/legislation/details/6474. The relevant articles are 61 and 64.

33. See Zhang Wenbo, "Lou Ye *Yiheyuan* ruwei Jiana? Shangxu shencha," *Xinjingbao*, April 20, 2006, http://www.southcn.com/ent/yulefirst/200604200174.htm, and Yin Wei, "Daoyan Lou Ye bochi chuanyan: Sheishuo *Yiheyuan* mei tongguo shencha?," *Xin wenhua bao*, May 9, 2006, http://www.chinanews.com/news/2006/2006-05-09/8/727270.shtml. After Cannes, the producers again tried to pass the film through censorship, but it was no longer accepted. See Pan Yuan, "Lou Ye *Yiheyuan* jianchi zaisongshen," Sina, July 28, 2006, http://news.sina.com.cn/o/2006-07-28/09549592470s.shtml.

34. Their offending films are *Blue Kite* (1993), *Beijing Bastards* (1993), *The Days* (1993), and *1966: My Time in the Red Guards* (1993), respectively.

35. Berry, *A History of Pain*, 341–42.

36. An early salvo is Dai Qing, "Raised Eyebrows for *Raise the Red Lantern*," trans. Jeanne Tai, *Public Culture* 5 (1993): 333–37.

37. See Paul Pickowicz, "Velvet Prisons and the Political Economy of Chinese Film-making," in *Urban Spaces in Contemporary China: The Potential for Autonomy and Community in Post-Mao China*, ed. Deborah S. Davis, Richard Kraus, Barry Naughton, and Elizabeth J. Perry (Cambridge: Cambridge University Press, 1995): 193–220. In a *New York Times Magazine* profile, Zhang Yimou was once described as "the great outsider." See Lynne Pan, "A Chinese Master," *New York Times Magazine*, March 1, 1992, 36.

38. For his troubles—watching a banned film and commenting on it—the author's piece was taken down even from the nationalist website guancha.cn, where it was originally posted. It can now be found at Ge Weiping, "*Yiheyuan*: Yong seqing yu zhengzhi boqu yishu zhiwai de kandian," Wuyouzhixiang, June 17, 2008, http://www.wyzxwk.com/Article/wenyi/2009/09/38112.html.

39. Jason McGrath, "Communists Have More Fun! The Dialectics of Fulfillment in Cinema of the People's Republic of China," *World Picture* 3 (2009), http://www.worldpicturejournal.com/WP_3/McGrath.html (italics in the original).

40. One may recall that Hou Hsiao-hsien's *A City of Sadness* (1989) was also criti-cized when it first appeared for romance dominating politics, being politically muddy, or actually supporting the government position. For a summary of such criticisms, see Robert Chi, "Getting It on Film: Representing and Under-standing History in *A City of Sadness*," *Tamkang Review* 29, no. 4 (1999): 47–84.

41. *Rhinoceros in Love* is a wildly popular play written by Liao Yimei and first directed in 1999 by her husband, Meng Jinghui. Hao Lei, who plays Yu Hong in *Summer Palace*, starred in the 2003 version of the play alongside Duan Yihong, who in the film plays the married man with whom Yu Hong has an affair.

42. Carma Hinton confirmed to me in a conversation that her documentary is often used without citation.

43. For a comprehensive examination of this formula in Chinese fiction from the 1920s to the 1990s, see Jianmei Liu, *Revolution Plus Love: Literary History, Wom-en's Bodies, and Thematic Repetition in 20th-Century Chinese Fiction* (Honolulu: University of Hawai'i Press, 2003).

44. According to Jianmei Liu, love in post–Cultural Revolution scar literature fre-quently brings about the return to the true self that was lost in the masses and is often portrayed as the key to solving social problems. See Liu, *Revolution Plus Love*, 24.

45. For a reading of melancholia in *Summer Palace*, see Yiju Huang's "By Way of Melancholia: Remembrance of Tiananmen Square Incident in *Summer Palace*," *Asian Cinema* 21, no. 1 (2010): 165–78.

46. Judith Butler, "Ruled Out: Vocabularies of the Censor," in *Censorship and Silencing: Practices of Cultural Regulation*, ed. Robert C. Post (Los Angeles: The Getty Research Institute, 1998), 256.

47. The two emendations are (1) not to designate the film as a coproduction but as a Chinese film and (2) to abbreviate a violent scene, specifically, cutting the number of times a character strikes another with a hammer to twice. The film had 20 percent French financial backing. See Julie Makinen, "Director Takes Chinese Censorship, Business Battles Public," *Los Angeles Times*, October 18, 2012.

4. THE ORTHOGRAPHY OF CENSORSHIP: PARTICIPATORY READING FROM PRINT TO THE INTERNET

1. The Chinese version is Chen Chen, "Youdai tianchong de kongge," trans. Wang Baorong, *Dangdai zuojia pinglun* 6 (2016): 52–61.

2. Jonathan Abel observes a similar dynamic in transwar Japan, with traces of censorship constituting a process he calls "archivization" wherein "the internalization of an explicit command to self-censor or at least self-redact left a public, visible, material marker of something removed: an archive of loss due to censorship." See Jonathan Abel, *Redacted: The Archives of Censorship in Transwar Japan* (Berkeley: University of California Press, 2012): 10.

3. Virginia Barry, *Red—the New Black: China-UK Publishing* (London: Arts Council England, 2007), 84–85.

4. For an informative account of how much writers were paid in the socialist period, see Perry Link, *The Uses of Literature: Life in the Socialist Chinese Literary System* (Princeton, NJ: Princeton University Press, 2000), 129–33. The literary journal *October*, also published by the Beijing Publishing House, had been awarded the periodical contract first, which is considered separate under Chinese copyright law.

5. In discussing the reception of Salman Rushdie's *The Satanic Verses* (1988), Aamir Mufti observes "forms of mass 'consumption' other than 'reading' in the narrower sense of that word," including rumors, media coverage, gossip, hearsay, and commentary. See Aamir Mufti, "Reading the Rushdie Affair: 'Islam,' Cultural Politics, Form," in *The Administration of Aesthetics: Censorship, Political Criticism, and the Public Sphere*, ed. Richard Burt (Minneapolis: University of Minnesota Press, 1994), 309.

6. Hao Jianguo, "'Shaanjun dongzheng' lushang de xing fengbo," *Huashangbao*, July 14, 2008, http://hsb.hsw.cn/2008-07/14/content_7030731.htm.

7. You Mianjin, "*Feidu* chongban: Rang wenxue de gui wenxue," *Xinjingbao*, July 30, 2009, http://culture.people.com.cn/GB/27296/9750065.html. {For the theory

that the ban came late so GAPP could profit more from the fines, see Xialin Xiao, Feidu *feishei* [Beijing: Xueyuan chubanshe, 1993], 112.}

8. Jiang Wenjuan, "Laobianji pilu *Feidu* zaojin neimu: Yiyejian tiantang bian diyu," *Qingnian zhoumo*, August 6, 2009, http://media.people.com.cn/GB/40606/9804080 .html.

9. As one scholar observes of *The Plum*: "Hundreds of years of critical discourse on the novel have focused on how the reader should respond to the sexual content of the novel." See Tina Lu, "The Literary Culture of the Late Ming (1573–1644)," in *The Cambridge History of Chinese Literature, vol. II: From 1375*, ed. Kang-I Sun Chang (Cambridge: Cambridge University Press, 2010), 110. The complete novel is available in a masterful English translation in five volumes by David Tod Roy.

10. For a study of native place in Jia's writings, see Yiyan Wang, *Narrating China: Jia Pingwa and His Fictional World* (New York: Routledge, 2006).

11. The debate on literary commercialization began in the late 1980s over Wang Shuo and his best-selling "hooligan literature." See Jing Wang, *High Culture Fever: Politics, Aesthetics, and Ideology in Deng's China* (Berkeley: University of California Press, 1996), 261–86.

12. All citations from the novel use page numbers or page ranges only. Unless otherwise noted, these citations draw from Jia Pingwa, *Ruined City*, trans. Howard Goldblatt (Norman: University of Oklahoma Press, 2016).

13. Xiao Xialin, ed., Feidu *feishei*, 140.

14. Duo Wei, Feidu *ziwei* (Zhengzhou: Henan renmin chubanshe, 1993), 155.

15. Xiao, Feidu *feishei*, 152.

16. Xiao, Feidu *feishei*, 236.

17. The buying of book numbers refers to another reform-era phenomenon in the publishing industry. No book can be published in China without an International Standard Book Number (ISBN), which only the then GAPP—now the National Administration of Press and Publication, under the control of the Central Propaganda Department—can issue. A bookstore, for instance, could sell a publishing house the rights to a work for a specified amount. The publishing house then attaches an ISBN to it and sells it back to the bookstore in a separate contract and for a greater amount than the original sale. The difference is the cost of the ISBN. See Barry, *Red—the New Black*, 81 and 89. The bookstore prints the title with the ISBN, and the book enters the market legally under the publishing house's name. Sometimes the bookstore and publishing house share production costs, responsibilities for marketing and distribution, and profits. See Mike Meyer, "The World's Biggest Book Market," *New York Times*, March 13, 2005. For more on unofficial publishing and distribution, see Shuyu Kong, *Consuming Literature: Best Sellers and the Commercialization of Literary Production in Contemporary China* (Stanford, CA: Stanford University Press, 2008), 65–94.

18. In the Chinese translation, the bracketed part is replaced by "1980s."
19. A concomitant debate that fed on and into the controversy surrounding *Ruined City* is expounded in the chapter "Ideologies of Popular Culture: The 'Humanist Spirit' Debate" in Jason McGrath, *Postsocialist Modernity: Chinese Cinema, Literature, and Criticism in the Market Age* (Stanford, CA: Stanford University Press, 2008), 25–58.
20. They include *What's Wrong with Jia Pingwa*; Ruined City, *Ruined Whom*; *Taste of* Ruined City; Ruined City *and "Ruined City Fever"*; *Riddle of* Ruined City, and—last but not least—Ruined City, *Oh* Ruined City.
21. The novel's clandestine lives had begun even before the ban. Jia stated in an interview that he has over seventy pirated versions in his collection. See Mu Tao, "Lüli," *Dangdai zuojia pinglun* 5 (2005): 27.
22. Li Pei, "Shiyunian hou *Feidu* zaiban yin guanzhu," *Nanfang ribao*, July 30, 2009, http://news.xinhuanet.com/book/2009-07/30/content_11796253_2.htm.
23. Kong, *Consuming Literature*, 47. For the transformation of Writers Publishing House from essentially an in-house publisher for CWA to a "best seller machine," see Kong, *Consuming Literature*, 43–54.
24. Peking University professor Chen Xiaoming's essay considers Jia's oeuvre as a whole. Sun Yat-sen University professor Xie Youshun's essay focuses on *Shaanxi Opera*. I discuss the third below.
25. Compare, for example, Jia Pingwa, *Feidu* (Beijing: Beijing chubanshe, 1993), 468, with Jia Pingwa, *Feidu* (Beijing: Zuojia chubanshe, 2009), 415.
26. Zhang Hong, "Jia Pingwa *Feidu* jiejin xinbanben shangjia," *Xinjingbao*, July 30, 2009, http://culture.people.com.cn/GB/22219/9750476.html.
27. Li Jingze, "Zhuang Zhidie lun," in Jia, *Feidu* (Beijing: Zuojia chubanshe, 2009): 1.
28. Li, "Zhuang Zhidie lun," 2.
29. Jianying Zha, *China Pop: How Soap Operas, Tabloids, and Bestsellers Are Transforming a Culture* (New York: New Press, 1995), 149.
30. For a translation of some of Xu Xu's representative writings, see *Bird Talk and Other Stories by Xu Xu: Modern Tales of a Chinese Romantic*, trans. Frederik H. Green (Berkeley, CA: Stone Bridge Press, 2020).
31. Xu Xu, " '. . . . .' '□□□□' lun," *Renjianshi* 4 (May 20, 1934): 21.
32. Lu Xun, *Lu Xun quanji*, 21 vols. (Beijing: Renmin wenxue chubanshe, 2005), 5:512.
33. The quintessential tale of Shanghai industrial and financial capitalism in the 1930s is Mao Dun's 1933 novel *Midnight*, trans. Hsu Meng-hsiung and A. C. Barnes (Beijing: Foreign Languages Press, 1979). For an overview and critique of scholarship on commerce and culture in republican-era Shanghai, see Wen-hsin Yeh, "Shanghai Modernity: Commerce and Culture in a Republican City," *China Quarterly* 150 (1997): 375–94.

34. Lu Xun, *Lu Xun quanji*, 6:162.
35. Lu Xun, *Lu Xun quanji*, 5:438.
36. Around the same time, by 1936, authorities in Japan began to ban from pub-lication *fuseji*, or "covering characters," used by writers and censors alike to redact writing, thereby making it harder to know where deletion had occurred (Abel, *Redacted*, 148). In the massive editing of books for collection in the Qing Emperor Qianlong's *The Emperor's Four Treasuries*, offending characters and sections had to be replaced with other characters. No blanks could remain. See R. Kent Guy, *The Emperor's Four Treasuries: Scholars and the State in the late Chien-lung Era* (Cambridge, MA: Harvard University Press, 1987), 193.
37. Although Qiu Jin became consecrated with the fall of the Qing dynasty in 1911, her legacy was fiercely contested, not least before the establishment of the Kuo-mintang government in 1927. See Hu Ying, "Qiu Jin's Nine Burials: The Making of Historical Monuments and Public Memory," *Modern Chinese Literature and Culture* 19, no. 1 (2007): 138–91, for an assessment of this contestation.
38. For a penetrating examination of historical nostalgia in the novel, see Carlos Rojas, "Flies' Eyes, Mural Remnants, and Jia Pingwa's Perverse Nostalgia," *positions: east asia cultures critique* 14, no. 3 (2006): 749–73.
39. Sheldon Lu reads the decay as an expression of fin de siècle malaise in "Lit-erature: Intellectuals in the Ruined Metropolis at the Fin de Siècle," in *China, Transnational Visuality, Global Postmodernity* (Stanford, CA: Stanford Univer-sity Press, 2001): 239–59.
40. In the Chinese translation, the bracketed part is "revolutionary tutors."
41. I am referring to the *livres philosophiques*, underground literature popular in the 1780s that was part pornography and part lampoon of monarchy and church, the subject of Robert Darnton's classic *The Forbidden Best-Sellers of Pre-Revolution-ary France* (New York: Norton, 1996).
42. The beginning of internet literature in Chinese can be traced back to Tiananmen. Jin Feng dates it to 1989, when overseas students in the United States started a news listserv that also distributed creative writing. See Jin Feng, *Romancing the Internet: Producing and Consuming Chinese Web Romance* (Leiden: Brill, 2013), 19–20. Michel Hockx likewise locates its beginning among overseas Chinese students but dates it to 1991 and the electronic magazine *Chinese News Digest*. See Michel Hockx, *Internet Literature in China* (New York: Columbia University Press, 2015), 30.
43. The first private Internet Service Provider (ISP) was founded in 1995, a year after China became wired. See Guobin Yang, "Political Contestation in Chinese Digital Spaces: Deepening the Critical Inquiry," *China Information* 28, no. 2 (2014): 135.
44. "CNNIC fabu di 15 ci hulianwang baogao," Sina, January 19, 2005, http://tech .sina.com.cn/it/2005-01-19/1354508840.shtml.

45. All citations from the novel, unless otherwise noted, are drawn from Hu Fayun, *Such Is This World@sars.come*, trans. A. E. Clark (Dobbs Ferry, NY: Ragged Banner Press, 2011), large-screen PDF edition.

46. For a useful overview of the subject, see Gudrun Wacker, "Resistance Is Futile: Control and Censorship of the Internet in China," in *From Woodblocks to the Internet: Chinese Publishing and Print Culture in Transition, Circa 1800 to 2008*, ed. Cynthia Brokaw and Christopher A. Reed (Leiden: Brill, 2010): 353–81. A benchmark study of the Chinese Internet in general is Guobin Yang, *The Power of the Internet in China: Citizen Activism Online* (New York: Columbia University Press, 2011).

47. Jia, *Ruined City*, 141.

48. Hu, *Such Is This World*, 3. The two books are Zhang Yihe's *Wangshi bingbu ruyan* (Beijing: Renmin chubanshe, 2004), a memoir of the Anti-Rightist Movement of 1957 by the daughter of the prominent "rightist" Zhang Bojun, and Chen Guidi and Wu Chuntao, *Will the Boat Sink the Water? The Life of China's Peasants*, trans. Zhu Hong (New York: PublicAffairs, 2006), a work of investigative reportage by a husband-and-wife team.

49. Hu, *Such Is This World*, 4. Among the other works on the list is another by Zhang Yihe, *Lingren wangshi* (Changsha: Hunan wenyi chubanshe, 2006).

50. Under Hu Fayun's first entry on his Sina blog—now removed—one internet user (Meng Ge Ma Li) in the comments section talks about the novel's "ban" piquing his interest: "Hearing that your work was banned, I hurriedly searched online and downloaded it. I came across your blog and took the liberty of entering. What glory to have your work among the eight banned books!" Another user (hqwxyz) is similarly motivated: "The CCP's Selection Department is truly a good guide to modern must-read books. I heard your work was banned and immediately bought a copy online. After reading the first few pages, I thought, 'Is this a publishing ploy? Even this book is banned?' Only half way through it did I realize how perceptive this department truly is." See Hu Fayun, "Ruyan ruyan nairuohe?," *Hu Fayun de BLOG*, November 21, 2006, http://blog.sina.com.cn/s /blog_4b4e30dd010005to.html. The "CCP's Selection [*xuan*] Department" is a pun on the Chinese Communist Party's Publicity (*xuan*) Department.

51. Hu, "Ruyan ruyan nairuohe?"

52. Shi Yan Wu Tian, "*Ruyan@sars.come* shanjie bufen," March 26, 2009, http:// tieba.baidu.com/p/556415421. This webpage is now removed, but interested readers can find a copy of Shi Yan Wu Tian's work under "Reference materials on Hu Fayun and *Such Is This World@sars.come*," Ragged Banner Press, http:// raggedbanner.com/HFY/HFY_ref.html.

53. Hu Fayun, "*Ruyan* zuozhe Hu Fayun de yidian shuoming ji beiwanglu," November 24, 2006, http://bbs.269.net/forum.php?mod=viewthread&tid=953271 (now removed).

54. Hu Fayun, "Fenghuang weishi meizhoutai *Tiantian huati* dui Hu Fayun de fangtan," *Hu Fayun de BLOG*, February 12, 2010, http://blog.sina.com.cn/s/blog _4b4e30dd0100giua.html (now removed).

55. Hu Fayun, "Yige meiyou jieshu de jiangzuo," *Hu Fayun de BLOG*, November 19, 2009, http://blog.sina.com.cn/s/blog_4b4e30dd0100fjj3.html. Hu was once able to post the eleventh lecture more than two years later in Hu Fayun, "Yipian 'simi bowen,'" *Hu Fayun de BLOG*, February 26, 2012, http://blog.sina.com.cn/s /blog_4b4e30dd0100x0z6.html, but it is now removed.

56. Hu, "Ruyan ruyan nairuohe?"

57. Shi Yan Wu Tian, "*Ruyan@sars.come.*"

58. Lao Jiao, "*Ruyan@sars.come* shanjie quxi," now removed, http://tieba.baidu.com /p/563429585.

59. Hu, "Ruyan ruyan nairuohe?" An interview—once available on his blog—that he conducted with the Hunan-based *Morning Weekly* is titled "Hu Fayun: Many topics in the unnamed forbidden zone can be gradually 'desensitized.'" See Hu Fayun, "Xuduo moming jinqu zhong de huati, shi keyi manman 'tuomin' de (yi)," *Hu Fayun de BLOG*, February 11, 2009, http://blog.sina.com.cn/s/blog _4b4e30dd0100bur5.html). Ironically, this entry is now "sensitized."

60. Hu Fayun, "Yige moshi de tonghua," *Hu Fayun de BLOG*, October 16, 2010, http://blog.sina.com.cn/s/blog_4b4e30dd0100ls52.html.

61. The blog entry "Today is the first day of heavy snow here" is simply an image of fifteen deleted titles. See Hu Fayun, "Jintian shi zher de diyichang daxue," *Hu Fayun de BLOG*, December 15, 2010, http://blog.sina.com.cn/s/blog_4b4e30dd0100nczs.html.

62. The original message breaks the characters of Liu Xiaobo's name into their components.

63. Carlos Rojas, *Homesickness: Culture, Contagion, and National Transformation in Modern China* (Cambridge, MA: Harvard University Press, 2015), 165.

64. Hu Fayun, "Mingri duanwu," *Hu Fayun de BLOG*, June 5, 2011, http://blog.sina.com .cn/s/blog_4b4e30dd0100rs4g.html.

65. Hu Fayun, "lby," *Hu Fayun de BLOG*, May 14, 2011, http://blog.sina.com.cn/s/blog _4b4e30dd0100raqv.html.

66. Hu, "lby."

67. The entry, now removed, is Hu Fayun, "Xinlang wangguan geiwo de meili de shengdan liwu," *Hu Fayun de BLOG*, December 26, 2010, http://blog.sina.com .cn/s/blog_4b4e30dd0100nljc.html. The essay is "Lin Zhao, how we love you." First labeled a rightist in 1957, Lin Zhao spent long bouts in prison and maintained her steadfast belief in human rights and freedom. She was secretly executed in 1968 at the age of thirty-five. She has since become a symbol for unrelenting opposition to political oppression and tyranny. An acclaimed documentary on her life is Hu Jie's *In Search of Lin Zhao's Soul* (2005).

68. Hu, "Yige moshi."

69. Hu Fayun, "Weizhe zheyang yisheng daoqian, wo xiang shuo—," *Hu Fayun de BLOG*, August 30, 2008, http://blog.sina.com.cn/s/blog_4b4e30dd0100aawj.html.

70. Hu Fayun, "Bu shengqi, zhiyou beimin," *Hu Fayun de BLOG*, October 9, 2011, http://blog.sina.com.cn/s/blog_4b4e30dd0100unul.html.

71. Hu Fayun, "Shanle jige Libiya de, Libiya yijing shengli zaiwang. Shanle jige 'Nayiye,' de, youhui zenyang ne?," *Hu Fayun de BLOG*, October 8, 2011, http://blog.sina.com.cn/s/blog_4b4e30dd0100unhy.html.

72. Hu Fayun, "Wuti," *Hu Fayun de BLOG*, June 4, 2011, http://blog.sina.com.cn/s/blog_4b4e30dd0100rrfc.html.

73. The entry, Hu Fayun, "2013 nian 06 yue 04 ri," *Hu Fayun de BLOG*, June 4, 2013, http://blog.sina.com.cn/s/blog_4b4e30dd01018okt.html, is now sensitized.

74. In a chapter on Mo Yan's *The Garlic Ballads*, I argue that the distinction between editing and censoring—and between revising and self-censoring—is not always easy to pinpoint. But the fact that editing and censoring sometimes blur does not mean the two are indistinguishable, a point I do not make sufficiently clear there. See Thomas Chen, "The Censorship of Mo Yan's *The Garlic Ballads*," in *Mo Yan in Context: Nobel Laureate and Global Storyteller*, ed. Angelica Duran and Yuhan Huang (West Lafayette, IN: Purdue University Press, 2014), 37–49.

75. Compare, for example, Hu Fayun, *Ruyan@sars.come* (Beijing: Zhongguo guoji guangbo chubanshe, 2006), 12, 28, 29, 72, 111, 128, and 236, with Hu, *Such Is This World*, 34, 65–66, 68, 141–43, 209, 239, and 427–28, respectively.

76. In addition to the passages to be discussed, compare Hu, *Ruyan@sars.come*, 63, 72, 118, 120–21, and 126–27, with Hu, *Such Is This World*, 124–25, 141, 221, 226, and 236–38, respectively.

77. Hu, *Such Is This World*, 224; translation slightly modified; Shi Yan Wu Tian, "*Ruyan@sars.come*."

78. Hu, *Such Is This World*, 226–27; Shi Yan Wu Tian, "*Ruyan@sars.come*."

79. Hu, *Such Is This World*, 230; Shi Yan Wu Tian, "*Ruyan@sars.come*."

80. Hu, *Such Is This World*, 477–78; translation slightly modified; Shi Yan Wu Tian, "*Ruyan@sars.come*."

81. Qin et al., "Q&A: Whistleblower Doctor Who Died Fighting Coronavirus Only Wanted People to 'Know the Truth,'" Caixin Global, February 7, 2020, https://www.caixinglobal.com/2020-02-07/whistleblower-doctor-who-died-fighting-coronavirus-only-wanted-people-to-know-the-truth-101512578.html.

82. Lily Kuo, "Coronavirus: Wuhan doctor speaks out against authorities," *Guardian*, March 11, 2020, https://www.theguardian.com/world/2020/mar/11/coronavirus-wuhan-doctor-ai-fen-speaks-out-against-authorities.

CONCLUSION: THE OTHER SIDE OF CENSORSHIP

1. "Hubei kaishi dui zuojia jinxing 'zhengnengliang' peixun," China Digital Times, March 9, 2020, https://chinadigitaltimes.net/chinese/2020/03/%E3%80%90%E7 %BD%91%E7%BB%9C%E6%B0%91%E8%AE%AE%E3%80%91%E6 %B9%96%E5%8C%97%E5%BC%80%E5%A7%8B%E5%AF%B9%E4% BD%9C%E5%AE%B6%E8%BF%9B%E8%A1%8C%E6%AD%A3%E8%83% BD%E9%87%8F%E5%9F%B9%E8%AE%AD/.

2. Fang Fang, "Ruyao chanmei, yeqing shougedu (7)," *Zuojia Fang Fang de boke*, February 1, 2020, http://fangfang.blog.caixin.com/archives/220631. Her diary has been translated into English as *Wuhan Diary: Dispatches from a Quarantined City*, trans. Michael Berry (New York: HarperVia, 2020).

3. Yan Lianke, "Jingci yijie, rang women chengwei you jixing de ren," Initium Media, February 21, 2020, https://theinitium.com/article/20200221-mainland-coronavirus -yanlianke/.

4. Sheng Keyi, *Death Fugue*, trans. Shelly Bryant (Artarmon: Giramondo, 2014), loc. 2990, Kindle.

5. Gu Yi, " 'Liusi' ershiliu zhounian zhi guonei tongxue de gongkaixin," China in Perspective, May 18, 2015, http://www.chinainperspective.com/ArtShow.aspx?AID =44088. An English translation can be found at "On the 26th Anniversary of Tian'anmen Massacre—an Open Letter to Fellow Students in Mainland China," China Change, May 27, 2015, https://chinachange.org/2015/05/27/on-the-26th -anniversary-of-tiananmen-massacre-an-open-letter-to-fellow-students-in -mainland-china/.

6. The Chinese version, removed from the *Global Times* website, can be found at *Huanqiu shibao*, "Jingwai shili shitu shandong balinghou jiulinghou," China Digital Times, May 26, 2015, https://chinadigitaltimes.net/chinese/20 15/05/%E3%80%90%E7%9C%9F%E7%90%86%E9%83%A8%E3%80%91%E5%A2 %83%E5%A4%96%E5%8A%BF%E5%8A%9B%E8%AF%95%E5%9B%BE%E7%85% BD%E5%8A%A8%E5%85%AB%E9%9B%B6%E5%90%8E%E4%B9%9D%E9%9B%B6 %E5%90%8E-2/. The English version is "Hostile forces target younger generation," *Global Times*, May 25, 2015, http://www.globaltimes.cn/content/923528.shtml.

7. *Global Times*, "Yu lishi ducuole, rensheng jiuhui qingru hongmao," Guanchazhe, May 5, 2016, https://www.guancha.cn/politics/2016_05_05_359139.shtml?web.

8. Elizabeth Redden, "Outrage Over University Press Caving in to Chinese Censorship," Inside Higher Ed, August 21, 2017, https://www.insidehighered.com /news/2017/08/21/cambridge-university-press-blocks-access-300-plus-articles -request-chinese-censors.

9. For a review of recent cases of foreign publishers bowing to pressure from the Chinese censorship regime, see Nicholas Loubere, "The New Censorship, the

New Academic Freedom: Commercial Publishers and the Chinese Market," *Journal of the European Association for Chinese Studies* 1 (2020): 239–52. An extensive investigation of the Chinese government's influence on the U.S. film industry is "Made in Hollywood, Censored by Beijing: The U.S. Film Industry and Chinese Government Influence," PEN America, August 5, 2020, https://pen .org/report/made-in-hollywood-censored-by-beijing/.

10. Shan Renping, "Jianqiao daxue chubanshe chuerfaner de beihou," *Huanqiu shibao*, August 24, 2017, https://opinion.huanqiu.com/article/9CaKrnK4RA9. The English version is "China Quarterly debate a matter of principle," *Global Times*, August 20, 2017, https://www.globaltimes.cn/content/1062304.shtml.

Bibliography

Abel, Jonathan. *Redacted: The Archives of Censorship in Transwar Japan.* Berkeley: University of California Press, 2012.

Anderson, Marston. *The Limits of Realism: Chinese Fiction in the Revolutionary Period.* Berkeley: University of California Press, 1990.

Assmann, Jan. "Collective Memory and Cultural Identity." Trans. John Czaplicka. *New German Critique* 65 (1995): 125–33.

Bao Pu 鲍朴, ed. *Zuihou de mimi: Zhongguo shisanjie sizhong quanhui "liusi" jielun wendang* 最后的秘密：中国十三届四中全会"六四"结论文档 [The last secret: The final documents from the June Fourth crackdown]. Hong Kong: New Century Press, 2019.

Bao, Ying. "Remembering the Invisible: Soundscape and the Memory of 1989." *Journal of Chinese Cinemas* 7, no. 3 (2013): 207–24.

Barmé, Geremie R. *In the Red: On Contemporary Chinese Culture.* New York: Columbia University Press, 1999.

Barry, Virginia. *Red—the New Black: China-UK Publishing.* London: Arts Council England, 2007.

Bei Tong. *Beijing Comrades.* Trans. Scott E. Myers. New York: The Feminist Press, 2016.

Beijing gonganju zhengzhibu 北京公安局政治部, ed. *Shoudu gongan ganjing pingbao jishi* 首都公安干警平暴纪实 [Record of the capital's public security police quelling the riot]. Beijing: Zhongguo shehui chubanshe, 1989.

Beijingshi sifaju fazhi jiaoyu jiaocai bianxiezu 北京市司法局法制教育教材编写组, ed. *Zhizhi dongluan pingxi fangeming baoluan falü wenti jieda* 制止动乱平息反

革命暴乱法律问题解答 [Answers to legal questions on the stopping of the turmoil and quelling of the counterrevolutionary riot]. Beijing: Beijing chubanshe,
1989.

Berry, Michael. *A History of Pain: Trauma in Modern Chinese Literature and Film.*
New York: Columbia University Press, 2008.

——, ed. *Speaking in Images: Interviews with Contemporary Chinese Filmmakers.*
New York: Columbia University Press, 2005.

Bloom, Michelle. "Transnational Chinese Cinema with a French Twist: Emily Tang
Xiaobai's 'Conjugation' and Jia Zhangke's 'The World' as Sinofrench Films." *Modern Chinese Literature and Culture* 21, no. 2 (2009): 198–245.

Bourdieu, Pierre. "Censorship and the Imposition of Form." In *Language and Symbolic Power*, ed. John B. Thompson, trans. Gino Raymond and Matthew Adamson, 137–159. Cambridge, MA: Harvard University Press, 1991.

Brady, Anne-Marie. *Marketing Dictatorship: Propaganda and Thought Work in Contemporary China.* Lanham, MD: Rowman & Littlefield, 2008.

Braester, Yomi. "Photography at Tiananmen: Pictorial Frames, Spatial Borders, and
Ideological Matrixes." *positions: east asia cultures critique* 18, no. 3 (2010): 633–670.

——. *Witness Against History: Literature, Film, and Public Discourse in Twentieth-
Century China.* Stanford, CA: Stanford University Press, 2003.

Brook, Timothy. *Quelling the People: The Military Suppression of the Beijing Democracy Movement.* Stanford, CA: Stanford University Press, 1999.

Brown, Jeremy. *June Fourth: The Tiananmen Protests and Beijing Massacre of 1989.*
Cambridge: Cambridge University Press, 2021.

Burt, Richard. "(Un)Censoring in Detail: The Fetish of Censorship in the Early Modern Past and the Postmodern Present." In *Censorship and Silencing: Practices
of Cultural Regulation*, ed. Robert C. Post, 17–42. Los Angeles: Getty Research
Institute, 1998.

Butler, Judith. "Ruled Out: Vocabularies of the Censor." In *Censorship and Silencing:
Practices of Cultural Regulation*, ed. Robert C. Post, 247–59. Los Angeles: Getty
Research Institute, 1998.

Calhoun, Craig. *Neither Gods nor Emperors: Students and the Struggle for Democracy in China.* Berkeley: University of California Press, 1994.

Calhoun, Craig, and Jeffrey N. Wasserstrom. "Legacies of Radicalism: China's Cultural Revolution and the Democracy Movement of 1989." *Thesis Eleven* 57 (1999):
33–52.

Cao, Yaxue. "The Historian of the Tiananmen Movement and the June Fourth Massacre—An Interview with Wu Renhua (Part Two of Two)." *China Change*, June
4, 2016. https://chinachange.org/2016/06/04/the-historian-of-the-tiananmen
-movement-and-the-june-fourth-massacre-an-interview-with-wu-renhua-part
-two-of-two/.

Che Muqi 车慕奇. *Beijing fengbo de qianqian houhou: Yige zhishifenzi de guancha, sikao* 北京风波的前前后后: 一个知识分子的观察・思考 [Beijing's turmoil from beginning to end: an intellectual's observation and reflection]. Beijing: Renmin Zhongguo chubanshe, 1990.

——. *Beijing Turmoil: More Than Meets the Eye*. Beijing: Foreign Languages Press, 1990.

Chen Chen 陈晨. "Youdai tianchong de kongge" 有待填充的空格 [Blanks to be filled]. Trans. Wang Baorong 汪宝荣. *Dangdai zuojia pinglun* 当代作家评论 [Contemporary Writers Review] 6 (2016): 52–61.

Chen Guidi, and Wu Chuntao. *Will the Boat Sink the Water? The Life of China's Peasants*. Trans. Zhu Hong. New York: PublicAffairs, 2006.

Chen Shenggeng 陈生庚, ed. *Lishi de beiwen: 1989 wujing budui zhizhi dongluan pingxi fangeming baoluan jishi* 历史的碑文: 1989武警部队制止动乱平息反革命暴乱纪实 [Inscriptions of history: record of the military police stopping the turmoil and quelling the counterrevolutionary riot in 1989]. Beijing: Jingji guanli chubanshe, 1989.

Chen, Thomas. "Blanks to Be Filled: Public-Making and the Censorship of Jia Ping-wa's *Decadent Capital*." *China Perspectives* 1 (2015): 15–22.

——. "The Censorship of Mo Yan's *The Garlic Ballads*." In *Mo Yan in Context: Nobel Laureate and Global Storyteller*, ed. Angelica Duran and Yuhan Huang, 37–49. West Lafayette, IN: Purdue University Press, 2014.

——. "An Italian Bicycle in the People's Republic: Minor Transnationalism and the Chinese Translation of *Ladri di biciclette/Bicycle Thieves*." *Journal of Italian Cinema & Media Studies* 2, no. 1 (2014): 91–107.

Chen, Xiaomei. "Singing 'The Internationale': From the 'Red Silk Road' to the Red Classics." In *The Oxford Handbook of Modern Chinese Literatures*, ed. Carlos Rojas and Andrea Bachner, 193–215. Oxford: Oxford University Press, 2016.

Chen, Yi. "Publishing in China in the Post-Mao Era: The Case of *Lady Chatterley's Lover*." *Asian Survey* 32, no. 6 (1992): 569–82.

Chi, Robert. "Exhibitionism: *Lust, Caution*." *Journal of Chinese Cinemas* 3, no. 2 (2009): 177–87.

——. "Getting It on Film: Representing and Understanding History in *A City of Sadness*." *Tamkang Review* 29, no. 4 (1999): 47–84.

——. "'The March of the Volunteers': From Movie Theme Song to National Anthem." In *Re-envisioning the Chinese Revolution: The Politics and Poetics of Collective Memories in Reform China*, ed. Ching Kwan Lee and Guobin Yang, 217–44. Stanford, CA: Stanford University Press, 2007.

——. "*The Red Detachment of Women*: Resenting, Regendering, Remembering." In *Chinese Films in Focus: 25 New Takes*, ed. Chris Berry, 152–59. London: BFI, 2003.

"China Quarterly Debate a Matter of Principle." *Global Times*, August 20, 2017. https://www.globaltimes.cn/content/1062304.shtml.

Chion, Michel. *The Voice in Cinema*. Trans. Claudia Gorbman. New York: Columbia University Press, 1999.

Chu Tian 楚天. "*Lan Yu* fangying xianchang ceji: Yiban chenggong yiban shibai" 《蓝宇》放映现场侧记：一半成功一半失败 [On-the-spot sidelight on *Lan Yu*'s screening: Half success, half failure]. Sohu 搜狐, January 2, 2002. https://web.archive.org/web/20020129105550/http://news.sohu.com/37/81/news147568137.shtml.

Chuan Fu 船夫. *Shinian xuechao jishi (1979–1989)* 十年学潮纪实 (1979–1989) [Record of ten years of student movements]. Beijing: Beijing chubanshe, 1990.

"CNNIC fabu di 15 ci hulianwang baogao." CNNIC发布第15次互联网报告 [CNNIC releases 15th internet report]. Sina 新浪, January 19, 2005. http://tech.sina.com.cn/it/2005-01-19/1354508840.shtml.

Cohen, Paul A. *History in Three Keys: The Boxers as Event, Experience, and Myth*. New York: Columbia University Press, 1998.

Conceison, Claire. "The Main Melody Campaign in Chinese Spoken Drama." *Asian Theatre Journal* 11, no. 2 (1994): 190–212.

Crevel, Maghiel van. *Chinese Poetry in Times of Mind, Mayhem and Money*. Leiden: Brill, 2008.

Cristini, Remy. "Gay Literature from China: In Search of a Happy Ending." *IIAS Newsletter* 31 (2003): 27.

Cyberspace Administration of China 国家互联网信息办公室. "Wangluo xinxi neirong shengtai zhili guiding" 网络信息内容生态治理规定 [Regulations on the governance of the ecology of internet informational content]. December 20, 2019. http://www.cac.gov.cn/2019-12/20/c_1578375159509309.htm.

Dai Qing. "Raised Eyebrows for *Raise the Red Lantern*." Trans. Jeanne Tai. *Public Culture* 5 (1993): 333–37.

Darnton, Robert. *The Forbidden Best-Sellers of Pre-Revolutionary France*. New York: Norton, 1996.

Denton, Kirk A. *Exhibiting the Past: Historical Memory and the Politics of Museums in Postsocialist China*. Honolulu: University of Hawai'i Press, 2014.

Duo Wei 多维, ed. Feidu *ziwei* 《废都》滋味 [Taste of *Decadent Capital*]. Zhengzhou: Henan renmin chubanshe, 1993.

Dutton, Michael. *Policing Chinese Politics: A History*. Durham, NC: Duke University Press, 2005.

Eng, David L. "The Queer Space of China: Expressive Desire in Stanley Kwan's *Lan Yu*." *positions: east asia cultures critique* 18, no. 2 (2010): 459–87.

Esherick, Joseph W., and Jeffrey N. Wasserstrom. "Acting Out Democracy: Political Theater in Modern China." *Journal of Asian Studies* 49, no. 4 (1990): 835–65.

Fang Fang 方方. "Ruyao chanmei, yeqing shougedu (7)" 如要谄媚，也请守个度（7）
[If you flatter, please show moderation (7)]. Zuojia Fang Fang de boke 作家方方的
博客, February 1, 2020. http://fangfang.blog.caixin.com/archives/220631.

——. *Wuhan Diary: Dispatches from a Quarantined City*. Trans. Michael Berry.
New York: HarperVia, 2020.

Fang Lizhi. *Bringing Down the Great Wall: Writings on Science, Culture, and Democracy in China*. Ed. and trans. James H. Williams. New York: Norton, 1990.

Feng, Jin. *Romancing the Internet: Producing and Consuming Chinese Web Romance*.
Leiden: Brill, 2013.

Foucault, Michel. *Discipline and Punish: The Birth of the Prison*. Trans. Alan Sheridan. New York: Vintage, 1995.

——. *The History of Sexuality, Volume 1: An Introduction*. Trans. Robert Hurley. New
York: Vintage, 1990.

Friess, Steve. "Testing China's Censors with a Gay Love Story." *New York Times*,
January 12, 2002.

Frye, Northrop. *Anatomy of Criticism: Four Essays*. Princeton: Princeton University
Press, 2020.

Ge Weiping 葛维屏. "*Yiheyuan*: Yong seqing yu zhengzhi boqu yishu zhiwai de kandian" 《颐和园》：用色情与政治搏取艺术之外的看点 [*Summer Palace*: Using
sex and politics to get attention outside of art]. Wuyouzhixiang 乌有之乡, June
17, 2008. http://www.wyzxwk.com/Article/wenyi/2009/09/38112.html.

Global Times. "Yu lishi ducuole, rensheng jiuhui qingru hongmao" 与历史赌错了
人生就会轻如鸿毛 [On the wrong side of history, life will be as insignificant
as a goose feather]. Guanchazhe 观察者, May 5, 2016. https://www.guancha.cn
/politics/2016_05_05_359139.shtml?web.

Gonganbu zhengzhibu xuanchuanbu 公安部政治部宣传部, ed. *Shizhongbuyu di
jianchi renmin minzhu zhuanzheng* 始终不渝地坚持人民民主专政 [Unswervingly uphold the people's democratic dictatorship]. Beijing: Qunzhong chubanshe, 1990.

Gongheguo weishi zhige: Shoudu jieyan budui yingmo shiji baogao wenxueji 共和国
卫士之歌：首都戒严部队英模事迹报告文学集 [Songs of the republic's guardians: Collection of reportage literature on martial law troops' heroic deeds in the
capital]. Beijing: Jiefangjun chubanshe, 1989.

Gongqingtuan Beijing shiwei 共青团北京市委, ed. *70 tian dashiji: Hu Yaobang
bingshi dao Zhao Ziyang jiezhi* 70天大事记：胡耀邦病逝到赵紫阳解职 [70 days'
major events: From Hu Yaobang's death due to illness to Zhao Ziyang's dismissal].
Beijing: Beijing chubanshe, 1990.

Gongqingtuan Beijing shiwei, Beijingshi xuesheng lianhehui 共青团北京市委,北京
市学生联合会, eds. *Zuguo mama qingting woshuo: Shoudu daxuesheng zai fengbo
hou de sikao* 祖国妈妈请听我说：首都大学生在风波后的思考 [Motherland,

please listen to me: Reflections of the capital's college students after the turmoil].
Chongqing: Chongqing chubanshe, 1990.

Gu Yi 古懿. "'Liusi' ershiliu zhounian zhi guonei tongxue de gongkaixin" "六四"二十
六周年致国内同学的公开信 [On the 26th anniversary of June Fourth, an open
letter to fellow students in mainland China]. China in Perspective, May 18, 2015.
http://www.chinainperspective.com/ArtShow.aspx?AID=44088.

Guangming ribao chubanshe bianjibu 光明日报出版社编辑部, ed. *Pingbao yingxiong pu: Pingxi Beijing fangeming baoluan yingmo shiji baogaoji* 平暴英雄谱: 平
息北京反革命暴乱英模事迹报告集 [A register of riot-quelling heroes: Collection
of reports on heroic deeds in quelling Beijing's counterrevolutionary riot]. Beijing:
Guangming ribao chubanshe, 1989.

Guojia jiaowei sixiang zhengzhi gongzuosi, Zhongguo jiaoyu baoshe 国家教委思
想政治工作司, 中国教育报社, eds. *"Jingying" yu dongluan* "精英"与动乱 [The
"elites" and the turmoil]. Beijing: Renmin jiaoyu chubanshe, 1989.

——. *Pantao "jingying" haiwai yanxing lu* 叛逃"精英"海外言行录 [Record of defected
"elites'" words and deeds overseas]. Beijing: Jiaoyu kexue chubanshe, 1990.

Guy, R. Kent. *The Emperor's Four Treasuries: Scholars and the State in the late
Chien-lung Era*. Cambridge, MA: Harvard University Press, 1987.

Habermas, Jürgen. *The Structural Transformation of the Public Sphere*. Trans.
Thomas Burger. Cambridge, MA: MIT Press, 1991.

Han, Rongbin. *Contesting Cyberspace in China: Online Expression and Authoritarian Resilience*. New York: Columbia University Press, 2018.

Hansen, Miriam. *Babel and Babylon: Spectatorship in American Silent Film*. Cambridge, MA: Harvard University Press, 1991.

——. "Early Cinema, Late Cinema: Permutations of the Public Sphere." *Screen* 34,
no. 3 (1993): 197–210.

——. "*Schindler's List* Is Not *Shoah*: The Second Commandment, Popular Modernism, and Public Memory." *Critical Inquiry* 22, no. 2 (1996): 292–312.

Hao Jianguo 郝建国. "'Shaanjun dongzheng' lushang de xing fengbo" "陕军东
征"路上的性风波 [The sex crisis in the "Shaanxi army's eastern expedition"].
Huashangbao 华商报 [Chinese Business View], July 14, 2008. http://hsb.hsw.cn
/2008-07/14/content_7030731.htm.

Hershkovitz, Linda. "Tiananmen Square and the Politics of Place." *Political Geography* 12, no. 5 (1993): 395–420.

Hillenbrand, Margaret. *Negative Exposures: Knowing What Not to Know in Contemporary China*. Durham, NC: Duke University Press, 2020.

Hockx, Michel. *Internet Literature in China*. New York: Columbia University Press,
2015.

Holquist, Michael. "Corrupt Originals: The Paradox of Censorship." *PMLA* 109, no.
1 (1994): 14–25.

"Hostile Forces Target Younger Generation." *Global Times*, May 25, 2015. http://www.globaltimes.cn/content/923528.shtml.

Hou, Rui. "The Commercialisation of Internet-opinion Management: How the Market Is Engaged in State Control in China." *New Media & Society* 22, no. 12 (2020): 2238–56. https://doi.org/10.1177/1461444819889959.

Hu Fayun 胡发云. *Ruyan@sars.come* 如焉@sars.come [Such Is This World@sars.come]. Beijing: Zhongguo guoji guangbo chubanshe, 2006.

——. *Such Is This World@sars.come*. Trans. A. E. Clark. Dobbs Ferry, NY: Ragged Banner Press, 2011. Large-screen PDF edition.

Hu, Ying. "Qiu Jin's Nine Burials: The Making of Historical Monuments and Public Memory." *Modern Chinese Literature and Culture* 19, no. 1 (2007): 138–91.

Hua Yuan 华原. *Tongshi mingjian: Zichanjieji ziyouhua de fanlan jiqi jiaoxun* 痛史明鉴: 资产阶级自由化的泛滥及其教训 [Mirror to a history of pain: The spread of bourgeois liberalization and its lesson]. Beijing: Beijing chubanshe, 1991.

Huang, Yiju. "By Way of Melancholia: Remembrance of Tiananmen Square Incident in *Summer Palace*." *Asian Cinema* 21, no. 1 (2010): 165–178.

Huanqiu shibao 环球时报. "Jingwai shili shitu shandong balinghou jiulinghou" 境外势力试图煽动八零后九零后 [Overseas forces attempt to incite post-80s, 90s generation]. *China Digital Times*, May 26, 2015. https://chinadigitaltimes.net/chinese/2015/05/%E3%80%90%E7%9C%9F%E7%90%86%E9%83%A8%E3%80%91%E5%A2%83%E5%A4%96%E5%8A%BF%E5%8A%9B%E8%AF%95%E5%9B%BE%E7%85%BD%E5%8A%A8%E5%85%AB%E9%9B%B6%E5%90%8E%E4%B9%9D%E9%9B%B6%E5%90%8E-2/.

"Hubei kaishi dui zuojia jinxing 'zhengnengliang' peixun" 湖北开始对作家进行"正能量"培训 [Hubei starts "positive energy" training for writers]. China Digital Times, March 9, 2020. https://chinadigitaltimes.net/chinese/2020/03/%E3%80%90%E7%BD%91%E7%BB%9C%E6%B0%91%E8%AE%AE%E3%80%91%E6%B9%96%E5%8C%97%E5%BC%80%E5%A7%8B%E5%AF%B9%E4%BD%9C%E5%AE%B6%E8%BF%9B%E8%A1%8C%E6%AD%A3%E8%83%BD%E9%87%8F%E5%9F%B9%E8%AE%AD/.

Hughes, Helen. "Crony Capitalism and the East Asian Currency and Financial 'Crises.'" *Policy* 15, no. 3 (1999): 3–9.

Iovene, Paola. "A Madwoman in the Art Gallery? Gender, Mediation, and the Relation Between Life and Art in Post-1989 Chinese Independent Film." *Journal of Chinese Cinemas* 8, no. 3 (2014): 173–87.

Jia Pingwa 贾平凹. *Feidu* 废都 [Ruined City]. Beijing: Beijing chubanshe, 1993.

——. *Feidu* 废都 [Ruined City]. Beijing: Zuojia chubanshe, 2009.

——. *Ruined City*. Trans. Howard Goldblatt. Norman: University of Oklahoma Press, 2016.

Jiang Pinchao 蔣品超, ed. *Liusi shiji* 六四詩集 [June Fourth poetry collection]. Monterey Park, CA: Liusi wenhua chuanbo xiehui, 2007.

Jiang Wenjuan 蔣文娟. "Laobianji pilu *Feidu* zaojin neimu: Yiyejian tiantang bian diyu" 老编辑披露废都遭禁内幕：一夜间天堂变地狱 [Former editor discloses the scenes behind *Decadent Capital*'s ban: In the blink of an eye heaven becomes hell]. *Qingnian zhoumo* 青年周末 [Youth Weekend], August 6, 2009. http://media .people.com.cn/GB/40606/9804080.html.

Jiangxi renmin chubanshe 江西人民出版社, ed. *Fangeming baoluan muduji* 反革命暴乱目睹纪 [Eyewitness account of the counterrevolutionary riot]. Nanchang: Jiangxi renmin chubanshe, 1989.

Jin Zhong 金鐘. "Wentan 'heima' Liu Xiaobo" 文壇「黑馬」劉曉波 [Dark horse of the literary scene, Liu Xiaobo]. *Jiefang yuebao* 解放月报 12 (1988). http://www .open.com.hk/old_version/1011p68.html.

Kehr, Dave. "At the Movies." *New York Times*, July 26, 2002.

Khatri, Naresh, Eric W. K. Tsang, and Thomas M. Begley. "Cronyism: A Cross-Cultural Analysis." *Journal of International Business Studies* 37, no. 1 (2006): 61–75.

Kong, Belinda. *Tiananmen Fictions Outside the Square: The Chinese Literary Diaspora and the Politics of Global Culture*. Philadelphia: Temple University Press, 2012.

Kong, Shuyu. *Consuming Literature: Best Sellers and the Commercialization of Literary Production in Contemporary China*. Stanford, CA: Stanford University Press, 2008.

Kraus, Richard Curt. *The Party and the Arty in China: The New Politics of Culture*. Lanham, MD: Rowman & Littlefield, 2004.

Kuo, Lily. "Coronavirus: Wuhan Doctor Speaks Out Against Authorities." *Guardian*, March 11, 2020. https://www.theguardian.com/world/2020/mar/11/coronavirus -wuhan-doctor-ai-fen-speaks-out-against-authorities.

Kwan, Stanley, dir. *Lan Yu*. 2001. Culver City, CA: Strand Releasing, 2003. DVD.

Lao Jiao 老礁. "*Ruyan@sars.come* shanjie quxi" 《如焉@sars.come》删节趣析（1）[Interesting analysis of *Such Is This World@sars.come* deletions (1)]. Now removed. http://tieba.baidu.com/p/563429585.

Laughlin, Charles. *Chinese Reportage: The Aesthetics of Historical Experience*. Durham, NC: Duke University Press, 2002.

Lee, Haiyan. "The Charisma of Power and the Military Sublime in Tiananmen Square." *Journal of Asian Studies* 70, no. 2 (2011): 397–424.

——. *Revolution of the Heart: A Genealogy of Love in China, 1900–1950*. Stanford, CA: Stanford University Press, 2007.

——. *The Stranger and the Chinese Moral Imagination*. Stanford, CA: Stanford University Press, 2014.

Li Jingze 李敬泽. "Zhuang Zhidie lun" 庄之蝶论 [On Zhuang Zhidie]. In Jia Pingwa 贾平凹, *Feidu* 废都 [Decadent capital], 1–9. Beijing: Zuojia chubanshe, 2009.

Li Jinkun 李锦坤, ed. *1989: Dongluan hou de huigu yu sikao* 1989：动乱后的回顾
与思考 [1989: Looking back and reflecting after the turmoil]. Tianjin: Tianjin
renmin chubanshe, 1989.

Li, Jinying. "From D-Buffs to the D-Generation: Piracy, Cinema, and an Alternative Public Sphere in Urban China." *International Journal of Communication*
6 (2012): 542–63.

Li Pei 李培. "Shiyunian hou *Feidu* zaiban yin guanzhu" 十余年后《废都》再版引
关注 [After more than 10 years *Decadent Capital*'s rerelease draws attention].
Nanfang ribao 南方日报 [Southern Daily], July 30, 2009. http://news.xinhuanet
.com/book/2009-07/30/content_11796253_2.htm.

Lim, Louisa. *The People's Republic of Amnesia: Tiananmen Revisited*. New York:
Oxford University Press, 2014.

Lim, Song Hwee. "Celluloid Comrades: Male Homosexuality in Chinese Cinemas of
the 1990s." *China Information* 16, no. 1 (2002): 68–88.

Link, Perry. *An Anatomy of Chinese: Rhythm, Metaphor, Politics*. Cambridge, MA:
Harvard University Press, 2013.

——. *The Uses of Literature: Life in the Socialist Chinese Literary System*. Princeton,
NJ: Princeton University Press, 2000.

Liu, Jianmei. *Revolution Plus Love: Literary History, Women's Bodies, and Thematic Repetition in 20th-Century Chinese Fiction*. Honolulu: University of Hawai'i Press, 2003.

Liu Jing 刘晶. "*Yiheyuan* qunzhong yanyuan jiti fuxie 37 ren bei songzhi yiyuan"
《颐和园》群众演员集体腹泻 37人被送至医院 [*Summer Palace* crowd actors
have collective diarrhea, 37 people taken to the hospital]. Sohu 搜狐, October
24, 2004. http://yule.sohu.com/20041024/n222651549.shtml.

Liu Xiaobo. "The Erotic Carnival in Recent Chinese History." Trans. Nick Admussen. In *No Enemies, No Hatred: Selected Essays and Poems*, ed. Perry Link, Tienchi Martin-Liao, and Liu Xia, 150–74. Cambridge, MA: The Belknap Press of
Harvard University Press, 2012.

——. *June Fourth Elegies*. Trans. Jeffrey Yang. Minneapolis, MN: Graywolf Press, 2012.

Long Xinmin 龙新民. "Dianshi yu yulun daoxiang" 电视与舆论导向 (Television and
the orientation of public opinion). *Qianxian* 前线 10 (1989): 43–46.

Loubere, Nicholas. "The New Censorship, the New Academic Freedom: Commercial Publishers and the Chinese Market." *Journal of the European Association for
Chinese Studies* 1 (2020): 239–52.

Lu, Sheldon. "Literature: Intellectuals in the Ruined Metropolis at the Fin de Siècle."
In *China, Transnational Visuality, Global Postmodernity*, 239–59. Stanford, CA:
Stanford University Press, 2001.

Lu, Tina. "The Literary Culture of the Late Ming (1573–1644)." In *The Cambridge
History of Chinese Literature, vol. II: From 1375*, ed. Kang-I Sun Chang, 63–151.
Cambridge: Cambridge University Press, 2010.

Lu Xun 鲁迅. *Lu Xun quanji* 鲁迅全集 [Complete works of Lu Xun]. 21 volumes. Beijing: Renmin wenxue chubanshe, 2005.

——. "Preface to *Outcry* (1923)." In *Jottings Under Lamplight: Lu Xun*, ed. Eileen J. Cheng and Kirk A. Denton, 19-24. Cambridge, MA: Harvard University Press, 2017.

Lull, James. *China Turned On: Television, Reform, and Resistance*. London: Routledge, 1991.

Ma, Ran. "Regarding the Grassroots Chinese Independent Film Festivals: Modes of Multiplicity and Abnormal Film Networking." In *China's iGeneration: Cinema and Moving Image Culture for the Twenty-First Century*, ed. Matthew D. Johnson, Keith B. Wagner, Tianqi Yu, and Luke Vulpiani, 235–53. New York: Bloomsbury, 2014.

Makinen, Julie. "Director Takes Chinese Censorship, Business Battles Public." *Los Angeles Times*, October 18, 2012.

Mao Dun. *Midnight*. Trans. Hsu Meng-hsiung and A. C. Barnes. Beijing: Foreign Languages Press, 1979.

McGrath, Jason. "Communists Have More Fun! The Dialectics of Fulfillment in Cinema of the People's Republic of China." *World Picture* 3 (2009). http://www.worldpicturejournal.com/WP_3/McGrath.html.

——. *Postsocialist Modernity: Chinese Cinema, Literature, and Criticism in the Market Age*. Stanford, CA: Stanford University Press, 2008.

Meyer, Mike. "The World's Biggest Book Market." *New York Times*, March 13, 2005.

Mu Tao 穆涛. "Lüli" 履历 [Curriculum vitae]. *Dangdai zuojia pinglun* 当代作家评论 [Contemporary Writers Review] 5 (2005): 24–30.

Mufti, Aamir. "Reading the Rushdie Affair: 'Islam,' Cultural Politics, Form." In *The Administration of Aesthetics: Censorship, Political Criticism, and the Public Sphere*, ed. Richard Burt, 307–39. Minneapolis: University of Minnesota Press, 1994.

Nakajima, Seio. "Film as Cultural Politics." In *Reclaiming Chinese Society: The New Social Activism*, ed. You-tien Hsing and Ching Kwan Lee, 159–83. New York: Routledge, 2009.

"On the 26th Anniversary of Tian'anmen Massacre—an Open Letter to Fellow Students in Mainland China." China Change, May 27, 2015. https://chinachange.org/2015/05/27/on-the-26th-anniversary-of-tiananmen-massacre-an-open-letter-to-fellow-students-in-mainland-china/.

Pagano, Michael S. "Crises, Cronyism, and Credit." *The Financial Review* 37, no. 2 (2002): 227–56.

Pan, Lynn. "A Chinese Master." *New York Times Magazine*, March 1, 1992.

Pan Yuan 潘媛. "Lou Ye *Yiheyuan* jianchi zaisongshen" 娄烨《颐和园》坚持再送审 [Lou Ye's *Summer Palace* persists in submission to censorship]. Sina 新浪, July 28, 2006. http://news.sina.com.cn/o/2006-07-28/09549592470s.shtml.

PEN America. "Made in Hollywood, Censored by Beijing: The U.S. Film Industry and Chinese Government Influence." PEN America, August 5, 2020. https://pen .org/report/made-in-hollywood-censored-by-beijing/.

Perlez, Jane. "Chinese Writer, Tackling Tiananmen, Wields 'Power to Offend.'" *New York Times*, October 10, 2014.

Perry, Elizabeth J. "Moving the Masses: Emotion Work in the Chinese Revolution." *Mobilization* 7, no. 2 (2002): 111–28.

Pickowicz, Paul. "Velvet Prisons and the Political Economy of Chinese Filmmaking." In *Urban Spaces in Contemporary China: The Potential for Autonomy and Community in Post-Mao China*, ed. Deborah S. Davis, Richard Kraus, Barry Naughton, and Elizabeth J. Perry, 193–220. Cambridge: Cambridge University Press, 1995.

Post, Robert C., ed. *Censorship and Silencing: Practices of Cultural Regulation*. Los Angeles: Getty Research Institute, 1998.

Qiao Youxuan 喬友萱, ed. *Beijing chunxia fengbo shilu* 北京春夏風波實錄 [Record of Beijing's spring-summer turbulence]. N.p.: Haihua chubanshe, 1989.

Qin, Jianhang, Gang Ding, Wei Han, and Denise Jia. "Q&A: Whistleblower Doctor Who Died Fighting Coronavirus Only Wanted People to 'Know the Truth.'" Caixin Global, February 7, 2020. https://www.caixinglobal.com/2020-02-07 /whistleblower-doctor-who-died-fighting-coronavirus-only-wanted-people-to -know-the-truth-101512578.html.

Redden, Elizabeth. "Outrage Over University Press Caving in to Chinese Censorship." Inside Higher Ed, August 21, 2017. https://www.insidehighered.com/news/2017/08 /21/cambridge-university-press-blocks-access-300-plus-articles-request-chinese -censors.

Repnikova, Maria, and Kecheng Fang. "Authoritarian Participatory Persuasion 2.0: Netizens as Thought Work Collaborators in China." *Journal of Contemporary China* 27 (2018): 763–79.

Roberts, Margaret E. *Censored: Distraction and Diversion Inside China's Great Firewall*. Princeton: Princeton University Press, 2018.

Robinson, Luke. *Independent Chinese Documentary: From the Studio to the Street*. London: Palgrave Macmillan, 2013.

Rojas, Carlos. "Flies' Eyes, Mural Remnants, and Jia Pingwa's Perverse Nostalgia." *positions: east asia cultures critique* 14, no. 3 (2006): 749–73.

——. *Homesickness: Culture, Contagion, and National Transformation in Modern China*. Cambridge, MA: Harvard University Press, 2015.

Rosenfeld, Sophia. "Writing the History of Censorship in the Age of Enlightenment." In *Postmodernism and the Enlightenment: New Perspectives in Eighteenth-Century French Intellectual History*, ed. Daniel Gordon, 117–45. New York: Routledge, 2001.

Rowe, William T. "The Public Sphere in Modern China." *Modern China* 16, no. 3 (1990): 309–29.

Ryan, Hugh. "The Controversial Chinese Gay Erotic Novel You Can Finally Read in English." *Vice*, March 16, 2016. https://broadly.vice.com/en_us/article/beijing -comrades-china-gay-erotica-online.

Saussy, Haun. "Crowds, Number, and Mass in China." In *Crowds*, ed. Jeffery T. Schnapp and Matthew Tiews, 249–69. Stanford, CA: Stanford University Press, 2006.

Schauer, Frederick. "The Ontology of Censorship." In *Censorship and Silencing: Practices of Cultural Regulation*, ed. Robert C. Post, 147–68. Los Angeles: Getty Research Institute, 1998.

Schoenhals, Michael. *Doing Things with Words in Chinese Politics: Five Studies.* Berkeley: Institute of East Asian Studies, University of California, Berkeley, 1992.

Shan Renping 单仁平. "Jianqiao daxue chubanshe chuerfaner de beihou" 剑桥大学 出版社出尔反尔的背后 [Behind the self-contradictions of Cambridge University Press]. *Huanqiu shibao* 环球时报 [Global Times], August 24, 2017. https:// opinion.huanqiu.com/article/9CaKrnK4RA9.

Sheng Keyi 盛可以. *Death Fugue.* Trans. Shelly Bryant. Artarmon: Giramondo, 2014.

——. *Siwang fuge* 死亡赋格 [Death fugue]. *Jiangnan* 江南 5 (2011).

Shi Yan Wu Tian 食砚无田. "*Ruyan@sars.come* shanjie bufen" 《如焉@sars.come》 删节部分[*Such Is This World@sars.come* deleted parts]. March 26, 2009. http:// tieba.baidu.com/p/556415421.

Sichuan ribao bianjibu 四川日报编辑部, ed. *Chengdu saoluan shijian shimo* 成都骚 乱事件始末 [The story of the disturbance in Chengdu]. Chengdu: Sichuan ren-min chubanshe, 1989.

Sorace, Christian P. *Shaken Authority: China's Communist Party and the 2008 Sich-uan Earthquake.* Ithaca, NY: Cornell University Press, 2017.

Strauss, Leo. *Persecution and the Art of Writing.* Glencoe, IL: The Free Press, 1952.

Tang, Xiaobing. "Why Should 2009 Make a Difference? Reflections on a Chinese Blockbuster." MCLC Resource Center, December 2009. https://u.osu.edu/mclc /online-series/tangxb/#fnb1.

Tsai, Chien-hsin. "In Sickness or in Health: Yan Lianke and the Writing of Autoim-munity." *Modern Chinese Literature and Culture* 23, no. 2 (2011): 77–104.

Tsao, Tsing-yuan. "The Birth of the Goddess of Democracy." In *Popular Protest and Political Culture in Modern China*, ed. Jeffrey N. Wasserstrom and Elizabeth J. Perry, 140–47. Boulder, CO: Westview Press, 1994.

Voci, Paola. "From the Center to the Periphery: Chinese Documentary's Visual Con-jectures." *Modern Chinese Literature and Culture* 16, no. 1 (2004): 65–113.

Vukovich, Daniel. "Uncivil Society, or Orientalism and Tiananmen, 1989." *Cultural Logic: A Journal of Marxist Theory & Practice* 16 (2009): 1–37. https://doi.org /10.14288/clogic.v16i0.191558.

Wacker, Gudrun. "Resistance Is Futile: Control and Censorship of the Internet in China." In *From Woodblocks to the Internet: Chinese Publishing and Print Culture in Transition, Circa 1800 to 2008*, ed. Cynthia Brokaw and Christopher A. Reed, 353–81. Leiden: Brill, 2010.

Wagner, Rudolf. *Inside a Service Trade: Studies in Contemporary Chinese Prose.* Cambridge, MA: Council on East Asian Studies, Harvard University, 1992.

Walder, Andrew G., and Gong Xiaoxia. "Workers in the Tiananmen Protests: The Politics of the Beijing Workers' Autonomous Federation." *Australian Journal of Chinese Affairs* 29 (1993): 1–29.

Wang, Ban. *Illuminations from the Past: Trauma, Memory, and History in Modern China.* Stanford, CA: Stanford University Press, 2004.

Wang, David Der-wei. *The Monster That Is History: History, Violence, and Fictional Writing in Twentieth-Century China.* Berkeley: University of California Press, 2004.

Wang Hui. *China's New Order: Society, Politics, and Economy in Transition.* Ed. Theodore Huters. Trans. Theodore Huters and Rebecca E. Karl. Cambridge, MA: Harvard University Press, 2006.

Wang Hui, Leo Ou-fan Lee, and Michael M. J. Fischer. "Is the Public Sphere Unspeakable in Chinese? Can Public Spaces (*gonggong kongjian*) Lead to Public Spheres?" *Public Culture* 6, no. 3 (1994): 598–605.

Wang, Jing. *High Culture Fever: Politics, Aesthetics, and Ideology in Deng's China.* Berkeley: University of California Press, 1996.

Wang, Juntao, and Anne-Marie Brady. "Sword and Pen: The Propaganda System of the People's Liberation Army." In *China's Thought Management*, ed. Anne-Marie Brady, 122–45. New York: Routledge, 2012.

Wang, Qi. *Memory, Subjectivity and Independent Chinese Cinema.* Edinburgh: Edinburgh University Press, 2014.

Wang, Yiyan. *Narrating China: Jia Pingwa and His Fictional World.* New York: Routledge, 2006.

Wang, Zheng. *Never Forget National Humiliation: Historical Memory in Chinese Politics and Foreign Relations.* New York: Columbia University Press, 2012.

Warner, Michael. *Publics and Counterpublics.* New York: Zone, 2005.

Wasserstrom, Jeffrey N. "History, Myth, and the Tales of Tiananmen." In *Popular Protest and Political Culture in Modern China*, ed. Jeffrey N. Wasserstrom and Elizabeth J. Perry, 273–308. Boulder, CO: Westview Press, 1994.

Watts, Jonathan. "Chinese Newspaper Editors Fired Over Tiananmen Square Ad." *Guardian*, June 7, 2007. https://www.theguardian.com/media/2007/jun/07/press andpublishing.china.

Williams, Raymond. *Marxism and Literature.* Oxford: Oxford University Press, 1977.

Worden, Andrea. "Missing Lei Feng." China Channel, March 5, 2021. https://china channel.org/2021/03/05/missing-lei-feng/.

World Intellectual Property Organization. "China: Regulations on the Administration of Movies." Last modified December 11, 2001. https://wipolex.wipo.int/en /legislation/details/6474.

Wu Hung. *Remaking Beijing: Tiananmen Square and the Creation of a Political Space.* Chicago: University of Chicago Press, 2005.

Wu Renhua 吳仁華. *Liusi shijian quancheng shilu* 六四事件全程實錄 [The complete record of the June Fourth incident]. Taipei: Yunchen wenhua, 2019.

Wu Songnian 吴松年, ed. *Shishi yu sikao: Zhongxuesheng shishi zhengzhixue wenda (1989 nian 5 yue—1990 nian 3 yue)* 时事与思考: 中学生時事政治学问答 (1989 年 5 月—1990 年 3 月) [Current affairs and reflection: Secondary school students' Q and A on current affairs politics]. Beijing: Xinhua chubanshe, 1990.

Xiao, Tie. *Revolutionary Waves: The Crowd in Modern China.* Cambridge, MA: Harvard University Press, 2017.

Xiao Xialin 萧夏林, ed. Feidu *feishei* 《废都》废谁 [*Decadent Capital*, decadent who?]. Beijing: Xueyuan chubanshe, 1993.

"Xi Jinping Asks for 'Absolute Loyalty' from Chinese State Media." *Guardian*, February 19, 2016. https://www.theguardian.com/world/2016/feb/19/xi-jinping-tours -chinas-top-state-media-outlets-to-boost-loyalty.

Xu Xu 徐訏. "' . . . . !' '□□□□□' lun" 「 . . . . 」 「□□□□□」 論 [On " . . . ." "□□□□□"]. *Renjianshi* 人间世 [This Human World] 4 (May 20, 1934): 19–21.

——. *Bird Talk and Other Stories by Xu Xu: Modern Tales of a Chinese Romantic.* Trans. Frederik H. Green. Berkeley, CA: Stone Bridge Press, 2020.

Xue Weirui 薛维睿. "Tiananmen shengqi shi: Cong yigeren de shidai dao jiushiliu ren de yishi" 天安门升旗史：从一个人的时代到九十六人的仪式 [History of flag-raising at Tiananmen: From the time of a single person to a 96-person ceremony]. *Fengmian* 封面, January 8, 2018. https://xw.qq.com/cmsid/20180108A04R9I00.

Yan Bin 严彬. "Sheng Keyi fangtanlu" 盛可以访谈录 [Interview with Sheng Keyi]. *Fenghuang dushu* 凤凰读书, May 12, 2014. http://www.xinhuanet.com// book/2014-05/12/c_126490827.htm.

Yan Lianke 阎连科. "Jingci yijie, rang women chengwei you jixing de ren" 經此疫 劫，讓我們成為有記性的人 [After the pandemic, let us become human beings with memory]. Initium Media, February 21, 2020. https://theinitium.com/article /20200221-mainland-coronavirus-yanlianke/.

Yang, Guobin. "Political Contestation in Chinese Digital Spaces: Deepening the Critical Inquiry." *China Information* 28, no. 2 (2014): 135–44.

——. *The Power of the Internet in China: Citizen Activism Online.* New York: Columbia University Press, 2011.

Yang Mo. *The Song of Youth*. Trans. Nan Ying. Beijing: Foreign Languages Press, 1964.

Ye Xuan 叶宣, ed. *Pingbao jishi* 平暴纪实 [Record of quelling the riot]. Taiyuan: Beiyue wenyi chubanshe, 1990.

Yeh, Wen-hsin. "Shanghai Modernity: Commerce and Culture in a Republican City." *China Quarterly* 150 (1997): 375–94.

Yin Wei 殷维. "Daoyan Lou Ye bochi chuanyan: Sheishuo *Yiheyuan* mei tongguo shencha?" 导演娄烨驳斥传言：谁说《颐和园》没通过审查？ [Director Lou Ye refutes rumors: Who says *Summer Palace* didn't pass censorship?]. *Xin wenhua bao* 新文化报, May 9, 2006. http://www.chinanews.com/news/2006/2006 -05-09/8/727270.shtml.

You Mianjin 游免津. "*Feidu* chongban: Rang wenxue de gui wenxue"《废都》重 版：让文学的归文学 [New edition of *Decadent Capital*: Let literature's belong to literature]. *Xinjingbao* 新京报 [The Beijing News], July 30, 2009. http://culture .people.com.cn/GB/27296/9750065.html.

Yu, Hongmei. "Visual Spectacular, Revolutionary Epic, and Personal Voice: The Narration of History in Chinese Main Melody Films." *Modern Chinese Literature and Culture* 25, no. 2 (2013): 166–218.

Zeng Wobu 曾我部. "Guan Jinpeng tan dongqing zhizuo *Lan Yu*: Wo bushi pai seqingpian" 关锦鹏谈动情之作《蓝宇》：我不是拍色情片 [Stanley Kwan discusses passionate film *Lan Yu*: I'm not making a porno]. *Nanfang dushibao* 南 方都市报 [Southern Metropolis Daily], December 10, 2001. http://ent.sina.com .cn/m/c/2001-12-10/66499.html.

Zha, Jianying. *China Pop: How Soap Operas, Tabloids, and Bestsellers Are Transforming a Culture*. New York: New Press, 1995.

Zhang Hong 张弘. "Jia Pingwa *Feidu* jiejin xinbanben shangjia" 贾平凹《废都》解 禁新版本上架 [Jia Pingwa's *Decadent Capital* unbanned; new edition for sale]. *Xinjingbao* 新京报 [The Beijing News], July 30, 2009. http://culture.people.com. cn/GB/22219/9750476.html.

Zhang, Rui. *The Cinema of Feng Xiaogang: Commercialization and Censorship in Chinese Cinema after 1989*. Hong Kong: Hong Kong University Press, 2008.

Zhang Wenbo 张文伯. "Lou Ye *Yiheyuan* ruwei Jiana? Shangxu shencha" 娄烨《颐 和园》入围戛纳？尚需审查 [Lou Ye's *Summer Palace* in competition in Cannes? Still in need of censorship review]. *Xinjingbao* 新京报 [The Beijing News], April 20, 2006. http://www.southcn.com/ent/yulefirst/200604200174.htm.

Zhang Yihe 章诒和. *Lingren wangshi* 伶人往事 [Performers past]. Changsha: Hunan wenyi chubanshe, 2006.

———. *Liu shi nü* 刘氏女 [The Woman Liu]. Guilin: Guangxi shifan daxue chubanshe, 2011.

———. *Wangshi bingbu ruyan* 往事并不如烟 [The past is not like smoke]. Beijing: Renmin chubanshe, 2004.

Zhang, Yingjin. "Narrative, Ideology, Subjectivity: Defining a Subversive Discourse in Chinese Reportage." In *Politics, Ideology and Literary Discourse in Modern China: Theoretical Interventions and Cultural Critique*, ed. Kang Liu and Xiaobing Tang, 211–42. Durham, NC: Duke University Press, 1993.

Zhao, Dingxin. *The Power of Tiananmen: State-Society Relations and the 1989 Beijing Student Movement*. Chicago: University of Chicago Press, 2004.

Zhen Xiaofei 甄晓菲. "Shishi feifei tongxinglian yingzhan" 是是非非同性恋影展 [Disagreements over gay film exhibitions]. *Nanfang zhoumo* 南方周末 [Southern Weekly], January 11, 2007. http://www.southcn.com/weekend/culture/200701110032.htm.

Zheng Nianqun 郑念群. *Zai jieyan de rizi li* 在戒严的日子里 [Days of martial law]. Beijing: Jiefangjun wenyi chubanshe, 1989.

Zhong Bu 钟步, ed. *Xinshiqi zuikeai de ren: Beijing jieyan budui yingxiong lu* 新时期最可爱的人: 北京戒严部队英雄录 [Those most worthy of our love in the new era: record of Beijing martial law troops' heroic achievements]. Beijing: Guangming ribao chubanshe, 1989.

Zhonggong Beijing shiwei bangongting 中共北京市委办公厅, ed. *Beijing zhizhi dongluan pingxi fangeming baoluan jishi* 北京制止动乱平息反革命暴乱纪事 [Chronicle of Beijing's stopping of the turmoil and quelling of the counterrevolutionary riot]. Beijing: Beijing ribao chubanshe, 1989.

Zhonggong Beijing shiwei xuanchuanbu 中共北京市委宣传部, ed. *Pingxi fangeming baoluan: Xuexi cailiao huibian* 平息反革命暴乱: 学习材料汇编 [Quelling the counterrevolutionary riot: Collection of study materials]. Beijing: Beijing qingnian chubanshe, 1989.

——. *Xuechao, dongluan, fangeming baoluan zhenxiang: Ziliao xuanbian* 学潮·动乱·反革命暴乱真相: 资料选编 [The truth behind the student movement, turmoil, and counterrevolutionary riot: Selected materials]. Beijing: Zhongguo qingnian chubanshe, 1989.

Zhonggong Beijing shiwei xuanchuanbu lilunchu 中共北京市委宣传部理论处, ed. *Xuexi Deng Xiaoping zhongyao jianghua chedi pingxi fangeming baoluan wenti jieda* 学习邓小平重要讲话彻底平息反革命暴乱问题解答 [Answers to questions on the study of Deng Xiaoping's speech about utterly quelling the counterrevolutionary riot]. Beijing: Beijing chubanshe, 1989.

Zhonggong Hubei shengwei xuanchuanbu 中共湖北省委宣传部, ed. *Pingbao "beiwanglu": Xuexi cailiao xuanbian* 平暴"备忘录": 学习材料选编 ["Memorandum" of the riot's quelling: Selection of study materials]. Wuhan: Hubei renmin chubanshe, 1989.

Zhonggong Liaoning shengwei gongchandangyuan zazhishe 中共辽宁省委共产党员杂志社, ed. *Pingxi fangeming baoluan 500 ti* 平息反革命暴乱500题 [500 questions on quelling the counterrevolutionary riot]. Shenyang: Liaoning daxue chubanshe, 1989.

Zhonggong zhongyang xuanchuanbu 中共中央宣传部, ed. *Jianjue yonghu Dang-zhongyang juece jianjue pingxi fangeming baoluan* 坚决拥护党中央决策坚决平息反革命暴乱 [Resolutely support the Party's Central Committee's decision to resolutely quell the counterrevolutionary riot]. Beijing: Renmin chubanshe, 1989.

Zhongguo jiaoyu baoshe, Beijing jieyan budui 中国教育报社, 北京戒严部队, eds. *Gongheguo weishi yinglie ji* 共和国卫士英烈集 [Collection of valiant deeds of the Republic's guardians]. Beijing: Zhongguo zhuoyue chubanshe, 1989.

Zhongguo renmin jiefangjun zonghouqinbu chechuanbu 中国人民解放军总后勤部车船部, ed. *Tiema chicheng wei Jinghua* 铁马驰骋卫京华 [The iron horse galloping to defend Beijing]. Beijing: Jiefangjun wenyi chubanshe, 1990.

Zhonghua renmin gongheguo sifabu xuanchuansi 中华人民共和国司法部宣传司, ed. *Chedi jielu fangeming baoluan de zhenxiang* 彻底揭露反革命暴乱的真相 [Utterly uncover the truth of the counterrevolutionary riot]. Beijing: Falü chubanshe, 1989.

Zhongyang dangxiao de jiben luxian yanjiu ketizu 中央党校党的基本路线研究课题组, ed. *Beijing fengbo zhenxiang he shizhi* 北京风波真相和实质 [The truth and essence of Beijing's turmoil]. Beijing: Dadi chubanshe, 1989.

Zhou, Yuxing. "Pursuing Soft Power Through Cinema: Censorship and Double Standards in Mainland China." *Journal of Chinese Cinemas* 9, no. 3 (2015): 239–52.

Zhu, Ying. *Chinese Cinema During the Era of Reform: The Ingenuity of the System.* Westport, CT: Praeger, 2003.

——. *Two Billion Eyes: The Story of China Central Television.* New York: New Press, 2012.

Zongzheng wenhuabu zhengwen bangongshi 总政文化部征文办公室, ed. *Jieyan yiri* 戒严一日 [One day of martial law]. 2 volumes. Beijing: Jiefangjun wenyi chubanshe, 1989.

Zongzhengzhibu xuanchuanbu, Jiefangjunbao bianjibu 总政治部宣传部, 解放军报编辑部, eds. *Hanwei shehuizhuyi gongheguo* 捍卫社会主义共和国 [Defend the socialist republic]. Beijing: Changzheng chubanshe, 1989.

Index

Calhoun, Craig, 187n48

Cambridge University Press, complicity with Chinese censorship, 173–74

Candide (Voltaire), 91

Cannes Film Festival, 103, 117, 118, 130

capitalism, 98, 100, 101, 106, 129

CCP (Chinese Communist Party), 5, 18, 23, 31, 64–65; *Global Times* tabloid, 169–71; job prospects as reason for joining, 97; national sovereignty restored by, 47, 48; *People's Daily* newspaper, 21, 39, 43–44, *43*, 66; as revolutionary remainder, 114

CCTV (China Central Television), 38, 42, 44; independent cinema in China and, 54; Shi Jian's connections to, 61

Celan, Paul, 90

censorship, 66, 127; academic reproduction of state censorship, 133; aesthetics shaped by, 51–52; carrot-and-stick (yes-no) approach to, 13–14, 44; censors as collective, 158; commercialization of, 98, 100; constitutive, 2; COVID-19, 11, 165; editing in relation to, 160, 203n74; as erasure and destruction, 49–50, 57, 90; extraterritoriality of, 173, 174–75; "fetish of censorship," 98–99, 119, 129, 175; film, 51, 114–15, 118–19; internet and, 150, 151, 152, 156–60; as joint production of censors and censored, 129–30; of Kuomintang government (1930s), 143, 160; made visible in edited film, 105; "material censorship" of the market, 6; in the neoliberal West, 3; of one government organ by another, 171; partial privatization of, 8; proscriptive

and prescriptive dimensions of, 5, 70, 93, 96; as realignment of opinion, 25; reconceptualization of, 2, 4–5, 15; reproduction of, 12, 53; as selling point for foreign viewers/consumers, 119; state propaganda as component of, 49, 63; as state propagation, 10, 12; as state violence, 113; structural versus regulative, 3; Tank Man and, 17; as twin project of prohibition and propagation, 15, 78; workarounds spurred by, 51, 56, 165

censorship, orthography of, 134, 165; ellipses, 134, 141; parentheses, 133, 134, 160–65. *See also* blank squares, for deleted words/characters

Charter 08 manifesto, 156

Chengdu Evening News, one-line ad in, 1

Chen Guidi, 201n48

Chen Kaige, 119

Chi, Robert, 113

China Quarterly, The, 173–74

China Queer Film Festival, 193n6

China Radio International Publishing House, 153, 163

China Youth University of Political Studies, 58

Chinese languages, traditional and simplified script, 21, 183n6

Chinese News Digest, 200n42

Chion, Michel, 191n20

Chyi Chin, 74, 76

City of Sadness, A (Hou Hsiao-hsien, 1989), 196n40

Clark, A. E., 161

Cold War, 3

Collected Writings of Ah Cheng, 164

Communist Party. *See* CCP (Chinese Communist Party)

"comrade" (*tongzhi*), as term of gay identity, 106, 194n17

Conceison, Claire, 188n64

confrontation, aesthetics of, 52

Conjugation [*Dongci bianwei*] (Tang Xiaobai, 2001), 10, 52, 53–54, 173; abortion metaphor, 77–78, *77*; Asian Games referred to, 70, 75–76; *Battle on Shangganling Mountain* referred to, 70–71; *Death Fugue* compared with, 83–84, 85, 89, 92; director as actor in, 68, *68*; disappeared body in, 72–82; Foot Finger figure as symbol of loss/disappearance, 74–78, 80, 81, 82, 83, 191n17; historical time as verb tenses, 68–72; limited circulation in China, 96, 97; movement as displacement/dispersal, 79–80, *80*; night and indoor settings of, 72–73; postproduction and distribution in Hong Kong, 82; significance of title, 68–70; sound design in, 73–74, 78; sound–silence contradiction as letimotif, 75, 77, 78; stories about disappearance, 80–82; *Summer Palace* compared with, 115–17, 122, 123, 126; underground status of, 99

consumption/consumerism, 99, 136, 147, 197n5

Contemporary Writers Review [*Dangdai zuojia pinglun*] (mainland literary journal), 132

counterproduction, 12, 13

"counterrevolutionary riot" narrative, 40, 42, 58, 79, 83, 172; forestalled challenges to, 58; reeducation of students in, 64; replaced by policy of silencing, 169

COVID-19 pandemic, 3, 11, 165, 167–68

Cui Jian, 121, 127

Cultural Revolution (1966–1976), 23, 129, 145, 183n8, 191n21; censored references to, 160–61; Hu Fayun's lectures on, 155; "turmoil" associated with, 21, 37

CWA (China Writers Association), 24, 84, 141, 185n28

Cyberspace Administration of China, 5

Death Fugue [*Siwang fuge*] (Sheng Keyi, 2011), 10, 51–52, 53, 84, 173, 189n1; artifice versus art in, 93–94; *Conjugation* compared with, 83–84, 85, 89, 92; on degradation and forsaking of poetry, 83–90; fugue as amnesia cause by trauma, 92; Holocaust connection to June Fourth, 90–91, 94, 95; *I Graduated* compared with, 83–84, 92; published in mainland China, 94, 99; reimagined places of past and future, 54; *Ruined City* compared with, 145; on silence after spiritual disorder, 83; *Summer Palace* compared with, 122; Swan Valley dystopia, 91–92; Tower Incident as allegory for Tiananmen, 84–85, 86, 168

democracy, 22, 23, 41, 91, 114. *See also* Goddess of Democracy statue

"Demons of the Chinese Literary Scene, The" (Lu Xun, 1934), 143

Deng Xiaoping, 20, 47, 190n14

Denton, Kirk, 14, 48

"Diary of a Madman" (Lu Xun, 1918), 82

Ding Dong, 153, 155

Discipline and Punish (Foucault, 1975), 2, 179n2

Doing Things with Words in Chinese Politics (Schoenhals), 25

Holquist, Michael, 2

Hong Kong, 82, 103, 137; British colonial rule in, 35, 187n45; return of sovereignty to China (1997), 190n12; "semiautonomy" of, 4; traditional Chinese script used in, 21

Hou Hsiao-hsien, 196n40

"How Can You Bear Seeing Me Sad?" (Huang Pin Yuan song, 1990), 104–5, 113

Hu, Jie, 202n67

Huang Jiguang, 66, 190n13

Huang Jingang, 66, 71, 97

Huang Pin Yuan, 104

Hu Fayun, 11, 12, 133, 148, 162, 163, 165; "Hu Fayun Bar" online fan forum, 154, 156; lectures on Cultural Revolution, 155; narration of censorship, 134, 153; Sina blog of, 156–60, 202n59. See also *Such Is This World@sars.come*

Hu Feng clique, campaign against (1955), 160, 162

Hu Jun, 104

Huxley, Aldous, 91

Hu Yaobang, 27

I Graduated [*Wo biye le*] (Wang Guangli, 1992), 10, 52, 53, 72, 173; ambient noise in soundtrack, 56; *Conjugation* compared with, 78; *Death Fugue* compared with, 83–84, 92; editing in, 57; five interview sections of, 58; flag-raising ceremony in, 60–61; as group portrait, 65; hand-held camera images in, 55; June Fourth interview section, 62–68; limited circulation in China, 96, 97; point-of-view shots in, 56; prelude of song and tinted images, 55; security apparatus in interludes, 58–61, *59*; state-produced documentary contrasted with, 55–56, 61–62; *Summer Palace* contrasted with, 115–17, 123; underground status of, 99

"illegal information," 5

imperialism, "Eight-Nation Alliance" of, 35

In Search of Lin Zhao's Soul (Jie Hu, 2005), 202n67

intellectuals, 22, 37, 44, 87, 99, 147, 180n14; public reputation of, 86; regained voices after military crackdown, 140; Tiananmen blamed on agitation of, 64

"Internationale, The" (communist anthem, Pottier), 113, 114, 194n23

internet, Chinese, 5, 9, 11, 135, 148–53, 171; Great Firewall, 150; internet opinion companies, 14; "internet sovereignty," 174

"Is the Public Sphere Unspeakable in Chinese?" (Wang and Lee, 1994), 8

Jiangnan (literary journal), 52, 84, 153, 154, 189n1

Jiangsu Phoenix Art Publishing House, 164

Jiang Zemin, 188n55, 189n68

Jia Pingwa, 11, 134, 136, 153, 162; critics of, 136–38, 141–43; performance of censorship, 139, 144. See also *Ruined City*

Ju Dou (Zhang Yimou and Yang Fengliang, 1990), 119

June Fourth, 1, 3, 42; Chinese Party-state narrative in wake of, 18, 19; civilians as true victims of, 29, 37, 62–63; collective decision not to

CPSIA information can be obtained
at www.ICGtesting.com
Printed in the USA
LVHW051259190722
723841LV00001B/95

9 780231 204019